INTERVENTION

RICHARD N. HAASS

INTERVENTION

THE USE OF AMERICAN MILITARY FORCE IN THE POST-COLD WAR WORLD

REVISED EDITION

A CARNEGIE ENDOWMENT BOOK

BROOKINGS INSTITUTION PRESS
Washington, D.C.

Copyright © 1999
THE BROOKINGS INSTITUTION
1775 Massachusetts Avenue, N.W.
Washington, D.C. 20036
www.brookings.edu

Intervention: The Use of American Military Force in the Post–Cold War World
was first published in 1994 by the Carnegie Endowment for International Peace.

Library of Congress Cataloging-in-Publication data:
Haass, Richard.
   Intervention : the use of American military force in the post-Cold War
world / Richard N. Haass.—Rev. ed.
     p. cm.
Includes bibliographical references (p.   ) and index.
   ISBN 0-87003-135-X (paper : alk. paper)
   1. Intervention (International law) 2. United States—Military
policy. 3. United States—Armed Forces. 4. International police. I.
Title.
   JZ6368 .H33 1999   99-006932
   355'.033573—dc21   CIP

9 8 7 6 5 4 3 2 1

The paper used in this publication meets minimum requirements of the
American National Standard for Information Sciences—Permanence of
Paper for Printed Library Materials: ANSI Z39.48-1984.

Typeset in New Caledonia

Printed by
R. R. Donnelley & Sons
Harrisonburg, Virginia

TO SAMUEL JOSEPH HAASS

TABLE OF CONTENTS

TABLE OF CONTENTS

It is now more than five years since the initial publication of *Intervention*. What makes this revised edition both necessary and desirable is the fact that the large number of diverse military interventions that characterized the first five years of the post–Cold War era proved not to be the exception. Military force continues to occupy a central place in American foreign policy and in international relations more generally. Anyone doubting this assertion need only stop to consider recent U.S. actions in Bosnia, Haiti, and Iraq, the 1996 Taiwan Straits crisis, the 1998 bombings of a terrorist camp in Afghanistan and an alleged chemical weapons plant in Sudan, and the 1999 war over Kosovo. It is just as important to consider the consequences when the United States determined not to use military force, as was the case in Rwanda.

The bulk of the book stands as it was initially written and published. It also includes a new afterword that describes and critiques the principal U.S. military interventions that have taken place since mid-1994. Once again, I attempt to draw lessons and provide guidelines. In addition, the appendices include the principal documents and statements that have informed several decades of public debate in the United States over the use of military force. The one addition to the original appendices is an important speech on the subject given in March 1996 by then National Security Advisor Anthony Lake.

The original acknowledgment holds. In addition, I would like to thank Ivo Daalder, Bates Gill, John Hillen, Jane Holl, Michael O'Hanlon, Gideon Rose, Stephen Stedman, and Robert Suettinger for reading and reacting to various drafts of the new material. I also want to thank Candice Geouge for ensuring that nothing was lost or changed (except intentionally) in marrying up the original edition to this one; Janet Walker for coordinating the manuscript process here at Brookings; Tanjam Jacobson for editing the new sections of the book; and Susan Woollen for working on the cover.

Richard N. Haass

Washington, DC
September, 1999

In the waning days of the Bush Administration, I was assigned the task of drafting a speech for the President. The speech was to constitute his final major public statement on national security issues. The subject was military intervention.

It was an obvious choice for the address. As commander-in-chief, George Bush had ordered U.S. forces into harm's way on numerous occasions, most dramatically in the Persian Gulf War, but also in Panama, the Philippines, and Liberia. U.S. forces had just entered Somalia; at the same time, the Bush Administration decided against involving military forces in Bosnia. There was confusion—why Somalia and not Bosnia?—and a growing debate about the proper role for U.S. military forces in the obviously complex and dangerous world emerging in the wake of the Cold War and the break-up of the Soviet Union.

I will leave to others to judge whether the speech delivered by President Bush at West Point on January 5, 1993, added to the debate. I came away from that experience with mixed emotions—pleased that we were able to articulate some serious views on an important and enduring public policy issue, frustrated that we had barely brushed the surface of an extraordinarily difficult and complex set of concerns.

Obviously, no speech could do justice to the subject of military intervention. I decided that I would return to it and attempt to produce a deeper and more comprehensive assessment. With time provided by the choices of the American voting public and the support of the Carnegie Endowment, I soon had the opportunity. This book is the result.

U.S. military intervention affects all Americans as well as count-less citizens elsewhere. I have tried to write not just for specialists but for anyone interested in the question of when military force is an appropriate policy tool for the United States. (For this reason, the appendices contain documents that are highly relevant but not always easy to find.) Throughout the book, I have labored to avoid two extremes: on the one hand, producing a set of hard rules that would attempt to dictate policy choices; on the other, avoiding all generalizations and simply saying, "it depends." The former would be unwise, while the latter would be unhelpful. My intent is to de-velop guidelines that both policymakers and citizens can use to de-cide when to favor the use of force and how best to use it for a broad range of foreign policy objectives.

This volume begins by looking at the post–Cold War world—what it is, why it is turning out this way, and what it holds for military in-tervention. Next, twelve cases are examined in which force was used (or, in some cases, not used) by the United States. The cases are taken largely from the post–Cold War period and provide background for the analysis that follows. In an effort to provide a common language, the text then goes on to define a broad range of purposes for which force can be used, and draws some lessons concerning both when and how we should use military force. The book shows how these ground rules could have been applied in the past and how they might be ap-plied to future interventions. Last, this study posits some policy con-sequences for the United States regarding where and how it should fight wars between states, where and how it should use force to af-fect conditions within states, and where and how it should seek to di-vide the labor of military intervention (with other countries, with re-gional bodies, or with the United Nations).

There may be utility in these conclusions for other would-be users of force. But the principal focus in this book is on the United States, with its own political system, interests, and military forces. For bet-ter or worse, the United States promises to be the world's sole su-perpower for the next chapter of history. Whether it determines to behave like one will depend in part on how Americans answer the question of when to intervene and how effectively they go about it.

INTERVENTION

CHAPTER ONE

THE DEBATE OVER INTERVENTION

o public policy issue is more controversial than the use of military force. As U.S. experience in Somalia and Bosnia in the early 1990s showed, it matters not whether we choose to intervene or stay aloof; the debate can be equally heated.

Such controversy is hardly new. Debates raged over U.S. entry into both world wars as well as over the conflicts in Korea and Vietnam. Questions of when, where, and how to intervene with military force inevitably raise basic questions of what our interests are in the world and what we are prepared to do on their behalf. Moreover, the use of military force is unlike most other forms of intervention, such as diplomacy, broadcasts, investment, or sanctions. It involves the immediate risk to life of everyone involved in the operation.

It is somewhat surprising, though, that the debate is taking place now, and with such intensity. There were grounds for supposing that the end of the Cold War would usher in a period of international relations in which political and military competition would diminish and the need to use force abroad would decline. By the onset of the 1990s, it looked as though a world was emerging in which democratic and market-oriented governments would dominate, in which age-old conflicts were being solved, and in which the United Nations was finally beginning to resemble the institution desired by its founders.[1] The Soviet Union and later Russia were working with the United States to manage conflicts; gone were the days when Moscow provided material and diplomatic backing for its clients while casting vetoes in the Security Council to frustrate Western initiatives. Neither Russia nor anyone else was able or willing to compete with the United States in the political-military realm on a global scale. It thus became possible for the Bush Administration to speak of building a new world order in which states did not threaten or use force to settle disputes and governments embraced democracy, human rights, and liberal economic policies.[2]

Things have turned out differently—very differently. To be sure, there are positive developments, including movement toward rapprochement in the Middle East, Cambodia, and South Africa, as well as considerable peace and prosperity in Latin America and East Asia. But there are many undesirable developments, including war in the Persian Gulf, continuing violence in Bosnia, a variety of humanitarian nightmares in Africa, and growing tensions on the Korean Peninsula. On balance, the post–Cold War world promises to be a messy one where violence is common, where conflicts within and between nation-states abound, and where the question of U.S. military intervention becomes more rather than less commonplace and more rather than less complicated.

FEATURES OF THE
POST-COLD WAR WORLD

The explanation for why there has been such violence, and why there could be even more in the future, is largely to be found in the nature of the Cold War and the effects of its passing. The Cold War, for all its risks and costs, and despite the reality of proxy wars and the potential for global holocaust, was not without its stabilizing aspects. "Duopolies," or systems based upon two poles, are simpler and easier to manage than those with multiple decision-making centers. Also, the Cold War was unique in that the fear of escalation to global nuclear war was an inhibiting factor for both superpowers. Rules of the road evolved that limited the direct use of force by both countries—not only in Europe, but also in regional conflicts anywhere, lest they create circumstances where direct confrontation between them could arise. These rules also placed limits on what either superpower could safely do in situations where the other had clear stakes. In the U.S.-Soviet relationship, competition was structured and circumscribed, formally in the case of arms control, informally in the case of regional competition.[3]

The end of the Cold War has altered much of this. First, the splitting up of blocs has resulted in a loss of political control. Decentralized decision-making and the diffusion of political authority increase rather than decrease the potential for international challenges and crises. It is unlikely, for example, that during the Cold War Iraq would have been left free by the Soviet Union, a principal source of its arms, to invade a country in a region known to be vital to the United States and the West. Similarly, it is far from certain that either China or Russia has the ability to persuade North Korea to forego the development of nuclear weapons, something that could set it on a collision course with the United States.

Second, with the relaxation of external threats and alliance systems, and the erosion of both empires and multinational states, nationalism has entered a new phase. Movements are defined more by ethnicity than by political ideology or territory, as various groups turn their energies inward, against populations within their borders. Such struggles are fast becoming commonplace. As Daniel Patrick Moynihan noted in a recent book, "Ethnic conflict does not require great differences; small will do."[4] The end to Europe's division and the demise of the Warsaw Pact provided an opportunity for Yugoslavs to redress long-held grievances. Similar "sorting out" of ethnic, political, and geographic questions can be seen in the former Soviet empire. The consequence is not only cross-border conflict, but also conflicts within former states or parts of them (often themselves new states), frequently resulting in massive flows of refugees and human suffering on a major scale.

Third, and closely related, is the revival of what might be called traditional great power politics. The world may not divide along an East-West axis, but powerful states in several regions have the ability to challenge the United States. Traditional friends and allies have demonstrated a greater willingness to stake out positions supportive of narrow national interests. More important, former adversaries are not necessarily assured partners. Russia and China have demonstrated a willingness and ability to conduct policies that run contrary to U.S. efforts and objectives.[5] While these countries no longer reflexively take an opposing view to U.S. positions, they still are engaged in power politics, pursuing their national interests as shaped by history, geography, culture, economics, and domestic politics.

Fourth, there is a relative weakening of the nation-state. Orwell's image of a future in which technology strengthened the organs of the state and its capacity to control its citizenry could not have been more wrong. Technology—television, computers, telephones, fax machines—increases the scope and impact of communications across state borders, making it much more difficult for governments to control what their citizens know and what others know about them. Moreover, the state is getting buffeted from "above" (from regional organizations, a stronger U.N. Security Council, a demanding International Monetary Fund) and from "below" (from nongovernmental organizations, corporations, and private individuals). These trends contribute to the difficulty and at times inability of existing governments to contend with challenges to their authority.

Fifth, the spread of advanced conventional and unconventional military technologies—chemical, biological, and nuclear, as well as the ballistic missiles to deliver them—is creating new instabilities. Those who possess unconventional weapons may be tempted to use them. Those who do not possess them, or those who see themselves as especially vulnerable to unconventional warfare, may be tempted to act against these capabilities before they can be fully deployed or employed by adversaries. Thus, there is not only a diffusion of political power, but a corresponding diffusion of military power— with greater potential for devastation if order breaks down.[6]

As a result of these developments, we are now living in a period of history that can be characterized as one of "international deregulation." There are new players, new capabilities, and new alignments, but as of yet, no new rules. As with almost any kind of deregulation, there are winners and losers. The result is a large number of new (if smaller) states and ethnic groups engaged in a seemingly endless struggle of competitive self-determination within and across boundaries. At the same time, the traditional sources of inter-state threats to peace continue to exist, except that they now have the potential to lead to conflicts much more violent in character.[7]

THE U.S. POSITION

The changes intrinsic to the post–Cold War world have created new, intense conflicts that complicate any prospective use of force by the United States. On the other hand, a number of political and technological developments enhance opportunities for the United States to use its military might effectively. The erosion of blocs and alliances makes it easier (in the political sense) to use force against individual states. There is little fear of direct conflict with another superpower growing out of a local confrontation with a third state, and less danger that a great power rival will furnish political, economic, and military support to a client embroiled with the United

States. The Bush Administration could make decisions about how to employ force against Iraq with far more latitude than earlier administrations enjoyed in regard to how Moscow and Beijing might react to possible escalations against North Korea or North Vietnam.

The Gulf War revealed that emerging technologies, in particular precision-guided munitions (PGMs), are creating new, more discrete opportunities for the United States to act militarily. Far fewer munitions can be used with equal or greater impact. The chance of unwanted (collateral) damage is less. Other technologies provide greater confidence of access to the airspace of another country at lower levels of vulnerability. Improvements in still other areas (from communications to intelligence) can enhance opportunities to use force effectively on modern battlefields.

But if there are new reasons as well as new opportunities for the United States to use force, there are no longer any clear guidelines for when and how to do it. The concept of "containment" provided some reference points for when force should be used. As George Kennan originally used it, "the main element of any United States policy toward the Soviet Union must be that of a long-term, patient but vigilant containment of Russian expansive tendencies . . . designed to present the Russians with unalterable counter-force at every point where they show signs of encroaching upon the interests of a peaceful and stable world."[8] Korea and Vietnam were the hallmarks of this era. Related calculations also affected how force should be used; indeed, an entire literature emerged about using force to signal adversaries of U.S. determination while also communicating a sense of limits, in order not to risk escalation to direct confrontation (and, with it, the danger of global nuclear war) with a rival superpower.

By contrast, in the foreseeable future, no single overarching foreign policy doctrine or touchstone is likely to command widespread popular and elite support. This is not for lack of imagination; rather it is an inevitable reflection of a more complicated world characterized by a diffusion of economic, political, and military power and relationships that resist easy or permanent categorization. In such a world, no intellectual edifice is likely to emerge that will suggest how specific local events are to be viewed and what the United States should do about them. Decision-making on a case-by-case basis—resembling debates during the pre–Cold War period—is all but unavoidable.[9]

But the problem confronting the United States is not just intellectual; it is also political. There is a strong sense in the country that domestic needs must come first and that the time has come for America to spend its peace dividend at home. With common definitions of national interest more elusive than ever, and with the external threat reduced in scale, building political consensus—both inside and outside the executive branch—around specific foreign policies is more difficult. At the same time, Congress not only remains highly assertive but is increasingly decentralized as an institution and hence more difficult to work with. Foreign policy-making is complicated further by the participation of individuals and groups holding very different views of U.S. priorities.[10] All this is taking place in a context of heightened media scrutiny and coverage. The net result is that policymakers have less latitude to pursue policies that are controversial, uncertain in outcome, and potentially expensive, as military interventions tend to be.

One should not exaggerate the relative simplicity or "clarity" of the Cold War.[11] The debates over U.S. policy in Korea and Vietnam revealed no agreement over how the doctrine of containment should be translated into specific policies. Prior to North Korea's invasion of its southern neighbor, there was little consensus that South Korea's independence constituted a vital U.S. interest; during the course of the war, especially after the massive Chinese intervention in late 1950, the debate over the limited nature of the U.S. strategy, designed to avoid engaging directly either China or the Soviet Union, was bitter.

The same was true for Vietnam. One view held that any use of force by the United States was unwise, that containment did not apply because what was at issue was less Soviet or Chinese expansion than local nationalism. Another view, found both in and out of government, disagreed not with the use of force per se but with how it was used, claiming that policies of gradualism and self-imposed limits should be jettisoned in favor of much more aggressive attacks on North Vietnam and neighboring sanctuaries.

Nevertheless, today's political environment is significantly different and, in important ways, more complex. All this creates opportunities for—and places special pressures and constraints on—the United States, the world's most powerful actor, arguably its only superpower. Liberated from the danger that military action will lead to confrontation with a rival superpower, the United States is now more free to intervene. Moreover, only the United States possesses the means to intervene decisively in many situations, in particular those that are more demanding militarily. Yet U.S. means are necessarily limited; there will always be more interests to protect than resources to protect them. The United States can do anything, just not everything. The need to choose remains inescapable. Questions of whether to intervene, as well as how, remain central.

Intervening too often poses an obvious danger. Any government indulging in what might be described as wanton uses of force would be guilty of acting irresponsibly, particularly toward those in uniform. Military intervention in any form is expensive. There is also the risk that indiscriminate intervention would leave the United States ill-prepared to meet inevitable contingencies; we cannot act in too many places at once. In addition, if an intervention fares poorly, or becomes a "quagmire," Americans could sour on their world role, triggering a renewed bout of isolationism at home and leaving the country ill-prepared to use force when it is really necessary. As James Schlesinger has pointed out, "America must be selective in its actions. It cannot take on all the world's troubles. The public will soon grow weary if this country takes on the role of world policeman, or world nanny, or international Don Quixote."[12]

At the same time, setting too high a bar against intervention has costs as well. Defining interests too narrowly or prerequisites for employing force too broadly would be tantamount to adopting a policy of isolationism. U.S. unwillingness to use force abroad could encourage mayhem overseas by those free of such qualms and accelerate arms proliferation, both by those who count on the United

States and those who oppose it. The United States would forfeit opportunities to affect world conditions and its interests for the better. In addition, unwillingness to intervene when it was warranted would prompt the American public to question the worth of funding and maintaining a modern military establishment.

The obvious challenge is how to get it just right. Every situation will pose a challenge. There will be no universal answer to the question of whether to intervene, and no answer will satisfy everybody in particular instances.

THE HISTORICAL DEBATE

Philosophers, scholars, practitioners, and journalists all have written and spoken about the subject of military intervention. For hundreds of years, experts have debated the political and legal grounds for going to war (*jus ad bellum*) as well as appropriate means of conducting wars (*jus in bello*). Much of what appears in today's newspapers and academic journals can be traced back at least in part to what someone wrote centuries ago. More important, today's debate is affected by these earlier contributions.

Christian "just war" theory, as first articulated by St. Augustine and as elaborated by Thomas Aquinas and others, dominated Western thought for centuries and provides a reference point for anyone speaking or writing on this subject. Wars are considered to be just if they are fought for a worthy cause, likely to achieve it, sponsored by a legitimate authority, undertaken as a last resort, and conducted in a way that uses no more force than is necessary or proportionate and that respects the welfare of non-combatants. Such thinking continues to enjoy authority far beyond the confines of the Church. The overall effect of this body of thought is to make it more difficult politically to go to war and more difficult militarily to fight one.[13]

A second influence on contemporary thinking are the jurists and legal scholars of the previous three centuries. Writing parallel to the

9

emergence and operation of the modern system of nation-states, they repudiated the amorality of Machiavelli and Hobbes, who tended to see war as inevitable and the decision to wage war for a wide range of purposes as an appropriate tool of statecraft. At the same time, these jurists were not content with the Church's approach to the just war, which they saw as too broad and too easily abused by allegedly legitimate authorities pursuing illegitimate ends.

"No other just cause for undertaking war can there be excepting injury received," wrote Hugo Grotius, arguably the most influential jurist to write on the subject.[14] Unlike the many thinkers who focused on refining the conduct of war, and unlike individuals such as Immanuel Kant who were dedicated to the more radical aim of abolishing war, Grotius sought to narrow the grounds under which force might be used legally by sovereign states. As such, he and others in the same tradition (notably Emmerich de Vattel in the eighteenth century) are fathers of one of the basic tenets of modern legal thinking and international relations, the right of self-defense, enshrined in the charters of both the League of Nations and the United Nations. The net impact of their work, like that of the principal religious scholars, has been to strengthen political and legal norms against the use of military force for purposes other than self-defense in relations between sovereign states.[15]

A third source of ideas affecting today's debate over intervention are the major strategists: Napoleon, Jomini, Clausewitz, Mahan, Hart, Fuller, Douhet, Mitchell, and others. With one principal exception—in the well-known words of Clausewitz, "war is not a mere act of a policy but a true political instrument, a continuation of political activity by other means"—their focus is more military than political, addressing how (as opposed to whether) to use force.[16]

Many of their fundamental ideas are familiar and continue to inform current military thinking. For example, a recent U.S. Army field manual lists nine principles of war—the importance of clear and attainable objectives, seizing and maintaining the initiative, massing one's combat power at decisive places and moments, employing one's forces to maximize economy, exploiting maneuver, unifying command, denying the enemy unexpected advantage through surprise, exploiting surprise oneself, and assuring simplicity in plans—all of which can be found in the classical literature.[17] Consistent with this body of writing, the Army's focus is on *how* to use the military instrument; the question of *whether* to use it, in contrast to doing something else or nothing at all, is largely left to others to consider and decide.

A fourth influence on today's thinking stems from work done primarily in the United States and Great Britain in the 1950s and 1960s. A number of defense thinkers, notably Henry Kissinger, Bernard Brodie, Morton Halperin, Thomas Schelling, and Robert Osgood, developed a literature devoted to war that was limited, in the words of Bernard Brodie, by "deliberate constraint."[18] Although the concept of limited war was not new—it was discussed at length by the traditional strategists and others and was implicit in the notion that war as an instrument of policy must be subservient to politics—analysts in the early years of the Cold War were motivated not simply by the primacy of politics but by the consequences of the nuclear revolution.

The premise of this body of work was that in the Cold War, with its inherent danger of escalation to nuclear exchanges on a global scale, the United States did not have the luxury to follow the optimal "all out" approaches articulated by the classical strategists. Instead, it was argued that the United States needed to develop doctrine and forces that would enable limited uses of conventional military force.[19] In this view, the doctrine of massive retaliation, a theory designed by the Eisenhower Administration to avoid future Korean War–like scenarios by threatening large-scale nuclear attacks to deter local non-nuclear challenges to U.S. interests, lacked credibility since the United States was in turn vulnerable to Soviet and Chinese nuclear attacks. In the writings of these academics, wars could and should be limited by the means employed, the goals, and/or the locale. Schelling in particular placed great emphasis on graduated or controlled escalation, a form of tacit bargaining based on the notion that, in the nuclear age, great power adversaries still shared an interest in avoiding escalation—an interest that motivated them to act with restraint. Military forces thus became instruments of communication as much as destruction.[20]

Vietnam provided a real-world laboratory for these views. Indeed, Vietnam and its "lessons" retain a powerful grip on how many Americans think about limited wars. But just as there is still no consensus about the Vietnam War itself, there is no consensus about what it purports to teach. The Vietnam experience has led some to believe that any foreign engagement will result in a quagmire and therefore ought to be avoided. Others conclude that we should not shy away from involvement and, more important, that any involvement should be carried out "without limits." Still others argue that Vietnam has no necessary lessons for today given all that is different in the world, and that it can be in the U.S. national interest to fight wars with limited means for limited ends.[21]

"Humanitarian intervention," the notion that outside parties have the right or even obligation to intervene to help peoples vis-à-vis their own governments or one another, represents a fifth influence on the contemporary debate over U.S. military intervention. This concept comes from a change in thinking that has created new pressures for the United States to use military force abroad to alter the domestic policies or change the leadership of other countries. It reflects the emergence of a new perspective about the inviolability of state sovereignty.

For the past several centuries, international law and most international relations theory was based on the premise that what takes place within the boundaries of a state is nobody else's business, and that for one state to insert itself into the internal affairs of another is a hostile act. This tenet of modern international society is designed to make inter-state violence less frequent. This thinking is enshrined in the United Nations Charter, which states, in Article 2 (4), that "All members shall refrain in their international relations from the threat or use of force against the territorial integrity or political independence of any state, or in any other manner inconsistent with the Purposes of the United Nations." This bias is reinforced in Article 2 (7), which states that "Nothing contained in the present Charter shall authorize the United Nations to intervene in matters which are essentially within the domestic jurisdiction of any state. . . ."[22]

One long-standing exception to this essentially unconstrained view of sovereign rights was put forward by John Stuart Mill. Widely if not universally accepted, Mill held that intervention by one state against another was permissible to help the people of a state throw off a foreign yoke. In short, counter-intervention was sanctioned. But Mill was careful to avoid advocating intervention in the absence of such provocation because it could lead to wars among the powers of the day and in any event would do little or no good as a people could not be saved from themselves.[23]

Today this highly circumscribed view of when external intervention is warranted in response to the internal situation of another state is giving way to a more expansive notion of humanitarian intervention. Although the change can be traced back decades to the U.N. Declaration on Human Rights and to the provisions of the Conference on Security and Cooperation in Europe (CSCE), both of which acknowledged human rights the state could not legally abridge, the new perspective has gained support in recent years. Today's critique is that intervention, including military intervention by outsiders, is legitimate and even necessary when a government severely represses the human rights of its own people or when the erosion of central governmental authority creates conditions in which innocent people are made vulnerable. Typical is the position endorsed by American Catholic Bishops in late 1993: " . . . the principles of sovereignty and nonintervention may be overridden by forceful means in exceptional circumstances, notably in the cases of genocide or when whole populations are threatened by aggression or anarchy."[24] It is now widely held that the international community was wrong in not doing more to thwart the efforts of Hitler in Germany or Pol Pot in Cambodia, who by their behavior forfeited the normal benefits and protection of sovereignty, and that it was right in intervening on behalf of Iraq's Kurds in 1991 and in Somalia in 1992.[25]

THE CONTEMPORARY DEBATE

The contemporary debate over military intervention is especially influenced by the many practitioners with experience in the executive or legislative branches. A number of prominent public figures—Caspar Weinberger, Gary Hart, George Shultz, Les Aspin, Colin Powell, George Bush, Bill Clinton, Madeleine Albright, Warren Christopher, William Perry—have expressed views on the question of when and how to use (or not use) force. Weinberger and Hart made their views known while the Cold War was still under way; others have done so since the Cold War's end. But all are of value, for they are the signposts informing the current debate and, in any case, what has stayed the same outweighs what has changed.

The most influential views, possibly because they were the first in the post-Vietnam era, were the guidelines articulated publicly in November 1984 by then-Secretary of Defense Caspar Weinberger. Weinberger posited six conditions that must be met before the United States commits its forces abroad. Three relate to *whether* force should be used: interests vital to the national interest of the United States or an ally must be at stake; there must be some reasonable assurance of congressional and popular support for the intervention; and the commitment of U.S. forces to combat should come only as a last resort. Weinberger's second three conditions relate to *how* force should be used: the United States should commit to force only if it is prepared to do so wholeheartedly and with the clear intention of winning; force should only be deployed on behalf of clearly defined objectives; and the size, composition, and disposition of the forces should be continually reassessed and where necessary adjusted as conditions change.[26]

Some eighteen months later, U.S. Senator Gary Hart put forward a similar list, which reflected the defense reform debate of the time and thus included some guidelines for employing force, such as a need for agreed command structure among the armed forces and operational simplicity and feasibility.[27] Like Weinberger's, Hart's guidelines, written in the aftermath of the Beirut tragedy and in the more distant shadow of Vietnam, had the intent (or at least the effect) of erecting tall barriers to the use of military force.

In the aftermath of the Persian Gulf War and amidst the debates over Bosnia and Somalia, others joined the debate. In his capacity as Chairman of the Joint Chiefs of Staff, Colin Powell discussed six questions that must be addressed before any decision or commitment to intervene is made: Is the political objective important, clearly defined, and understood? Have all other non-violent policy means failed? Will military force achieve the objective? What will the cost be? Have the gains and risks been analyzed? Once the situation is altered by force, how will it develop further and what will the consequences be? Powell emphasized the third concern, that is, determining beforehand that the use of military force is matched carefully to political objectives. Similarly, he has gone on record as being uncomfortable with policy that emphasizes keeping involvement limited rather than achieving a specific outcome. If force is to be used, he favors using it overwhelmingly to accomplish the mission.[28]

In fall 1992, before becoming Secretary of Defense, Chairman of the House Committee on Armed Services Les Aspin summarized his perception of the four critical elements of Powell's and the military's approach to using force: that force must be a last resort, that it must be used for clear purposes, that there must be a basis for withdrawal, and that it must be used in an overwhelming manner. Aspin then went on to take issue with this approach, characterizing it as an "all or nothing" school that would sharply curtail the use of military force for foreign policy purposes. Instead, he leaned toward what he described as a "limited objectives" school, one that supports more expansive use of military force by the United States for political purposes.

Aspin did not agree that limited uses of force create pressures for escalation and continued involvement. He argued instead that the collapse of the Soviet Union and the end of the Cold War enable the United States to use limited force for limited purposes. Even if the desired purpose is not achieved, the United States can "walk away" (thereby avoiding escalation and possible quag-mire) with little or no adverse consequences beyond the immedi-ate situation. In addition, he argued that new technologies make it possible in some circumstances for the United States to use com-pellent force, that is, to strike targets in one place (say, the capital city of an adversary) to influence behavior elsewhere (on a battle-field, for example). In particular, he cited the emergence of precision-guided munitions as an important development that allows strikes to be carried out with minimal risk to U.S. forces and with minimum collateral damage. In Aspin's views, these twin develop-ments—the end of the Cold War and the emergence of smart mu-nitions—increase the scope for limited uses of military force for political purposes.[29]

George Bush articulated his views on the use of military force in the waning days of his presidency. Against the backdrop of de-cisions to intervene militarily in Somalia and to avoid intervention in Bosnia, Bush argued for a case-by-case approach in deciding when and where to use force. He argued *against* using interests as an absolute guide, noting that "military force may not be the best way of safeguarding something vital, while using force might be the best way to protect an interest that qualifies as important but less than vital." Instead, Bush set out five requirements for mili-tary intervention to make sense: force should only be used, he said, where the stakes warrant it, where and when it can be effective, where no other policies are likely to prove effective, where its ap-plication can be limited in scope and time, and where the poten-tial benefits justify the potential costs and sacrifice. Multilateral support is desirable but not essential. What is essential in every case is a clear and achievable mission, a realistic plan for accom-plishing the mission, and realistic criteria for withdrawing U.S. forces once the mission is complete.[30]

More recent contributions to this debate have been provided by several senior members of the Clinton Administration, including the President himself. Secretary of State Warren Christopher, testifying in April 1993 before the Senate Committee on Foreign Relations, provided four prerequisites for the use of military force by the United States: clearly articulated objectives, probable success, likelihood of popular and congressional support, and a clear exit strategy.[31] Unlike the views of Congressman Aspin, but more similar to both Powell and Bush, Christopher was marshalling arguments that weighed against direct U.S. military intervention in Bosnia.

Most Clinton Administration pronouncements on the use of force have been concerned with U.S. support for or involvement in multilateral military efforts. In September 1993, for example, Madeleine Albright, the Permanent Representative of the United States to the United Nations, put forward a series of questions that need to be addressed before the United States would support U.N. peacekeeping operations. She listed five questions: Is there a real threat to international peace and security? Does the proposed mission have clear objectives and can its scope be clearly defined? Is a cease-fire in place, and have the parties to the conflict agreed to a U.N. presence? Are the financial resources needed to accomplish the mission available? And can an end point to U.N. participation be identified?[32]

Just four days later, President Clinton used the occasion of his annual address to the U.N. General Assembly to restate these questions, making clear that his purpose was to make it harder for the world body to launch such efforts. "The United Nations simply cannot become engaged in every one of the world's conflicts. If the American people are to say yes to U.N. peacekeeping, the United Nations must know when to say no."[33] And by May 1994, when the Administration issued its policy statement on "multilateral peace operations," the number of criteria that had to be met or considered had grown to eight in the case of U.N. operations for which the United States was asked to vote, fourteen if the United States was expected to participate in peaceful operations, and seventeen if U.S. participation was likely to involve combat.[34]

These pronouncements and documents have all affected current thinking about the use of military force; however, none is adequate. Each was shaped in part by recent or ongoing conflicts and political contexts in which policymakers sought to justify policies of intervention or non-intervention.

We now have new and more recent experience with military intervention, acting alone or in concert with others. Some of this experience is in "traditional" ways of resisting aggression by one state against another; some involves the more modern form of humanitarian intervention. This experience needs to be incorporated—or at least taken into account—in our thinking. It appears we cannot get away from the dilemmas of limited war, whether the limits are of means, ends, or both. The post–Cold War world requires its own consideration of military intervention, one that reflects the political and technological characteristics of this period in history.

CHAPTER TWO

RECENT CASES OF U.S. INTERVENTION

The United States has frequently used military force—broadly defined—both during and since the end of the Cold War.[1] Force is used every day for deterrence; examples include maintaining strategic nuclear forces on some sort of alert, stationing large numbers of forces in Europe and Korea, and the U.S. Navy sailing the high seas to signal U.S. interests and a readiness to act on their behalf.

The focus here, however, is on those uses more commonly understood as interventions. *Armed inter-*

ventions entail the introduction or deployment of new or additional combat forces to an area for specific purposes that go beyond ordinary training or scheduled expressions of support for national interests. This definition encompasses two quite different forms of military activity. The first is best termed "classic," that is, the use of force by the United States against another state or its military forces for essentially military purposes dealing with the state's potential or actual behavior beyond its borders. Classic uses of force can involve resisting aggression, denying a state control over the territory of another, or destroying emerging military capabilities. The second form of military endeavor involves the use of military forces for the purpose of affecting the internal situation in or politics of another state. Some have argued that only the latter type constitutes an intervention per se; in this study, however, "intervention" and "use of force" are used to cover both types of military undertakings.[2]

Many military interventions took place during the Cold War. Korea and Vietnam were by an order of magnitude the two largest such efforts. But any listing of significant U.S. military interventions during the height of the Cold War would also include the 1958 dispatch of nearly 15,000 marines to Lebanon in the aftermath of a coup in Iraq that overthrew the monarchy and brought Arab radicals to power; the support of Cuban exile forces that culminated in the 1961 Bay of Pigs debacle; the deployment in spring 1965 of more than 20,000 troops to the Dominican Republic to assist government troops in suppressing an uprising that the Johnson Administration feared would lead to "another Cuba"; the Nixon Administration's decision in December 1971 to send a carrier task force to the Indian Ocean to signal India (as well as China and the Soviet Union) that no further dismemberment of Pakistan would be tolerated; and the undertaking by the Ford Administration to reclaim the merchant vessel *Mayaguez* after it was seized by the Cambodian government in May 1975.

In the 1980s, there were the unsuccessful effort by the Carter Administration to rescue American hostages in Iran; the two deployments of marines to Lebanon in 1982; the October 1983 rescue effort cum pacification in Grenada; the April 1986 bombing of suspected terrorist sites in Libya; the positive response to Kuwait's request to place U.S. flags on tankers in the Persian Gulf area during the 1987–88 tanker war; and the 1989 operation in Panama designed to break Noriega's hold.

The pace of interventions has, if anything, picked up in the current decade. The Persian Gulf War is the major but not the only example. Several years later, U.S. forces remain involved in and over Iraq. The United States has also intervened—or debated whether to intervene—in the former Yugoslavia, Somalia, Haiti, and Rwanda.

During these same decades, other states have also undertaken military interventions in pursuit of their own perceived national interests. A quick sample would include Turkey in Cyprus; Cuba in Angola; the Soviet Union in Hungary, Czechoslovakia, and Afghanistan; China in Vietnam; Vietnam in Cambodia; both Israel and Syria in Lebanon; India in Pakistan (giving rise to Bangladesh) and then again in the Maldives and Sri Lanka; and Great Britain against Argentina in the Falklands/Malvinas conflict.

This study, however, focuses on U.S. military interventions in the 1980s and 1990s. It does so for several reasons: the ending of the Cold War and the emergence of a new geopolitical context in which the United States is pre-eminent and in which the danger of global war is much reduced; the availability of new technologies, military and otherwise; and the obvious impact of these more recent experiences on thinking in and about the United States.

Twelve interventions are described briefly below, forming the basis for subsequent discussion. In each case, an effort has been made to address similar questions, including an assessment of the U.S. interests at stake, the purposes and objectives behind the intervention, assumptions about the adversary and how much force would be required, the kind and amount of force actually used, consideration afforded public and congressional support, the involvement of other countries and organizations, and factors affecting when force was first used and when it was halted or intended to come to an end. The purpose is not to write the definitive history of any of these interventions but to provide sufficient information to facilitate comparison and permit the drawing of conclusions.

U.S. HOSTAGES IN IRAN[3]

On November 4, 1979, some nine months after the Ayatollah Khomeini had seized power in Iran in the final phase of a revolution that had ousted the Shah of Iran, a mob stormed the U.S. Embassy in Tehran and took more than sixty Americans hostage. On April 24, 1980, after nearly half a year of diplomacy and sanctions had proven fruitless, the Carter Administration launched a military operation to rescue the hostages.

The operation itself was modest—purposefully so. Secrecy was paramount as surprise was deemed essential. Except for Egypt (through which access was required by U.S. forces travelling to Iran), no allies were involved; Congress was not consulted. Concern for the welfare of the hostages led to a decision to mount a rescue mission rather than undertaking coercive use of force designed to persuade Iran to free the captives (which could have prompted Iran to harm them) or some larger effort (which could have led to a larger conflict). President Carter described the operation as a "mission of mercy—not a military attack."[4]

The planned operation involved several stages, the first of which was rendezvousing six C-130 transport planes (taking off from Egypt) and eight carrier-based RH-53 helicopters at a remote desert site where refueling and final preparations for the trip to a location just outside Tehran were to take place. From there the troops involved in the actual rescue operation—some 90 of the 180 involved in the mission—were to proceed by truck to the embassy compound and the Foreign Ministry, where several additional hostages were being held. The plan was based more on surprising an Iranian guard force judged to be unprofessional and vulnerable than on overwhelming the Iranians with brute force.

It never got that far. Two of the eight helicopters that left the USS *Nimitz* never made it to the first desert site, victims of bad weather and failing machinery. A third helicopter was unable to leave the site when it developed mechanical problems. The commander on the scene recommended to his superiors that they abort the mission because a minimum of six helicopters was believed necessary to carry out the mission. The recommendation was accepted. Further tragedy ensued when a helicopter and a transport plane collided as they were departing the site to return home. Eight soldiers died. The hostages, who were subsequently dispersed around Iran to preclude any future rescue mission, remained in captivity until January 20, 1981. No further military intervention was attempted, whether to rescue them directly, to coerce Iran to let them go, or to punish Iran after their release.

LEBANON [5]

In September 1982, two weeks ahead of schedule, 800 U.S. marines departed Beirut, their mission accomplished. The marines had been part of a multinational force of U.S., French, and Italian forces invited to Lebanon to facilitate the withdrawal of Palestine Liberation Organization (PLO) forces from Beirut. The withdrawal was triggered by the PLO's inability to repel Israel's invasion. The United States was willing to participate in the withdrawal, less as a favor to the PLO than as a means of eliminating the PLO's military presence in Beirut. U.S. participation was also seen as a step that could help end the fighting in Lebanon, which would contribute to that country's future and to peace in the region.

A month later, 1,200 marines — soon to grow to 1,800 — were back. Once again, they were joined by European counterparts, in this case some 4,000 French, Italian, and British troops. This time their experience was different. It lasted some 18 months, until February 1984. Far from being a success, this second multinational force (MNF) failed to accomplish anything of value and suffered significant casualties in the process.

The second MNF was sent in the wake of the assassination of Lebanon's President-elect and the massacres of Palestinian civilians in refugee camps by Lebanese Phalangists. The commitment was for a long term and explicitly supported by the U.S. Congress. Although the intervention was provided a set of rationales—to bolster Lebanon's struggling government, to restore Lebanon's armed forces so that they could disarm the various militia threatening public order, to bring about an environment that would lead to the withdrawal from Lebanon of all foreign forces, including those of Israel and Syria—the U.S. decision to re-enter Lebanon was less a considered policy decision than an impulse to "do something" to demonstrate U.S. concern (and to assuage American guilt) over what had taken place in the refugee camps despite U.S. promises that Palestinians would be safe after the PLO's departure.

Once there, U.S. forces did little more than hunker down in fixed, vulnerable positions near Beirut airport. By August 1983, less than a year after their arrival, they were exchanging fire with various factions in Lebanon's civil war; by September, U.S. warships and carrier-based fighter aircraft were bombing these same factions and Syrian air defense units so the Lebanese Armed Forces could maintain control of the heights overlooking the airport. The marines and the MNF as a whole had come to be perceived as a hand-maiden of Lebanon's Christian-dominated government, which had signed a controversial peace agreement with Israel the previous May. As a result, the MNF became a de facto participant in Lebanon's internecine struggles. On October 23, 1983, 241 marines became victims of those struggles, killed when a truck carrying some 12,000 pounds of TNT rammed into their barracks. Four months later, in early 1984, amidst increasing domestic opposition to their continued presence, the marines were "re-deployed," little more than a euphemism for being withdrawn.

GRENADA [6]

The Reagan Administration's decision to invade Grenada in October 1983—immediately after the Beirut tragedy—developed almost as quickly as the crisis that prompted the decision. Grenada was a small Caribbean island nation known to few Americans. Its brief experience with independence was stormy. Matters reached a nadir in mid-October 1983 following a coup that ousted the regime of Maurice Bishop. By October 19, Bishop was dead. Five days later, U.S. forces came ashore.

The public justification for the U.S. intervention emphasized the need to protect the lives of Americans on Grenada (some 600 medical students) believed endangered by the chaos and to respond to requests for assistance from the island's Governor-General and the Organization of Eastern Caribbean States (OECS).[7] It is not clear, however, that the students were in imminent danger; if they were, the scope of the U.S. intervention far exceeded any rescue mission. Moreover, the requests for assistance appear to have been prompted at least in part by the Administration. The motivation behind the use of force seems more a result of perceived opportunity: to replace a government friendly toward Cuba and the Soviet Union with one more pro-Western and democratic, to prevent the use of Grenada and its airport by either Cuba or the Soviet Union to further their peacetime or wartime interests in the region, and to show that the United States could still act effectively in the world in the aftermath of the Beirut debacle.

The intervention itself, code-named *Urgent Fury*, consisted primarily of U.S. troops, with token participation by neighboring states. The small (initially only 3,000) attacking force encountered unexpected difficulty in overcoming local resistance and took more casualties than anticipated. Despite poor intelligence, a host of communications problems, and apparent inter-service rivalries that hampered efficient planning and operations, the U.S.-led forces prevailed quickly. By December, most of the U.S. contingent was able to withdraw. Initial public and congressional skepticism in the United States (and congressional unhappiness over the lack of prior consultation) was overtaken by satisfaction with the results, a sense of relief that the students were "saved," and the quick departure of most U.S. forces.

LIBYA [8]

U.S. relations with Libya, strained for decades, deteriorated sharply in the 1980s. Clashes, both diplomatic and military, developed over expansive Libyan claims to territorial waters in the Gulf of Sidra, an extension of the Mediterranean Sea. (In one incident in August 1981, two Libyan aircraft were shot down by U.S. military aircraft.) Even more of a factor was Libyan support for international terrorism. In January 1986, the Reagan Administration responded by declaring a state of national emergency with Libya, a technical characterization that allowed the Administration to institute strict economic sanctions.

Matters came to a head beginning in March 1986. Following a build-up of U.S. naval forces in the Mediterranean, U.S. probes of disputed waters led to new incidents in the Gulf of Sidra. Then, on April 5, a bomb exploded in a West Berlin discotheque frequented by U.S. service personnel, killing one American soldier and injuring more than sixty others. Soon after, the U.S. government announced that it had indisputable evidence of Libyan involvement in the La Belle discotheque bombing.

The U.S. military strike against Libya came on April 15, 1986. The action was intended to retaliate punitively for Libya's role in the Berlin bombing (as well as support for terrorism in general) and to reduce Libya's capacity and will to carry out additional terrorist attacks in the future. Secretary of Defense Caspar Weinberger explained U.S. aims this way: "The President's goal was to preempt, or disrupt, and discourage further Libyan operations abroad and to teach Qaddafi a lesson that the practice of state-sponsored terrorism carried a high cost."[9] Working against these goals was a desire to minimize civilian casualties (for fear of losing the international support that would be necessary to isolate Libya) and a decision to minimize risk to the airmen involved in the raid (for fear that one or more would be taken prisoner by the Libyans and exploited for propaganda purposes). Both considerations kept the operation modest in size and narrowly focused. Because secrecy was at a premium, congressional leaders were only briefed after the planes were en route to Libya.

The strike involved U.S. aircraft based in Britain and on several carriers in the Mediterranean Sea. Five targets were chosen; four were terrorist-related, one was tied to air defense assets that posed a risk to the safety of U.S. crews. One of the four terrorist-related targets, the Azziziyah barracks, was also where many of Libya's leaders were based. (This last feature was meant to underline the coercive message and jeopardize Qaddafi's hold on power if not his life. Attacking high-value economic targets, including Libyan oil installations, was ruled out for fear of losing international support.) There was a high percentage of mechanical breakdowns and missed targets; mission effectiveness was degraded because of the long routes necessitated when France and Spain denied overflight. Some collateral damage to Libyan citizens and the French Embassy resulted when several U.S. bombs missed their targets.

Although the operation was widely considered successful at the time—damage to the targets was extensive, no planes were lost, and a signal was sent—its long-term impact is difficult to gauge. Libyan support for terrorism seemed to diminish; the State Department noted that Libyan-sponsored terrorism dropped from nineteen attacks in 1986 to only seven in 1987.[10] But there was no decisive policy shift away from terrorism. Indeed, within two years of the U.S. attack, the Qaddafi government carried out the destruction of Pan Am flight 103, resulting in the deaths of 270 innocent people.

PROTECTION OF GULF SHIPPING [11]

In late 1986, with the Iran-Iraq war still raging and with Iran increasingly threatening Arab states helping Iraq, Kuwait turned to both the Soviet Union and the United States for help in protecting its shipping. Months later, in spring 1987, the Reagan Administration agreed to provide assistance. It did so without imposing a time limit and despite considerable congressional opposition to getting involved in an operation that many feared would drag the United States into the seemingly endless Iran-Iraq war. By July 1987, U.S. warships and helicopters (joined by those of several European allies) were escorting formerly Kuwaiti tankers now reflagged as American.

U.S. motivations were wide-ranging, and included a desire to prevent the expansion of Iranian influence, something fully consistent with the pro-Iraqi tilt of U.S. foreign policy at the time; to deny the Soviet Union a major foothold in the Gulf; to act on behalf of U.S. interests in the free flow of Gulf oil and the principle of freedom of navigation; and to take actions that would be welcomed by moderate Arab states who were surprised and angry with revelations of the sale of arms by the Reagan Administration to Iran.

The actual use of force—Operation *Earnest Will*—was limited to convoying tankers, attacking Iranian patrol boats that were sowing mines, and carrying out modest punitive attacks on Iranian oil installations in retaliation for damages suffered by U.S. ships as a result of mines. The mission lasted just over a year—the Iran-Iraq war ended in the summer of 1988—and resulted in only limited damage to U.S. vessels.

Two ironies are worth noting. The greatest casualties suffered by the United States in the Gulf at the time came at the hands of an attack not by Iran but by Iraq on the USS *Stark* just days before the reflagging mission commenced. Second, the U.S. military action that most impressed Iranians—the destruction of an Iranian civil airliner in mid-1988 by the USS *Vincennes*—resulted from error, not calculation.

PHILIPPINES [12]

In early December 1989, with the attention of the world on the summit in Malta of Presidents Bush and Gorbachev, the decision was made by the Bush Administration to respond to requests for assistance from the government of Corazon Aquino in the Philippines, where some military leaders were attempting a coup d'etat. Government authorities requested the United States bomb airfields and bases controlled by the rebels; U.S. officials, however, considered such action unnecessarily provocative and entangling. Instead, two U.S. warplanes (F-4s, based inside the country) flew over the captured facilities. The U.S. aircraft did not fire, nor were they fired upon. Congress was notified after the intervention was completed.

The U.S. action had several purposes: to express support for the legitimate government, to maintain order and protect U.S. lives, to intimidate the rebels, and to ensure that only government-controlled aircraft would be able to fly. The aim was to achieve these ends without getting enmeshed in internal politics any more than necessary. The U.S. intervention was motivated by a desire to stand by a democratically-elected friend in a country where the United States maintained bases of declining but still considerable strategic importance.

It is difficult to measure precisely the impact of the U.S. intervention. The only thing that can be said for sure is that no rebel aircraft flew once U.S. planes appeared—they had conducted bombing and strafing missions prior to the U.S. action—and that the coup collapsed the following day. Nevertheless, the record suggests that the quick if modest U.S. response had a powerful psychological and political impact on both sides of the contest. This is perhaps attributable more to Philippine political culture, and the unique status the United States enjoyed in the Philippines at the time, than to the nature of the military operation itself.

PANAMA [13]

Some two weeks after the Philippine intervention, U.S. military forces intervened in the domestic affairs of another country. In Panama, as in the Philippines, the United States found itself entwined with a country with which it enjoyed a special relationship. On this occasion as well, the result was mostly positive. There, however, the similarity ends. The Philippine intervention was modest by any standard; the U.S. action in Panama in late 1989 was the largest military engagement of U.S. forces up to that point since Vietnam.

The intervention had its roots in the long and tangled history of U.S. relations with Panama, in the growing estrangement (going back several years) between the United States and Panamanian Defense Force (PDF) head Manuel Noriega, in Noriega's involvement in narcotics trafficking, and in Noriega's decision to nullify the results of the May 1989 election in which opposition candidates were denied their apparent victory and instead were attacked by PDF-supported "dignity battalions." The Bush Administration sought Noriega's ouster, calling for the people to overthrow him and instituting diplomatic and economic sanctions as added pressure. Despite these efforts, Noriega appeared entrenched. U.S. indictments issued in February 1988 for narcotics trafficking further reduced any incentive for him to compromise or step down.

In May 1989, the United States deployed nearly 2,000 additional U.S. troops to join the approximately 10,000 forces stationed in Panama. Against a backdrop of growing congressional criticism of Noriega's regime, the Bush Administration introduced a host of additional political and economic sanctions. The criticism increased following an unsuccessful coup attempt in October 1989, during which the U.S. military did not get involved because it did not have adequate intelligence about the intentions of the plotters. In mid-December, the Noriega-controlled Assembly declared war on the United States and renewed PDF-sanctioned harassment of American service personnel and their dependents. On December 19, the U.S. military launched an ambitious mission to neutralize the PDF and arrest Noriega. Congressional leaders were informed after the decision had been made and hours before operations commenced.

Operation *Just Cause* apparently surprised Noriega, not because he had no warning, but because he had discounted it. Possibly, repeated U.S. exercising had numbed him to intelligence reports. A more likely explanation was that he doubted U.S. willingness to act. The fact that the United States acted alone, without the military participation or even diplomatic support of others, added to the surprise. The United States employed what can only be described as overwhelming force given the relative weakness of the adversary; from the outset, U.S. forces took the initiative via intense attacks against a wide range of targets throughout Panama. Some 25,000 U.S. forces were involved, as were a large number of aircraft, including the F-117 stealth bomber.

Within days, organized resistance disappeared and the principal mission of rendering the PDF impotent was achieved. The secondary goal of capturing Noriega proved more difficult, but was accomplished within two weeks. Thus within a short time U.S. objectives were achieved: protecting the lives of U.S. citizens and the security of the Panama Canal, apprehending Noriega, and seating Panama's elected government. Forces involved in the invasion were withdrawn by mid-February 1990, less than two months after deploying.

THE PERSIAN GULF WAR [14]

The Persian Gulf conflict is in reality shorthand for multiple interventions. The immediate crisis can be dated from mid-July 1990, when Iraqi troops began their fateful build-up along Kuwait's border. For the most part, U.S. officials (including this author) discounted the likelihood of conflict; instead, it was widely thought that the Iraqi activity was intended to pressure

Kuwait on a number of matters, most importantly levels of oil production and price.

Alone among the Gulf states, the United Arab Emirates (UAE) approached the United States to ask for a demonstration of U.S. support. The Bush Administration proposed (and the UAE accepted) to conduct an exercise involving in-flight refueling by U.S. tankers of UAE combat aircraft. The United States asked other Gulf states, including Kuwait, if they would like to participate in a similar exercise as a signal to Iraq of their ties to the United States and their capacity to resist any Iraqi aggression. All demurred on the grounds that diplomacy was sure to work and that such an exercise risked bringing about the very crisis it was designed to avoid. The U.S.-UAE exercise went ahead. So too did negotiations. Indeed, by late July, it appeared that Saudi Arabia had succeeded in bringing Iraqis and Kuwaitis together for a series of meetings that would resolve the crisis.

The sense of relief was short-lived. On August 2, 1990, Iraq invaded Kuwait. Encountering little resistance, Iraqi forces quickly occupied the entire country—although Iraq failed to capture Kuwait's leadership or the bulk of its armed forces. Additional Iraqi forces poured into Kuwait; still other forces moved south within Iraq towards its border with Kuwait. To many it appeared that Iraq was preparing to invade Saudi Arabia. Even if not, it was thought that an Iraq that controlled Kuwait could intimidate Saudi Arabia and the other Gulf states—and as a result dominate the world's energy markets.

On August 8, President Bush announced that U.S. forces would be deployed to Saudi Arabia. Four U.S. goals were articulated for Operation *Desert Shield:* Kuwait's liberation; the restoration of Kuwait's government; the security and stability of Saudi Arabia and the entire Gulf region; and the protection of U.S. citizens. Underlying these objectives was the view that how the United States and the West reacted to Iraq's invasion of Kuwait would have a significant impact upon the character of post–Cold War international relations. Iraq's invasion and occupation of Kuwait was viewed as an attack upon the core principles of international order. In addition, there were more immediate concerns relating to energy interests and the well-being of America's traditional friends in the Middle East.[15]

The purpose of *Desert Shield* was to deter any Iraqi use of force against Saudi Arabia or others in the region while (it was hoped) political and above all economic sanctions persuaded Saddam Hussein to withdraw from Kuwait. At the same time, the U.S. military presence provided the foundation for an offensive military strategy if it became necessary. In time, *Desert Shield* involved over five hundred thousand U.S. troops and several hundred thousand additional soldiers from more than twenty-five contributing nations.

Another reason for using force was to enforce sanctions. It was believed that no oil embargo could work if based simply on the willingness of governments not to purchase.[16] Instead, the U.S.-led coalition decided that pipelines had to be closed (the principal Saudi and Turkish outlets were thus shut pursuant to U.N. Security Council Resolution 661) and tankers prohibited from leaving Iraq filled with oil. This in turn required a naval force, dubbed the Multinational Interdiction Force, which operated pursuant to Security Council Resolution 665.

By mid-autumn 1990, the deterrent strategy was in place. The Administration was confident it could accomplish the task of defending Saudi Arabia, but it was not certain that *Desert Shield* combined with sanctions would bring about Iraq's complete and unconditional withdrawal from Kuwait as required by U.N. Security Council Resolution 660.

In addition, there was growing concern that the passage of time would on balance work to the coalition's disadvantage. Although the United States and its partners were increasing their military strength and readiness, the diverse coalition (which included Israel and numerous Arab and Islamic states) was vulnerable to political divisions. Iraq was busy reinforcing its conventional military presence in and near Kuwait and developing unconventional weapons, activity that threatened to raise the costs to U.S. and allied forces if it proved necessary to liberate Kuwait by force. The passage of time also added to the personal and material costs of occupation borne by Kuwaitis.

On November 8, 1990, the Bush Administration announced that it had achieved the ability to defend Saudi Arabia, but that it would increase sharply (by a factor of two, from nearly 250,000 to 500,000) the size of its presence in Saudi Arabia and the region. The rationale was twofold: to compel or intimidate Iraq into fulfilling the relevant U.N. resolutions and, failing that, to put into place the means of liberating Kuwait by force.[17] As in August, Congress was informed of the decision as troops were dispatched to Saudi Arabia.

Against this backdrop, the pace of diplomacy quickened on several tracks. First, the Administration sought and gained international support on November 30, 1990, for U.N. Security Council Resolution 678, authorizing U.N. member states to use "all necessary means" to liberate Kuwait if Iraq was still in non-compliance with previous resolutions as of January 15, 1991. Second, the Administration sought and, after an intense struggle, received de facto authorization from Congress in early January to carry out the U.N. resolution. Third, there was one last chance at diplomacy when Secretary of State James Baker met with Iraqi Foreign Minister Tariq Aziz in Geneva on January 8, 1991.

With the success of the first two tracks and the failure of the third, the U.S.-led coalition launched Operation *Desert Storm* in mid-January 1991. *Desert Storm* was fought in two phases. The first was an air-only phase involving strategic use of air power, both to destroy key targets (command and control facilities, electricity grids, unconventional weapons production facilities, etc.) and to prepare the battlefield (by subjecting Iraqi troops to sustained bombardment and by destroying aircraft and tanks that could be used in any ground phase of the war). After six weeks of using advanced aircraft (including stealth and cruise missiles) to attack numerous Iraqi targets in both Kuwait and Iraq itself, the coalition initiated a ground campaign in late February. With control of the air complete, and with room for maneuver assured, U.S.-led coalition forces destroyed the bulk of Iraq's army. The ground phase of the fighting (which in reality was a combined ground, air, and sea effort) required only a hundred hours. It proved to be much less difficult—and U.S. and allied casualties were significantly less—than anticipated.

By the end of February, with Kuwait liberated and the Iraqi armed forces and support establishment decimated, the fighting stopped. The Iraqi political establishment was still in place and several army divisions or their equivalent were still intact. But it was calculated that any military benefits resulting from continued fighting would be modest. In addition, the Bush Administration judged that the purposes of the intervention had been accomplished, and that any further military effort—for example, to continue the air campaign or to occupy parts or all of Iraq in an effort to remake its government—would endanger U.S. and coalition forces and meet domestic and international resistance. Further fighting would also risk Iraq's unity, and a unified Iraq was considered desirable for regional stability.[18]

GULF WAR AFTERMATH: NORTHERN AND SOUTHERN IRAQ [19]

Senior Bush Administration officials expected that surviving Iraqi troops would return home in March 1993 and, together with their fellow citizens, rise up against the government of Saddam Hussein. Things did not work out that way. Instead, two challenges to Saddam's authority materialized: an Iran-backed Shia uprising in the south and a Kurdish uprising in the north. Saddam put them both down, beginning in the south, appealing to anti-Iranian and nationalist sentiments to forge popular support, especially among Sunni-dominated military and intelligence personnel. The United States remained aloof from these uprisings. Its political and legal mandates (from the United Nations, the coalition, Congress, and the American people) did not extend to such undertakings. Getting involved in Iraq's civil conflicts on behalf of parties with unclear objectives (or objectives the United States did not share, such as the break-up of Iraq) risked an open-ended commitment of U.S. forces, one that could end in a quagmire.

In early April, however, it was clear that the defeat of the Kurds in the north was turning into a rout. Millions of Kurds were streaming toward and across the border with Turkey, where they faced starvation, exposure, or both. Television and press accounts created public and congressional as well as international calls for a response. Normal relief efforts were overwhelmed. On April 5, President Bush announced a military airlift to drop supplies. After only ten days, it was clear that this effort—the largest U.S. relief operation ever mounted—could not resolve the Kurdish refugee crisis. As a result, on April 16, the United States overcame its reluctance to get involved more directly and announced, together with France, Great Britain, and Turkey, the creation of a security zone in the far north of Iraq from which all Iraqi military forces were barred, and a much larger "no-fly" zone (north of the 36th parallel) in which no Iraqi aircraft would be permitted to fly. No limit was set on how long the zones would remain in place.[20]

These measures brought about the return of the Kurds from the border areas of Turkey and Iran, as well as relative calm and considerable political autonomy to the northern part of Iraq. Meanwhile, the situation in the south began to deteriorate. In spring 1992, there was evidence that Iraq had used fixed-wing aircraft in operations designed to intimidate the largely Shia people of the south. There were also reports of increased repression in violation of U.N. Security Council Resolution 688. Finally, in August, the United States (acting on behalf of the coalition and pursuant to various Security Council resolutions) established a no-fly zone south of 32 degrees to facilitate monitoring of (and, indirectly, to promote) Iraqi compliance with U.N. requirements. As in the north, the zone was to remain in place indefinitely.[21]

For several months thereafter, Operation *Provide Comfort* in the north of Iraq and Operation *Southern Watch* in the south seemed to maintain an uneasy calm over the country. This ended in early January 1993, with the movement of Iraqi radars, missiles, and aircraft into the no-fly zones. On several occasions, U.S. aircraft took limited action against Iraqi aircraft and ground installations. In addition, the Clinton Administration launched two dozen cruise missiles in a unilateral operation against Iraq's intelligence headquarters in June 1993 to retaliate against what appeared to be an Iraqi attempt to assassinate former President Bush. In late 1993 and early 1994, mounting evidence of Iraqi repression of the so-called marsh Arabs in the south in violation of Security Council Resolution 688 (but not the no-fly zone) did not effect a U.S. military response.

FORMER YUGOSLAVIA [22]

A complete history of the Yugoslavia crisis (or more accurately crises) beginning in 1991 would be too much for our purposes here. At the same time, the role played by outside military forces, particularly the United States, has been modest. Still, it is important to include the situation in the former Yugoslavia, if only because the debate over what the United States and the West might have done illuminates so many questions relevant to this study.

It is difficult to know when to date the beginning of the crisis; one could easily go back to the post–World War I origins of what was the modern Yugoslav Republic or even earlier. Suffice to say, the Republic could not withstand the end of the Cold War, the associated demise of its Communist Party, and the loss of national cohesion that stemmed from an end to the Soviet threat and the collapse of a strong central government. The Serbian-dominated federal army could not contain the centrifugal forces stemming from nationalistic, religious, cultural, and economic differences and divisions; to the contrary, the army became an agent of long-frustrated Serbian nationalism and hence a part of the problem that quickly spelled the disintegration of what was Yugoslavia.

The beginning of the end of the former Yugoslavia came in June 1991, with the declarations of independence by Slovenia and Croatia, two of the six component republics of the former federal state. (The others were Bosnia, Serbia, Montenegro, and Macedonia.) The Yugoslav army made a brief attempt to crush Slovenia's move;

whether because of surprising Slovenian strength or a lack of Serbian will—there was only a negligible Serbian minority in Slovenia to identify with—the Serbs decided to back off and accept Slovenian independence.

Things did not go as well in Croatia, where the population was 12 percent Serbian. Serbian forces (recruited mostly from outside Croatia) gained the upper hand, seizing control of approximately one-fourth of Croatia's territory; Croatia turned to the United Nations, which in spring 1992 dispatched peacekeeping forces (U.N. Protection Forces, or UNPROFOR) to monitor the negotiated ceasefire. UNPROFOR met with some success, although fighting continued to break out sporadically later that year and in 1993.

The real Yugoslavia crisis, and the one that stimulated a great debate in the United States, began in March 1992 with the formal declaration of independence by Bosnia-Herzegovina. It was a step resisted by Bosnia's Serbs, who were boycotting its national parliament at the time. Bosnia, the most ethnically and religiously mixed of the former Yugoslav states, took this fateful action months after first Germany and then the European Community recognized both Croatia and Slovenia.

The Bosnians felt they had no good choice. Their dilemma was accurately described by one observer: "Trying for recognition was likely to bring on civil war; not trying would mean becoming part of a Serbian rump state, with 'ethnic cleansing' and the expulsion of Muslims."[23] Intense fighting materialized, as Serbia moved quickly to take control of the would-be Bosnian state that the United States and the European Community recognized in April 1992.

Against a backdrop of Serbian military gains and ethnic cleansing of predominately Muslim areas, the U.N. Security Council extended the mandate of UNPROFOR to Bosnia in June 1992. Eventually, 7,500 European peacekeeping troops were sent, initially to monitor one of the many ceasefires. In August, the Security Council authorized (in Resolution 770) member states to use "all measures necessary" to facilitate the delivery of humanitarian assistance; in October, Security Council Resolution 781 established a no-fly zone over Bosnia (but not as yet the means to enforce it).

As fighting continued, the international community (acting through the United Nations) took a number of measures. These included an embargo on arms to all the protagonists (that in reality favored the Serbs given their alternative sources of supply); economic sanctions levied against Serbia and Montenegro; dispatching a small number of U.N. peacekeepers to Macedonia to help prevent the crisis from spreading further; and diplomatic initiatives to partition Bosnia. The Vance-Owen plan, named for its two principal architects, U.N. envoy Cyrus Vance and European Community envoy Lord David Owen, was the most prominent such endeavor. It sought to create a new, loosely federated Bosnia consisting of ten areas, three predominantly Muslim, three Croatian, three Serbian, and one (around Sarajevo) mixed.

The U.S. response to developments in Bosnia during both the Bush and Clinton administrations was restrained by virtually any measure. In part, this was the result of a lack of consensus and clarity about the nature of U.S. interests, the nature of the conflict, and the potential effectiveness of external intervention. For some, Bosnia represented a humanitarian tragedy with few or no strategic U.S. interests—interests viewed as less important than avoiding a falling out with pro-reform leaders in Russia who could not afford to ignore pro-Serbian public opinion at home. Others felt the United States had an interest in strengthening the norm against external aggression and in avoiding both the spread of violence elsewhere in Europe and a poor precedent for the post–Cold War world. Similarly, there was disagreement over whether Bosnia represented a civil conflict or a more traditional inter-state conflict. In light of international recognition of the independence of Bosnia-Herzegovina, the conflict was technically a war between states. Many, however, viewed it as essentially a civil war, given its ethnic dimension and the newness of the separation.

The biggest disagreements in the debate, however, were over policy options. Some people clearly favored indirect or even direct military involvement by the United States and the Europeans, to provide arms to the Bosnian Muslims and/or to strike Serbian targets to coerce them into halting their aggression. Others doubted the potential effectiveness of these actions and feared that their lack of success would lead the United States ever more deeply into a conflict that outsiders could not solve.

The debate came to a head in May 1993, when Secretary of State Warren Christopher travelled to Europe. He proposed selectively lifting the embargo to allow arms to reach the Bosnians and a possible use of air power against the Serbs—the option was dubbed "lift and strike"—to coerce Serbia into ceasing hostilities and accepting a cantonized Bosnia along lines somewhat more favorable to the Bosnians than those developed by Owen and Vance. The lift and strike option found little favor with the Europeans, who feared it would result in retaliation against their troops on the ground and interrupt what few relief supplies were reaching the Bosnian people. They were also concerned that the more ambitious and assertive policy being proposed would undermine prospects for the Vance-Owen diplomatic effort. Meanwhile, the Vance-Owen plan was widely criticized in the United States for rewarding aggression. While it offered Bosnia's Muslims considerably more territory than they then controlled, it also offered them considerably less than what they had before the fighting began. Confronted with European opposition to U.S. proposals but uncomfortable with what the Europeans were supporting, the Clinton Administration backed off pushing any approach.

In early August, U.S. diplomacy was more forceful, this time gaining NATO approval for limited strikes against Serbia if it continued to block the flow of food and other supplies into the Bosnian capital of Sarajevo. But the impact of this development was diluted by what it represented. Implicit in the summer 1993 U.S. proposal was acceptance of the new status quo on the ground, namely, a de facto partition of Bosnia with Serbs and Croats controlling the lion's share of the territory. Roll-back to the status quo ante bellum had been effectively jettisoned as an objective. Strikes were never authorized, as Serbia always seemed to pull back from the sort of blatant, extreme measures against the Bosnian population that risked provoking NATO action.

For nearly two years, the United States and NATO eschewed carrying out substantial military undertakings, including the use of air attacks to destroy Bosnian-Serb weapons and disrupt supply routes. Strategic air attacks on Serbia either to punish or coerce were ruled out, as was arming the Bosnian Muslims. The rhetoric employed by the Clinton Administration was more assertive than that employed by its predecessor; the policy for the most part was not.

The low level of U.S. military involvement in the former Yugoslavia during this time assumed several forms. U.S. naval and air forces participated in U.N. sanctions enforcement efforts designed to pressure Serbia and Montenegro (who had joined to form the Federal Republic of Yugoslavia, a self-declared successor of the former Yugoslavia not recognized by the West). In mid-1992, U.S. aircraft flew supplies of food and medicine into Sarajevo; beginning in February 1993, the United States began to drop food and medicine by air to alleviate shortages caused by the inability of UN-PROFOR to overcome Bosnian Serb interference with relief efforts. As of mid-April 1993, U.S. military aircraft participated in NATO's enforcement of a no-fly-zone (Operation *Deny Flight*) authorized two weeks earlier by Security Council Resolution 819. And in July 1993, the United States sent 300 troops to Macedonia to join 700 Scandinavian troops under U.N. auspices to deter spread of the war in that direction.

Matters changed somewhat after February 5, 1994, in the wake of a mortar attack on a Sarajevo marketplace that left sixty-eight dead and caused many in Congress and the public at large to demand action. Citing four "distinct interests"—avoiding a broader European war, preserving NATO's credibility, stemming refugee flows, and a humanitarian stake in stopping the strangulation of Sarajevo and the slaughter of innocents in Bosnia—President Clinton adopted a new tack, one endorsed by NATO and the United Nations. The result was the creation of a zone extending twenty kilometers from the center of Sarajevo in which heavy artillery and mortars would not be permitted. All parties were given until February 21 to either withdraw such weapons from the exclusion zone or hand them over to U.N. personnel; any weapon found in violation would be destroyed by U.S. aircraft operating in concert with NATO and the United Nations. Compliance proved to be near complete. No air strikes were launched, although air power was employed a week after the deadline passed when four Serbian fixed-wing aircraft found to be in violation of the no-fly zone (established earlier over the entire country) were destroyed by U.S. F-16 aircraft deployed as part of Operation *Deny Flight*.[24]

At the same time, both the United States and Russia undertook diplomatic initiatives. Russian peacekeeping forces took up positions in territory previously held by Serbs, and Russian diplomats made explicit their opposition to any air strikes against Serbian positions. Simultaneously, U.S. diplomats fostered a federation of Bosnian Croats and Muslims and became much more active proponents of a settlement that would recognize ethnic partition and most Serbian military gains.[25]

This is how matters stood until late March 1994, when Serbian forces began shelling the 65,000 mostly Muslim inhabitants of Gorazde, a city just southeast of Sarajevo. The attacks were especially significant because Gorazde was one of six Bosnian cities designated as safe areas by the United Nations in Security Council Resolution 824. Moreover, under the terms of Security Council Resolution 836 (passed in June 1993), member states were allowed to use force to protect U.N. personnel under attack in any safe area.

The initial reaction of the Clinton Administration was to rule out, publicly and explicitly, the use of force to protect Gorazde.[26] (Indeed, even before the siege of Gorazde, both Secretary State Warren Christopher and Secretary of Defense William Perry had gone on record opposing any replication elsewhere of the Sarajevo formula. Perry went so far as to argue that airpower would not be effective against Serb infantry and might cause civilian casualties.[27]) Then, amidst much public criticism and powerful television images, the Administration reversed course.[28] Against a backdrop of continued Serbian attacks, and working with NATO and the United Nations, the United States struck twice. On April 10, two U.S. F-16 aircraft attacked a Serbian tank and a "command center" just outside Gorazde; a day later, a U.S. F-18 attacked several Serbian armored vehicles.

The highly limited attacks failed to persuade the Serbs to lift their siege of Gorazde. A week and a half later, and more than three weeks after the Serbian offensive began, NATO (at U.S. behest) issued an ultimatum to the Serbs, ordering them to stop their attacks, pull back from Gorazde, and stop interfering with relief efforts. NATO threatened to attack if these conditions were not met.[29] As in Sarajevo, the Serbs complied enough to escape NATO attack, although fighting continued and even intensified in other areas of Bosnia. At the same time, new diplomatic efforts designed to bring about a political settlement were initiated by a "contact group" consisting of the United States, Russia, France, Britain, and Germany. These efforts culminated in July 1994 when the warring parties were handed a proposed map that created a loosely-federated, independent Bosnia in which Serbs would control 49 percent of the territory (down from the 70 percent they controlled) and the Muslim-Croat federation 51 percent (an improvement over their situation at the time, but substantially less than they began with). Diplomatic prospects faded quickly, however. Bosnian Serbs rejected the proposed plan, and when they violated the terms of the zone around Sarajevo, NATO initiated new airstrikes against the offending weapons. Bosnia's Serbs and Muslims both intensified their fighting around Sarajevo.[30]

SOMALIA [31]

Throughout 1992, the situation in Somalia deteriorated steadily. Governmental authority was minimal. Rival armies and bands fought constantly and interfered with international humanitarian efforts. A growing number of Somalis were suffering from malnutrition and dying of starvation. In mid-August, the United States announced that it was prepared to provide military airlift to transport a 500-person U.N. force to Somalia pursuant to U.N. Security Council Resolution 751 to help provide the security needed to deliver food and other relief services and supplies. The United

States also announced it would use military airlift to deliver food and other relief supplies.

In the following months, television pictures and other eyewitness reports showed that the relief effort was not making much difference. Despite the airlift and the presence of some 3,500 U.N. troops (UNISOM I), hundreds of thousands of Somalis died; possibly millions more faced the same fate. When U.N. Secretary General Boutros Boutros-Ghali asked the United States to do more, it agreed. President Bush announced on December 4, 1992, that, pursuant to U.N. Security Council Resolution 794, U.S. forces would " . . . create a secure environment in the hardest hit parts of Somalia so that food can move from ships over land to the people in the countryside now devastated by starvation."[32] Bush stressed that the U.S. mission was limited, particularly in the political sphere. It would open supply routes, get food moving, and prepare the way for a U.N. peacekeeping force which, as soon as it could be arranged, would be given responsibility for maintaining order. The thinking was that a short, U.S.-dominated humanitarian phase would give way to a longer, U.N.-dominated political effort.

As President Bush reported in his message to Congress on December 10, the rationale for the U.S. effort was humanitarian; no strategic interests were at stake. The Senate did not pass a joint resolution authorizing the deployment until February 4, 1993; the House did not act until May. But Operation *Restore Hope* began months earlier on December 9, when the first U.S. troops landed in Somalia. It was a largely U.S.-run and manned operation under U.N. auspices. Major airfields, ports, and land routes were seized; local bands mostly held on to their weapons. The U.S. troops faced some sniper-fire and rock throwing but no organized resistance. Food and medicine were delivered on a large scale, saving hundreds of thousands of lives.

By mid-January 1993, U.S. troop levels peaked at around 25,000. Less than three months later, U.S. force levels had shrunk to half that amount with troops from other countries filling the gap. The timetable for the formal handover to the U.N. successor force (UNISOM II) got pushed back several times from mid-winter to early May, when approximately 25,000 troops from more than 30 countries took the place of the U.S. force. Even so, the U.S. withdrawal was less than total; a residual combat force of some 1,300 U.S. combat troops remained in and around Somalia under U.S. command (in addition to 3,000 U.S. logistics troops under U.N. command) to help deter and deal with challenges that might arise.

U.S. involvement did not end there. Within months the Clinton Administration found itself far more deeply involved in Somalia than either it or the Bush Administration had anticipated. U.S. patrols of Mogadishu became more frequent. In early June, against a backdrop of slowly mounting violence between some of the clans and external forces, a contingent of Pakistani forces detailed to the United Nations was ambushed. Two dozen Pakistani soldiers were killed, allegedly by the forces of Somali warlord Mohammed Farah Aideed. Seeing the U.N.'s credibility at stake, the Security Council passed a new resolution (837), calling for the arrest and punishment of those responsible, and mounted (with the United States) military operations aimed at weakening and if possible capturing Aideed. What followed were more aggressive American attacks on Aideed positions and higher casualty rates for both U.S. and U.N. troops. Outbreaks of fighting, increasingly resulting in civilian deaths, became the norm.

The Clinton Administration, fearing that all that had been accomplished to date was in jeopardy, articulated a more ambitious set of objectives for Somalia. Speaking in late August 1993, Secretary of Defense Les Aspin stated that U.S. requirements prior to withdrawal included restoring calm to south Mogadishu, progress in disarming the warlords, and the establishment of credible local police forces in major population centers.[33] The new policy amounted to nothing less than nation-building, but the forces introduced to implement these expanded goals were modest. No new authority was requested from Congress. The turning point in the intervention came on October 3, 1993, when eighteen U.S. soldiers were killed in a single engagement. Poor coordination between U.S. and U.N. authorities exacerbated a situation in which the U.S. troops found themselves outnumbered by local forces.[34]

(There were 1,700 U.S. combat forces in Somalia at the time, backed up by only a handful of helicopters and gunships.) Although hundreds of Somalis were killed in the encounter, the perception was of U.S. failure—a view reinforced by television images of a dead soldier being dragged through the streets of Mogadishu and pictures of a captured U.S. airman. A major public outcry and congressional debate ensued. Many in Congress, already unhappy after three U.S. soldiers died when their helicopter was shot down on September 25, demanded an immediate or at least near-term withdrawal of U.S. forces.

Four days later, on October 7, President Clinton announced a new policy: the United States would increase its military presence in and around Somalia (by over 5,000 troops and 100 armored vehicles) for a period of just under six months. At the end of that time, virtually all U.S. troops would be withdrawn. Distancing himself from what had become the de facto purpose of U.S. policy— "It is not our job to rebuild Somalia's society or even to create a new political process that can allow Somalia's clans to live and work in peace"—Clinton stated four objectives behind the decision to send more troops for a limited period: to protect troops and bases, to keep open key roads and ports, to pressure those who would attack the supply routes or U.S. forces, and to provide a context for a Somali political process.[35]

On the ground, patrols of Mogadishu largely ended, as did the effort to find and arrest Aideed. (The Security Council made this official on November 16, when it called for the establishment of a commission to investigate the attacks on the Pakistani peacekeepers.) Emphasis returned to brokering a political solution that would include Aideed and his followers, a change symbolized by the U.S. decision just weeks later to fly Aideed on a U.S. military transport to a peace conference in Ethiopia. The enlarged U.S. presence became little more than an inactive group of soldiers preoccupied with self-protection and counting the days until March 31, 1994.[36]

HAITI [37]

After decades of violent autocratic rule, it appeared to many observers that Haiti and its six million inhabitants turned a corner in December 1990 with the clear-cut election of the Rev. Jean-Bertrand Aristide. But Aristide, who was inaugurated as Haiti's President in February 1991, ruled for less than eight months, ousted that September in a coup led by military leaders.

Despite controversy surrounding Aristide stemming from charges that he tolerated or even encouraged violence against his political opponents, the United States and other members of the Organization of American States (OAS) reacted with dismay to his overthrow. Economic sanctions were imposed by the OAS almost immediately. The principal effect of this isolation was to increase the hardship of daily life for average Haitians, some of whom were also targets of political terror. Many Haitians tried to flee by any possible means to the United States. In May 1992, the Bush Administration deployed the Coast Guard to prevent Haitian immigrants from reaching U.S. waters.

Although he had criticized the Bush Administration for this policy during the 1992 campaign, President Clinton and his administration kept U.S. immigration measures in place out of fear that hundreds of thousands if not millions of Haitians would take the dangerous voyage to the United States. At the same time, the Clinton Administration intensified diplomatic efforts to arrange for the return of Haiti's ousted President. U.N. sanctions entered into force in June. These efforts appeared to come to fruition in early July 1993, when Haitian leaders meeting under U.N. auspices at Governors Island agreed to restore the elected government and President Aristide himself by October 30.

As part of the handover of power, just over two hundred U.S. and Canadian soldiers were dispatched by ship to Haiti with the mission of training Haiti's security forces and participating in some engineering projects. (Authorized by U.N. Security Council Resolution 867 of September 1993, they were part of a combined police and military contingent set to number nearly 1,300.) They arrived outside Port-au-Prince in early October, but were ordered not to disembark when mobs—reportedly paid thugs—gathered at the port. The forces, operating under authority derived from Chapter 6 of the U.N. Charter, had no mandate to use force other than in self defense. Emboldened by events in Somalia, Haiti's military rulers decided not to honor the commitments made at Governors Island; just as clearly, the Clinton Administration, reeling from the deaths of eighteen soldiers in Somalia, determined not to place these non-combat forces in a vulnerable position. The ship was withdrawn and sent to Guantanamo. In its place, the Administration sent six warships to the area to enforce U.N. sanctions that were re-imposed when Haiti's military rulers violated the Governors Island commitment. The hope was that this embargo of Haiti would create conditions for renewed diplomacy and the restoration of democracy.

The hope went unrealized. By spring 1994, it was increasingly apparent that renewed sanctions had no positive effect. Haiti's military leaders were able to insulate themselves from the effects of sanctions, a task made easier by the porous nature of Haiti's border with the Dominican Republic. U.S. attempts to negotiate Aristide's peaceful return came to naught. Meanwhile, Aristide languished in Washington, while the bulk of Haiti's people struggled to survive. The Clinton Administration's response to these developments was to propose still stronger sanctions, instituted by the U.N. Security Council on May 21. But the result of tougher sanctions and new U.S. procedures for screening Haitian refugees was a massive outflow of Haitians seeking to come to the United States. By mid-July 1994, U.S. policy looked to sanctions and the threat of a U.S.-led invasion to persuade Haiti's rulers to leave before the refugee problem grew too large to manage. At the same time, both to back up sanctions and to provide an alternative to them, U.S. diplomatic and military preparations for an invasion of Haiti became more intense and visible.

CHAPTER THREE

THE VOCABULARY OF INTERVENTION

T he phrases "use of force" or "military intervention" are necessarily broad and encompass a host of possibilities, as the case studies in the previous chapter illustrate. Some uses of force reflect more than one motive, in part because bureaucratic consensus to act often can only be achieved if people are free to sign on to a policy for their own reasons. Nevertheless, it is important to be as precise as possible about the purposes of an intervention. The differences among various kinds of military interventions go to the heart of the question of whether force should be used in a given situation and how it can be used effectively.

Interventions differ in their scale, composition, duration, intensity, authority, and, above all, objective. They need not involve "shooting"; to the contrary, shooting is only one way to use military force. Interestingly, the distinction that is generally *not* useful is the one most commonly heard, that is, "offensive versus defensive." Not only is this distinction primarily in the eyes of the beholder, it also breaks down in the real world. The same weapon system can be used both ways. Moreover, one can and normally does have tactical offensive operations taking place within an overall defensive strategy, and tactical defensive efforts within the context of an overall offensive strategy. As a result, the distinction is best set aside or, if used, should be done so with the knowledge that it may be impossible to sustain.

Military interventions can be classified according to the following purposes: deterrence, prevention, compellence, punishment, peacekeeping, war-fighting, peace-making, nation-building, interdiction, humanitarian assistance, and rescue. In addition, indirect uses of force provide military assistance without engaging in direct intervention.

DETERRENCE

The standard definition of deterrence is " . . . the persuasion of one's opponent that the costs and/or risks of a given course of action he might take outweigh its benefits."[1] The movement and use of military forces is obviously a critical component of a deterrence strategy. Forces can be positioned, deployed, and/or exercised to signal the existence of interests and the readiness to respond militarily if those interests are either threatened or attacked. Deterrence involves a prophylactic use of threatened force, designed to persuade an adversary not to take a particular action.

Deterrence can be the purpose behind long-term deployments, such as the U.S. military presence on the Korean Peninsula or in

Europe since the end of World War II. Such deployments are structural, to remain until the political map or international situation fundamentally changes. The decision to place several hundred U.S. troops in Macedonia in early 1993 and the maintenance of air forces in southern Turkey to discourage Iraq from attacking its Kurdish population are more recent examples of this phenomenon.

Deterrence can also take the form of a response to a specific or tactical situation that emerges suddenly—say, the perceived threat to shipping in the Persian Gulf in the late 1980s when the United States decided to "reflag" Kuwaiti vessels, or the stationing of U.S. and coalition forces in Saudi Arabia under *Desert Shield* to deter Iraqi aggression against Saudi Arabia following the invasion of Kuwait. An unsuccessful example of such "tactical" (as opposed to "strategic") deterrence was the U.S.-UAE tanker exercise that failed to dissuade Iraq from invading Kuwait.

It is also possible to point to situations in which tactical deterrence was not used; for example, forces might have been inserted into Kuwait in July 1990 to deter the Iraqi invasion or into Bosnia in 1991 to deter the Serbs. U.N. Secretary General Boutros Boutros-Ghali describes such interventions as "preventive deployments."[2]

PREVENTIVE ATTACKS

Preventive uses of force are those that seek either to stop another state or party from developing a military capability before it becomes threatening or to hobble or destroy it thereafter. For the target country, preventive attacks are the proverbial bolt out of the blue. An example is Israel's attack against Iraq's Osirak nuclear reactor complex in 1981. The *Desert Storm* coalition's attacks against Iraqi unconventional warfare capabilities inside Iraq involved preventive employment of force; the capabilities targeted were not yet in a state of development to affect the course of this battle. Similarly, preventive action is often discussed as a possible course of action to destroy North Korea's nuclear capability.

Preventive attacks have several inherent shortcomings. To begin with, they can be difficult to conduct successfully. A good deal of information is needed just to know what exists and to assess its significance—information that can be hard to come by. Such programs tend to be surrounded by walls of secrecy and may use tunnels, camouflage, etc. to divert suspicion. Even more precise information (information that is instantly outdated if something is moved) is needed to target a capability. Also necessary is the capacity to carry out the mission, which tends to demand surprise and great accuracy. In addition, an attack—say, on a nuclear or biological research or weapons facility—may cause substantial harm to innocent civilians in the area. Perhaps most important, it is impossible to know in advance how the object of the attack will respond; a preventive attack, even if successful, might be the beginning rather than the end of the confrontation. It is in part for this reason that the United States has thus far refrained from attacking North Korean nuclear facilities; even if successful, it could start a large conventional conflict.

Closely related to preventive uses of force are *preemptive* actions. The difference is one of timing and context. Preemptive uses of force come against a backdrop of tactical intelligence or warning indicating imminent military action by an adversary; they may constitute actions or attacks before the other side acts or attacks or even after hostilities have begun but before the targeted forces have been introduced into battle. Israel's air strikes against its Arab neighbors in June 1967 are an example. So too are the U.S. preemptive rescue mission in Grenada in 1983 and to some extent the U.S. invasion of Panama in 1989.

Preemptive and preventive strikes are similar in that they can raise political problems with skeptical publics, both domestic and those of neutrals and allies. It is important to be able to demonstrate the necessity of acting, to make the case that the costs and risks of striking were less than those of holding back, and to prepare for any possible retaliation.

COMPELLENCE

Compellent uses of force are discrete, consciously limited uses of force designed to sway decision-making. Compellent interventions seek to destroy some carefully chosen targets of value (in the eyes of the people or leadership of the targeted country) or at least demonstrate an ability to destroy such targets. The goal is to persuade the adversary to alter his calculus, to re-assess whether his offending actions are worth the potential cost, and to change his behavior as a result.

It is important not to confuse compellence with deterrence. Robert Art provides the following guide: "The distinction between compellence and deterrence is one between the active and passive use of force. The success of a deterrent threat is measured by its not having to be used. The success of a compellent action is measured by how closely and quickly the adversary conforms to one's stipulated wishes."[3]

Of the two, compellence generally tends to be the more difficult course of action to carry out successfully. As Thomas Schelling has pointed out, "Compellence . . . usually involves initiating an action . . . the overt act, the first step, is up to the side that makes the compellent threat."[4] But if compellence requires more of the one initiating the action, it also asks more of the recipient. In this regard, Scott Sagan makes an important observation: "A state that is deterred can deny that it ever had the intention of attacking another; a state that is coerced into changing its behavior, however, often faces the loss of prestige that comes from having publicly succumbed to pressure from another power."[5] As a result, successful compellence can require a complementary set of concessions, real or face-saving, to make it politically possible for the adversary to comply.

Historical analysis suggests that compellence is more likely to succeed if the goal is specific and relatively modest—to persuade an adversary to stop doing something—than if the goal is more ambitious, say, to have an adversary reverse what it has already done. Bringing about a change in the adversary's general behavior, or in his nature or political composition, is even more difficult to achieve. Other critical factors that appear to determine the prospects for compellence are the perceived balance of interests (compellence tends not to work if the issue is of greater importance to the adversary) and the immediate (as opposed to potential) military equation.[6]

Depending upon the targets selected, a compellent use of force may have residual military benefits, for example, destroying forces that could be brought to bear on a battlefield; but this is secondary. The goal could be to target and possibly destroy something the other side values (e.g., facilities closely tied to the political and/or military leadership, key economic installations, or something that would weaken the leadership in the eyes of its public) or simply to show willingness and ability to attack any of these things. The United States tried this (albeit half-heartedly) in Lebanon against various militia and the Syrians in 1983. It is also the approach suggested by some analysts for the former Yugoslavia in the form of air strikes against selected targets in Belgrade. Compellence also motivated the summer 1994 exercises designed in part to persuade Haiti's military leaders to give up power or risk being invaded and overthrown.

As in the case of deterrence, the success of compellent uses of force depends entirely upon the target of the intervention. What is relevant is not the force used but the reaction to it. It is impossible to know in advance whether a given use of force will have the desired effect. If it does not—if the unwanted behavior persists—the choice becomes one of admitting failure, with all the immediate and long-term costs this could entail, or escalating, either by resorting to greater amounts of force in the hope of achieving compellence or by undertaking another form of intervention.

One traditional example or mode of compellence is gunboat diplomacy. The classic definition comes from James Cable: "Gunboat diplomacy is the use or threat of use of limited naval force, otherwise than as an act of war, in order to secure advantage, or to avert loss, either in the furtherance of an international dispute or else against foreign nationals within the territory or the jurisdiction of their own state."[7] The definition is somewhat too narrow; there is no reason for it to be confined to naval forces. Modern air forces can perform much the same function, as demonstrated by the United States in the Philippines. But the relative lack of recent case studies suggests that the days of gunboat diplomacy may be waning, possibly because of the proliferation of military power, doubts about U.S. credibility in the aftermath of several unsuccessful interventions (or decisions not to intervene), and the emergence of world public opinion that is less amenable to such demonstrations of force. The likely consequence is that for compellence to work it will require actual uses of military force, and considerable ones at that.

PUNITIVE ATTACKS

Punitive actions are uses of military force designed to inflict pain and cost, that is, to make the opponent pay a price for his behavior. They do not reverse what has been done by the adversary, whether because matters cannot be reversed (say, a terrorist incident), because the direct use of force does not look advantageous, or because a restoration of the status quo ante is deemed insufficient. Nor can punitive attacks guarantee any particular future behavior by the target country. Indeed, they can stimulate further hostile action or discourage it; the result cannot be predicted with confidence. It is partly out of concern that punitive attacks against Iran for its hostage taking would trigger further hostilities that the Carter Administration decided against such attacks.

Punitive attacks require something not always available: clear evidence of who was responsible for the offending action. Such proof is necessary to persuade skeptical publics in the United States and in other countries. It is noteworthy that the Clinton Administration eschewed punitive actions in the wake of the February 1994 bombing of the Sarajevo marketplace when it could not point to evidence that would confirm its suspicions of Serbian responsibility. By contrast, the Clinton Administration did undertake a punitive attack against Iraq in 1993 when it received persuasive evidence of Iraqi complicity in an attempt to assassinate President Bush. Similarly, the Reagan Administration bombed Libya when it determined that Libya was responsible for a terrorist attack in Berlin.

Punitive actions are quintessentially political in nature. They are designed to make a point, not change the situation created by the adversary's provocation. But unlike a compellent use of force, in which the object or target of the exercise in effect determines whether the force used is effective, punitive uses of force leave the initiative in the hands of the party actually intervening. The determination of "how much is enough" becomes arbitrary, designed as much to satisfy oneself (and one's own public) as anything else.

Punitive attacks can be proportionate or disproportionate. In the case of the June 1993 retaliation against Iraq for mounting an attempt on President Bush's life, the Clinton Administration emphasized the proportionate nature of its response. The Reagan Administration carried out proportionate, i.e., modest, strikes when Iran interfered in a small way with Gulf shipping. Proportionate responses reflect the realities of coalition politics; anything deemed disproportionate risks creating problems for coalition solidarity.

Whatever the scale of the attack, it is meant to send a message not only to the target, but also to friends, adversaries, and the domestic public. The motive may be to satisfy a need for vengeance and retribution. Punitive actions can also take on a compellent or deterrent quality, especially if they are disproportionate to what was done by the adversary. For years, for example, Israel's stated policy was to respond with substantial uses of forces to terrorist attacks. The U.S. raid on Libya in 1986 is an example of a punitive attack that also had — or sought to have — a compellent or deterrent aspect. In such circumstances, public presentation of the purposes behind the attack becomes most important, and often is the only thing that differentiates a punitive from a deterrent or compellent use of force.

PEACEKEEPING

Peacekeeping involves the deployment of unarmed or at most lightly-armed forces in a peaceful environment, normally to buttress a fragile or brittle political arrangement between two or more contending parties. Peacekeeping takes place under Chapter 6 of the U.N. Charter, which addresses "pacific settlement of disputes," in contrast to Chapter 7, which addresses enforcement actions requiring "action with respect to threats to the peace, breaches of the peace, and acts of aggression." Peacekeepers might be called upon to monitor a separation of forces, monitor or verify troop withdrawals, or even supervise or provide security during an election. Peacekeepers also are increasingly called upon to perform additional and more demanding functions; many of these go beyond the traditional definition and capabilities of peacekeepers and therefore deserve separate consideration.[8]

Peacekeepers are impartial. They are also relatively passive, i.e., they are more monitors and observers than true keepers of the peace in that their ability to keep peace depends almost entirely upon consent. They use force only as a last resort and only for purposes of self-defense. As William Durch and Barry Blechman have wryly noted, "Peacekeeping operations cannot get off the ground without the support of the great powers, and can't do well *on* the ground without the support of all local parties."[9]

Peacekeeping thus involves the use of force in a largely consensual framework in which there are *at most* only periodic, relatively isolated, and small-scale breakdowns of the peace. By definition, such challenges are not conducted or backed by governments or principal parties to the agreement.[10] If they were, something more than peacekeeping, namely peace-making, would be called for.

Peacekeeping has become something of a growth industry. One recent study counted thirteen peacekeeping operations undertaken by the United Nations between 1948 and 1978, none during the next decade, and twenty since 1988.[11] The United States participated in seven of these at one time or another, although the number of operations mounted (as well as the number including U.S. participation) is lower if the measure is peacekeeping as defined here rather than the broader definition used by the United Nations and others, which includes more demanding operations under the rubric of peacekeeping.[12] None of the twelve cases examined in this volume represents an example of peacekeeping— although some started out as peacekeeping but became something more, ending badly as a result. The Clinton Administration has spoken of its willingness to contribute to a peacekeeping force in Bosnia, but only if a political and territorial settlement is accepted by all parties and promises to hold. Prospects are not good for meeting these requirements; if forces are nevertheless inserted, their mission would be substantially more demanding than peacekeeping and they should proceed accordingly.

WAR-FIGHTING

At the opposite end of the spectrum from peacekeeping is warfighting. This is the high end of intervention, and involves fullfledged combat operations. Such fighting is still limited in one or more ways—in terms of geography, the means employed, and/or the ends to which they are employed. Nevertheless, what distinguishes war-fighting is that it brings to bear whatever forces are available and deemed necessary to dominate the confrontation by attacking enemy forces on the battlefield and those forces located elsewhere that could be introduced to affect it.

The Korean War was an example of war-fighting, although with significant self-imposed restraint. Vietnam was an example as well, although there the restraint was so pronounced that at times the U.S. effort constituted something less, more like peacemaking as defined below. More recent and less restrained examples of war-fighting were Grenada (on a modest scale), Panama, and *Desert Storm.*

PEACE-MAKING

Peace-making is an imprecise and misleading term, probably because it is associated with both peace and peacekeeping, when in fact it has little to do with either. Indeed, some analysts have suggested the whole notion should be jettisoned because it creates a perception so at variance with reality.[13] Some in the U.S. military prefer the phrase "aggravated peacekeeping."[14] Still others define peace-making to encompass a host of activities, including diplomacy and sanctions, designed to help bring about conditions of peace.[15]

Here, the term peace-making is used to cover those activities falling between peacekeeping and war-fighting, in environments characterized by the U.S. military as neither "permissive" nor "hostile" but "uncertain."[16] What distinguishes it from ordinary warfare is mostly context. Moreover, unlike pure war-fighting, where the goal is to inflict significant destruction on the adversary, peace-making is carried out with measurable restraint. Much greater emphasis is placed on limiting the scope of the combat (rather than trying to solve the problem with a massive use of force) and on restoring or creating an environment in which resistance to a peace accord will become marginal and allow peacekeepers to operate.

The reason for accepting military constraints tends to derive from the inherent messiness of the situation, particularly the absence of a single adversary and a defined battlefield in which the adversary(ies) can be engaged on a significant scale. Peace-making often involves one or more local parties to the dispute that are friendly or neutral and a geographical context in which the hostile parties cannot be isolated from them. The option of war-fighting is thus either not available or brings with it severe costs.

It is also important to distinguish peace-making from more modest forms of intervention, particularly peacekeeping. *Peacekeeping* is appropriate where all the major parties to the dispute accept an arrangement and the presence of outside troops; any challenges to the peace will at most be marginal and done without the support of a major protagonist. *Peace-making*, on the other hand, assumes that at least one of the principal protagonists opposes the status quo, the presence of outsiders, or both. Unlike peacekeepers, peace-makers therefore must be heavily armed and be prepared to overcome considerable resistance. On the other hand, peace-makers are not able to call upon the full arsenal of modern weaponry for intense or sustained warfare. They work in a non-consensual environment in which the threats are limited in strength, frequency, and duration. It is a transitional activity that if successful should give way to true peacekeeping and/or nation-building.

The requirements of peace-making must not be underestimated. As one observer correctly points out, "It is in the gray area between peacekeeping and all-out war-fighting that the United Nations has gotten itself into serious trouble. The trouble stems from the fact that the United Nations has misapplied perfectly good tools to inappropriate circumstances."[17] The U.S./U.N. intervention in Somalia became one of peace-making in spring and summer 1993, but failed in part because the forces were capable of little more than peacekeeping. The same can be said of the second multinational force sent to Lebanon. Peace-making is an option for Bosnia, but the requirements for implementing it would be extraordinarily large because the three protagonists are heavily armed, deeply divided, and intensely committed.

It is also useful to distinguish between peace-making and *policing*. Police missions involve the deployment of forces in a quasi-hostile environment in which terrorism and small arms are the essential threats. They do not require consent by any party or parties. Nor do they require a peace to keep, enforce, or make. What the British are doing in Northern Ireland is the best example. Policing is a damage-limiting operation, designed neither to defeat opposition nor to solve underlying causes. As a result, it tends to be open-ended; it seeks to place a ceiling on violence to provide a constructive backdrop in which diplomacy can operate, or at least in which daily life is made tolerable for most of the inhabitants.

NATION-BUILDING

Nation-building (or "peace building" in the lexicon of the U.N. Secretary General) is an extremely intrusive form of intervention, one that seeks to bring about political leadership and, more important, procedures and institutions different from those that exist. In the case of the United States, nation-building seeks to encourage and sustain democratic and free-market practices. The effort requires a monopoly on the use of force until authorized indigenous units can be created to assume this responsibility. It can have the purpose of (and require) occupation.[18]

Nation-building is an option for dealing with failed states (that is, those where order breaks down because it has no widely accepted and functioning central authority) once resistance is overcome through peace-making or exhaustion. Similarly, nation-building is an option for dealing with defeated states; indeed, nation-building is what the United States did in Germany and Japan after World War II. It is what the United States did on a far more modest scale in Grenada and Panama. The Bush Administration eschewed this course of action in Iraq in spring 1991 and later in Somalia and Haiti. The Clinton Administration experimented with this option in Somalia before returning to more modest aims. It would be an option for Haiti if the United States (working with or without others) first defeated and then disarmed the military.

INTERDICTION

Interdiction involves the discrete and direct use of force to prevent specified equipment, resources, goods, or persons from reaching a battlefield, port, or terminal. It can be done to enforce sanctions; examples include the maritime multinational force (MNF) operating vis-à-vis Iraq since summer 1990 and the earlier multinational effort against Rhodesia. It can also be done for law enforcement purposes; for example, the U.S. Coast Guard and other agencies practice interdiction to limit the influx of narcotics or illegal aliens into the United States. Haiti is an example of interdiction used to keep goods out of Haiti and Haitians out of the United States. Interdiction can be done from the air as well as the sea, for example, to prevent reinforcement of hostile forces in the theater of operations.

HUMANITARIAN ASSISTANCE

Humanitarian operations involve the deployment of forces to save lives without necessarily altering the political context. Humanitarian operations can entail the delivery of basic human services where the central authority is unable or unwilling to do so, the evacuation of selected peoples (e.g., the first deployment of marines to evacuate the PLO from Beirut), or the protection of a people from governmental or nongovernmental forces.

Humanitarian interventions, narrowly defined, can be either *consensual* (requiring unarmed or lightly-armed personnel) or *imposed* (requiring heavily armed troops). A consensual humanitarian operation is one conducted within a permissive environment where uniformed forces are involved only for technical reasons, i.e., they possess skills and capabilities to lift/sustain personnel in difficult conditions. This type of effort routinely occurs after natural disasters; it was also the sort of effort mounted by the United States in July 1994 to assist Rwandan refugees in Zaire and elsewhere who had left their homes during their country's civil war.

An imposed humanitarian intervention, by contrast, is one carried out in an uncertain or hostile environment. It is humanitarian in that its aims are narrow, to provide food and/or other life-sustaining supplies (as well as protection) to peoples. It does not seek to change the overall political authority, but rather to minimize suffering until either the authority changes or its policies change. But it is a military operation in that force must be available to protect those delivering the aid, to deter and defend against attacks on both the forces involved and on civilians, and to retaliate by punishing those who interfere and reducing or eliminating their capacity to interfere. This sort of operation has been carried out in Northern Iraq since mid-April 1991 and was introduced around Sarajevo in early 1994. It is also what French forces did inside Rwanda beginning in late June 1994.

A number of options exist if a humanitarian operation designed to deliver food and other supplies in a consensual environment encounters resistance. It can be suspended (as often happened in Bosnia) or be carried out indirectly, using airdrops (as was tried in Iraq in April 1991 and in Bosnia in 1992). Forces can also take active measures to protect those carrying out the operation as well as those being helped. The principal alternative is to overcome resistance with some other form of military intervention, such as peace-making, compellence, and/or war-fighting. In Somalia, for example, the United States undertook a humanitarian operation that evolved into something more (peace-making) when resistance was encountered; the problem was the failure of the United States and the United Nations to either scale back the mission or provide the forces to back up the new mission. Yugoslavia (UNPROFOR II) has been an example of how humanitarian intervention encounters difficulty when it operates in a non-consensual environment but is unwilling to adopt more aggressive forms of intervention.

RESCUE

Rescue operations are a form of humanitarian intervention, but sufficiently special to merit separate treatment. They are actions sharply limited in scale and, more important, purpose, taken in what must be assumed to be a hostile environment. Hostage rescue missions, including the failed 1980 Carter Administration attempt to rescue the U.S. hostages in Iran, are an example. So too is extracting potential hostages. Liberia is a textbook case. Against a backdrop of escalating civil conflict and mounting threats to the

U.S. embassy and U.S. personnel and citizens, the United States dispatched naval and marine forces to Liberia in June 1990. Some Americans were evacuated right away using commercial aircraft in a relatively permissive environment; over one thousand others were not evacuated until August, when the situation was far more complicated and required well-armed marines to assert visible control of the embassy area.[19]

What makes both the Iranian hostage rescue attempt and Liberia classic rescue missions was the absence of any direct or indirect involvement in internal politics. Rescue missions are narrowly focused; Grenada was not a rescue mission but something broader.

INDIRECT USES OF FORCE

An indirect use of force involves providing military assistance in the form of training, arms, intelligence, etc., to another party so that it may employ force directly for its own purposes. An indirect use of force involves military instruments, but it is not a military intervention per se, although it can quickly lead to such intervention. The Nixon and Reagan doctrines emphasized this approach, which reduces the need for the United States to intervene directly. (There was an important difference, however. The Nixon Doctrine provided a basis for assisting friendly governments facing hostile neighbors; the Reagan Doctrine provided a rationale for aiding friendly groups opposing hostile governments.) Normal security assistance is a routine example of the indirect approach. U.S. assistance to resistance fighters in Afghanistan and Nicaragua were perhaps the most dramatic examples of "covert" indirect use of force. The possibility of indirect use of force in Bosnia, by selectively relaxing the embargo to permit military aid to reach the Bosnian Muslims, has been debated in the United States as well as internationally but never agreed to.

Indirect uses of force—essentially providing arms and training to various protagonists—are not without their drawbacks or limitations: they can take time before having an impact, they can prolong or expand fighting, and there is no guarantee that the provider or benefactor will not be called upon or pressured to intervene directly if those being helped fare poorly. Indirect activities need to overcome logistical problems—getting the arms there, providing the necessary training in a safe setting, and so on. Being called upon to intervene directly is in fact likely if the other side escalates in reaction to the decision to provide indirect support to their adversary. Also, indirect uses of force give less control to the side providing the assistance; there is no assurance as to how the material will be used either immediately or in the future. What indirect efforts thus offer is a trade-off: less involvement in exchange for less influence over events.

The Afghan resistance worked as well as it did for several reasons—the fact that Pakistan provided sanctuary, topography that favored guerilla tactics over large-scale engagements, the commitment of the Afghan resistance fighters, limits on the Soviet commitment; these characteristics are not easily or readily duplicated. Getting arms to Bosnian Muslims, for example, would have required working with and through the Croatians, a problem until they formed a federation in early 1994. Such a course of action by the United States and other Western countries would also require some time before having the desired impact—time that might have been used by the Serbs or others to increase the pressure on the Bosnian side. In Lebanon, the same factional problems that defined the situation precluded effective training of a national military. And Haiti showed that training on the scene is not possible when order breaks down. In short, indirect uses of force may limit one's investment or exposure but they also tend to limit the results.

CHAPTER FOUR

WHETHER TO INTERVENE

T wo types of guidelines affect the use of force. The first set addresses the question of *whether* to use force. They help determine what kinds of situations lend themselves to being affected by an intervention. In particular, they help determine what interests are involved and whether they are sufficiently important to justify sacrificing blood and treasure on their behalf. The second set of guidelines addresses the question of *how* to use force. These guidelines are concerned with tactics, with operational approaches to the use of force, with useful or necessary political concomitants. This chapter addresses the question of whether; the following chapter addresses the question of how.

The two sets of considerations are separated for the sake of analytical clarity. *But the question of whether to use force can never be divorced from the question of how to use it effectively. If there is no satisfactory answer to the latter question, there can be no commitment to the former.* The decision to use force should never be made in the abstract; it must be grounded in implementation considerations. As one editorial thoughtfully noted, "A justified intervention needs a genuinely deserving victim to rescue; a wise one needs a solid prospect of a success and an interest of one's own to be served in the process."[1] Or, as others have pointed out more succinctly, an intervention must be both worth doing and doable. However stated, the point that cannot be lost is this: *judgments of desirability cannot be made divorced from assessments of feasibility.*

One additional caution is needed. There should be no absolutes in this area. A definitive set of rules would unnecessarily tie the hands of policy makers. A government should not be compelled to act if all its criteria are met, any more than it should be prevented from acting even if some criteria are not. Moreover, criteria established in the abstract can never anticipate particular contexts; the devil will always be in the details. No measurement can ever substitute for judgment. Also, there is no reason to signal requirements for acting in advance; like all red lines, this only invites adventurism up to that line, which can embolden foes and unnerve friends. Although there is no proof, it seems likely that Dean Acheson's public speech in January 1950 leaving South Korea outside the U.S. defense perimeter at least contributed to North Korea's decision to invade months later.

Nevertheless, it is essential to think in advance about the question of military intervention. Such consideration can assist in the planning of forces, help to prepare the public and Congress, signal allies and adversaries, and shape diplomatic undertakings. Just as important, the guidelines in this and the next chapter provide a set of questions and a yardstick by which any proposed intervention can be assessed. The answers need not determine policy, but any departure from the guidelines ought to be carefully considered and justifiable.

INTERESTS ARE ONLY A GUIDE

In principle, it is useful to identify national security interests—strategic, political, moral, humanitarian, economic, environmental, and so on—and to weigh them both absolutely and relative to one another. As Hans Morgenthau wrote more than forty years ago, "To establish a hierarchical order, an order of priorities, among all possible objectives of a nation's foreign policy must be the first step in framing a rational foreign policy."[2] Not surprisingly, one often encounters lists of interests ranked as vital, major (or important), minor, and peripheral.

In reality, though, such lists are of little use. People have grown numb to claims of "national interests" and "vital interests" when in actuality far less is at stake. More fundamentally, the term is of limited value because determinations are necessarily subjective and reflect (or betray) one's philosophy and values. Indeed, as Alexander George has observed, " . . . 'national interest' has become so elastic and ambiguous a concept that its role as a guide to foreign policy is highly problematical and controversial. Most thoughtful observers of U.S. foreign policy have long since concluded that the 'national interest' concept unfortunately lends itself more readily to being used by our leaders as political rhetoric for *justifying* their decisions and gaining support rather than as an exact, well-defined criterion that enables them to determine what actions and decisions to take."[3]

This is not to argue that the concept has no validity. The more important an interest is, the stronger the initial presumption that force is an appropriate policy tool if the interest is threatened or if the opportunity exists to advance it. But the point should not be pressed further. To draw a direct connection or parallel between the importance of an interest and a willingness to intervene on its behalf would be wrong. An interest can be widely viewed as extremely important but military force may not be the best or most appropriate tool to promote or protect it; alternatively, an interest can be only moderately important but intervening militarily might be judged to be relatively "cheap and easy" and worth it. Western reluctance to use direct military force on behalf of the peoples of Czechoslovakia (1968), Afghanistan (1979), and China (1989) are all examples of the former; the decision to enter Somalia to provide humanitarian relief in 1992 is a case of the latter. More generally, military force may simply be inappropriate or even irrelevant to a particular dispute, as is often the case in the economic realm.

Military force is but one policy option and but one form of intervention. If war is an extension of politics, it is also only one way of pursuing political ends, and needs to be weighed against the others. Prior cost-benefit assessment must bear scrutiny: with any commitment of public resources, force should only be used if it promises to provide benefits that outweigh the costs of acting. In the words of Colin Powell, " . . . the use of force should be restricted to occasions where it can do some good and where the good will outweigh the loss of lives and other costs that will surely ensue."[4] Also, an intervention should be undertaken only if it is likely to provide benefits that outweigh the costs of not acting and if the intervention is likely to yield a better ratio of benefits to costs than other available policies.

Narcotics provides an example in which force may not be the best tool despite the important interests at stake. In the "war against drugs," military force became central to U.S. policy in the 1980s in two aspects: destroying overseas production areas/facilities and interdicting shipments en route to the United States. Both the Defense Department and the Coast Guard budgets reflected this priority. Yet it is not at all clear that such efforts were effective, either in their own right or in comparison to other ways the resources might have been spent (for example, limiting demand or increasing local policing and incarceration). This was the judgment of the Clinton Administration, which decreased the use of military force in the control of narcotics.

In the twelve cases presented previously, it is difficult to argue that any—except the Gulf War—constituted a vital U.S. interest. Some of the others—Panama, protection of shipping in the Gulf—could be said to represent important interests; in most of the others, including Grenada, the Philippines, Lebanon, Haiti, and Somalia, the United States had only relatively minor interests. (The importance of U.S. interests in the former Yugoslavia remains a matter of considerable debate.)

This assessment does not mean the United States was necessarily right to use force in the Gulf or wrong to use it in Somalia. The point is simply that the question of whether to intervene is one in which the use of force must be weighed against other approaches, including diplomatic, economic, or political sanctions or speeches.

TOLERANCE FOR COSTS REFLECTS THE INTERESTS AT STAKE

There is an important relationship between interests and the ability to intervene successfully. The ability to sustain an intervention over time and, more importantly, despite human and financial costs, is linked directly to the perceived importance of the interests at stake. In the absence of widely perceived national interests, elite and popular tolerance of the costs of intervention is much diminished. Widespread doubt that the United States had important interests at stake in Vietnam made continued participation in that war impossible. The abrupt departure of U.S. troops from Lebanon was triggered by the Reagan Administration's assessment that the public was not prepared to pay relatively high costs for such uncertain interests and prospects. (These examples also demonstrate that attempts to use the intervention as its own justification for continuing—the notion that previous sacrifices of blood and treasure necessitate soldiering on even in the absence of intrinsic interests worth more than the costs—will not succeed for long if at all.) Similarly, public reluctance helped pushed the Clinton Administration into recasting the Somalia intervention (which was based upon "soft" humanitarian interests rather than "hard" national interests) to reduce the exposure of U.S. forces and to place a time limit on their presence. This same calculation explains in part the reluctance of both the Bush and Clinton administrations to get involved in Bosnia.

The opposite is also true. Interventions are more sustainable if leaders can point to clear and important national (as opposed to universal humanitarian) interests. Both world wars as well as the Korean War are testament to this. So too was the Gulf War; the Bush Administration entered the conflict able to point to vital national interests whose existence led U.S. officials to feel confident that they could continue the military effort even if substantial casualties materialized.

None of this is meant as an argument per se against intervention when interests are modest. But any such intervention must be extremely short or, if this is not possible, designed so that risks and costs are modest. The interventions in northern and southern Iraq as well as the steps taken in Bosnia in February and April 1994 are consistent with this point. The problem with the Bosnian interventions is that the desire to minimize risks and costs appears at the same time to have minimized the effectiveness of the actions taken.

THE PURPOSE OF THE INTERVENTION MUST BE CLEAR

It is essential to know the purpose behind any intervention and how the proposed use of force will accomplish or at least contribute to that end. The inability to readily define the precise mission of a proposed intervention is prima facie evidence that the intervention is ill-advised. The second deployment of marines to Lebanon is a classic and tragic illustration of a deployment without a clear mission. The contrast with the Gulf War, with its specific aim of liberating Kuwait, could not be more dramatic.

It is equally important that the mission is appropriate for military forces. As Samuel Huntington has written, " . . . if American forces have to be used, they should be used to achieve military objectives . . . Military forces are designed to defeat opposing military forces; they are not very useful in the pursuit of most other goals."[5] Even if one does not go so far as Huntington—military forces can be used for broader purposes than he suggests—the purpose of the intervention must not only be clear but also be sufficiently precise to ensure that prospective missions and forces have a good chance of accomplishing the goal.

It is equally important to be extremely careful about changing objectives once an intervention has begun. Changing objectives mid-stream should receive no less scrutiny than the original decision to intervene. It is interesting to contrast the serious thought the Truman Administration gave to the initial decision to resist and roll back the North Korean invasion of the South with the less careful scrutiny it gave to the ultimately reckless decision to head north of the 38th parallel even after liberation of the South was achieved. Nearly half a century later, the Clinton Administration went from a policy of humanitarian aid in Somalia to one of peace-making and nation-building without examining seriously the wisdom of the change or the requirements that flowed from it.

A clear contrast to these examples is the Bush Administration's decision of late February and early March 1991 not to go beyond the liberation of Kuwait and occupy Iraq or get directly involved in its internal struggles. This does not mean that the Bush Administration was correct at the time. Nor is this meant to imply that it is never right to change goals—opportunities should on occasion be exploited, just as unexpected difficulties need to be taken into account. But such decisions should be taken with great care. They should not be made simply because officials are caught up in the flush of tactical success or unnerved by tactical failure.

THE ADVERSARY'S RESPONSE MUST BE ANTICIPATED

An initial use of force will probably be to one's own comparative advantage, especially if there is the element of surprise. (There are exceptions, such as the unsuccessful attempt to rescue American hostages in Iran, but most interventions initially favor the active side.) But there is little reason to assume the situation will stop at that point, or that the adversary will not shift the next phase of the struggle to areas/means of its comparative advantage. Japan won a clear tactical triumph at Pearl Harbor, but this battle set in motion an American response that years later led to Japan's defeat.[6]

It is always difficult to predict that a certain use of force will persuade the adversary to stop doing what you want stopped and not prompt new, unwanted actions. This is the cardinal reason to be careful with both preventive and preemptive attacks and with compellence. It is as simple—and as basic—as the difference between winning a battle and winning a war. It only takes one party to initiate hostilities, but it takes everyone involved to bring hostilities to an end.

These considerations also place a premium on intelligence—on knowing as much as possible about the adversary, about its strengths and weaknesses, its values and priorities. Eliminating uncertainty and knowledge gaps is impossible, but there is no reason for such unknowns to be unnecessarily large. Lebanon, Somalia, and even Grenada are examples of the tragedy that can result from underestimating an adversary or misreading the complexity of a situation. Haiti is another example of how misreading a situation can allow unrealistic options—in this case, the dispatch of essentially unarmed instructors into a volatile environment—to move ahead.

In many situations, relative staying power is critical. For engagements that promise to be protracted, it is essential to assess U.S. ability to sustain the confrontation relative to the adversary's. Such an assessment must include political, economic, and psychological calculations as well as military factors. This is not meant to suggest that intervening, much less "staying the course," are always correct—they are not—but to point out that such relative assessments are critical in determining the likely costs of intervening relative to the interests at stake. As is often the case, Clausewitz is worth contemplating on this point:

To discover how much of our resources must be mobilized for war, we must first examine our own political aim and that of the enemy. We must gauge the strength and situation of the opposing state. We must gauge the character and abilities of its government and people and do the same in regard to our own. Finally, we must evaluate the political sympathies of other states and the effect the war may have on them. To assess these things in all their ramifications and diversity is plainly a colossal task.[7]

Incentive to "stay the course" tends to increase for a party in direct proportion to geographic proximity and the perceived importance of interests at stake. Thus civil or internal struggles are closer and almost always more important to the protagonists (who may include not just those directly involved but also their kith and kin in some nearby motherland) than to outsiders separated by ethnicity and distance. These factors help explain why Syria and the militia it backed proved so tenacious in Lebanon, or why capturing Aideed proved so difficult in Somalia. It also explains the strength of the commitment of both Greeks and Turks to Cyprus or of Serbs in Serbia to Serbs in Bosnia.

Democracies can have a hard time enduring a conflict as costs mount—witness the impact of the Boer War on Britain or of the Vietnam conflict on the United States. Even relatively small tactical defeats accompanied by loss of life—the bombing of the marine barracks in Beirut, the failed operation in Somalia—can undermine domestic support for continuing an operation. Again, the key variable here tends to be the value of interests relative to costs. The United States can stay involved either if costs are low or if interests are high. What cannot be sustained are high-cost, low-interest engagements.

NEITHER VICTORY NOR AN EXIT DATE SHOULD BE PREREQUISITES

Before undertaking an intervention, there may a desire to determine precisely how long it will take, what it will accomplish, and how much it will cost. Similarly, there may be a desire for clear "success" or "winning." This is both understandable and good policy. What is less justifiable, and often counter-productive, is to require either certainty of victory or certainty of exiting by a specific date as preconditions for intervention.

The requirement of victory—that is, using force only for the purpose of winning—applies to a small number of situations that generally fall into two types: a) war-fighting, when realizing battlefield objectives is the appropriate aim, or b) in such defined interventions as rescue missions and preventive strikes. In many other situations, however, especially peacekeeping, peace-making, and humanitarian undertakings, but also in compellence and punitive strikes, more limited goals may be entirely appropriate. These goals can include preventing a situation from deteriorating, preventing a situation from materializing, or creating a context in which diplomacy is more likely to make headway. As a result, there should be allowance for limited uses of force for limited aims. As will be seen, what is critical is to make sure any limits on the force match both the aims and the circumstances.

Similarly, a decision to intervene should not require a simultaneous decision to withdraw or otherwise cease intervening by a specific date (as the Clinton Administration made when it announced its intention to depart Somalia by March 31, 1994). This is not to be confused with defining in advance the criteria for stopping or ending an intervention. This can help the military plan and can help erect a bulwark against open-ended or ever-expanding involvement. The end point should be tied to some achievable situation on the ground or to reaching acceptable political arrangements. The Gulf War is a model of clear objectives and flexible timetables; there was no promise of victory or withdrawal by any particular date. Other successes that shared this characteristic include the Gulf reflagging effort and the interventions in Panama and Grenada.

The crucial point is to avoid a specific end point or certain date for ending the commitment regardless of local developments. Artificial boundaries on a U.S. intervention run the risk of emboldening adversaries, who need only to wait until the deadline has passed, and unnerving allies. The rare exceptions to this rule could include discrete events (a punitive action or something narrow and specific, such as facilitating the evacuation of the PLO from Beirut) or situations in which a handoff of responsibility can be assured (to another external actor, a local protagonist, or some mixture of the two).

None of this is a call for vagueness. One must be realistic about what the intervention will entail in terms of manpower, human and material cost, and duration. What is needed is a strategy for seeing the commitment through—a *sustainability strategy;* this is possible if and so long as the interests promoted are visibly greater than the costs likely to be incurred.

POPULAR AND CONGRESSIONAL SUPPORT ARE DESIRABLE BUT NOT NECESSARY

One of former Defense Secretary Caspar Weinberger's six tenets is that the President should only commit forces abroad if he is confident that Congress and the country will be supportive. Some who hold this view mean that the President should abide by the provisions of the War Powers Resolution requiring Congress to approve any commitment of forces to situations of likely or actual hostilities after sixty days; others mean something less formal. Both perspectives are potentially short-sighted.

Presidents need some discretion and flexibility; they do not always have the opportunity to take a poll or consult widely before acting. Certain missions which require absolute surprise to succeed—hostage rescues, for example—all but preclude prior consultations.

However, only interventions that promise to be short and relatively inexpensive (and above all successful) can be safely carried out with little prior effort to garner public or congressional support.

Interventions tend to rise and fall on their merits. Success will create support that may not have existed beforehand—Grenada and the protection of Gulf shipping are cases in point—while failure will drain any support that might have existed (for example, Lebanon and Somalia). George Shultz made this point eloquently in a 1984 speech that was widely viewed as his critique of the Weinberger approach: "There is no such thing as guaranteed public support in advance. Grenada shows that a president who has the courage to lead will *win* public support if he acts wisely and effectively. And Vietnam shows that public support can be frittered away if we do not act wisely and effectively."[8]

Leaders should be prepared to lead, which can entail getting out in front of public and elite opinion if the situation warrants. At the same time, any president would be foolhardy not to do everything possible (largely through the use of the bully pulpit) to narrow the gap between the likely costs of policy and what Congress and the public are prepared to support. In general, a president should consult in an effort to get informal or formal congressional support for military undertakings that promise to be time consuming and costly, as the Bush Administration finally did in the Gulf War. The Clinton Administration erred in not obtaining congressional support for its more ambitious approach to Somalia.

A useful rule of thumb is that the need for advance, formal congressional support (although *not* the war powers legislation itself, for reasons discussed below) increases in proportion to the scale of the proposed intervention. The same would apply to U.S. support for or participation in U.N. efforts. A president who does not consult with Congress or its leaders before embarking on a major intervention is foolish, but a president who requires a formal commitment from Congress before intervening anywhere will likely find himself intervening rarely if at all.

This raises fundamental questions about the wisdom of the current legislation on war powers. As the law now stands, the Executive can commit U.S. forces to combat situations for sixty (or, in certain circumstances, ninety) days. After that time, forces can only remain overseas if Congress votes to extend the undertaking.[9] This requirement is seriously flawed, for it places the burden of action on those who want to continue with a policy (that is, the particular intervention) rather than on those who want to change it. This reinforces questions about U.S. staying power. A better approach would be to allow Congress to vote (by simple majority or preferably two-thirds majority, thus overriding a presidential veto) to bring the forces back home if it chooses.

Better still would be to scrap the statute, one that has never been implemented as intended. Presidents report to the Congress "consistent with" rather than "pursuant to" the law in order to shield themselves from its provisions, traditionally viewed as unwise or even unconstitutional. With or without a law, in most circumstances, the inherent and unavoidable politics of decisions to intervene with military force demand that presidents consult beforehand with Congress or its leadership and, depending upon the nature and scope of the intervention in question, get some informal or even formal expression of support.

DETERRENCE IS NOT COST FREE AND NOT ALWAYS AN OPTION

Deterrence is almost always preferable to fighting a war. But the decision to deter is one that should only be taken with great care, for with it comes the responsibility to make good on the commitment. Otherwise, not only are the immediate interests lost but one's credibility everywhere is brought into question. Moreover, deterrence is not without costs even if it succeeds, as it ties down forces and drains resources that are then not available for other contingencies.

Using force as a deterrent is easier said than done. It is not always an option; in some situations, local politics preclude stationing U.S.

forces in the country. The Persian Gulf has normally been such a case, in the sense that U.S. forces were desired by America's friends "over the horizon" but out of sight to domestic audiences that might oppose them. Alas, they were also invisible to external foes. Also, as crises develop, there is pressure not to introduce forces that might deter for fear they might provoke; precisely this concern led Gulf states (other than the UAE) to turn down U.S. offers to conduct military exercises in late July 1990. As one post-mortem on the Gulf War concluded, "[E]xtended deterrence is a tricky business. It will not always be possible for the United States to issue clear deterrent threats, and half-hearted ones may not work."[10]

The real question is what is required for deterrence to be effective? One study concludes that " . . . deterrence is likely to hold when a potential attacker is faced with the prospect of employing an attrition strategy, largely because of the associated exorbitant costs and because of the difficulty of accurately predicting ultimate success in a protracted war."[11] Still another assessment lists four minimum conditions if deterrence is to work: "A state must clearly define its commitment to defend a particular interest, communicate that commitment to the potential aggressor, possess a sufficiently potent military capability to increase costs on the adversary that exceed his potential gains, and demonstrate its resolve to implement the threat in spite of short-term costs to itself."[12] One influential study suggests that local military capabilities (as opposed to potential or overall force levels based upon inventory) are a critical factor in determining the likelihood that deterrence will succeed.[13]

These conclusions are consistent with the case studies in this volume. Efforts to dissuade Saddam Hussein from invading Kuwait failed, probably for reasons including a lack of local U.S. military capability and uncertainty in Saddam's mind about the depth of the U.S. commitment to Kuwait. *Desert Shield* and the stronger U.S.-Saudi relationship appear to have made a different and far more successful impression in that Saddam did not move against Saudi Arabia. The 1987–88 reflagging operation in the Gulf succeeded for similar reasons. It is too soon to judge whether the presence of several hundred lightly-armed U.S. forces in Macedonia will have any effect; the absence of substantial on-the-scenes capability rather than just a symbolic or trip-wire presence suggests that it may not. The potential problem with this deployment is exacerbated by the vagueness of the U.S. commitment to Macedonia and the possibility that instability will result not from an outbreak of classic aggression across borders but from within.[14]

THE ADVERSARY IS NOT THE ONLY AUDIENCE

Any use of force (or decision not to use force) will have an impact that transcends the immediate situation. Consequences will follow: politically and economically at home, for the military as an institution, for the perceptions of friends and allies, and for the thinking of actual and would-be adversaries. It is true that in the post-Soviet world there is little danger of any conflict leading to the global level as was feared during the Cold War, but this does not mean that all situations have become discrete and all decisions can be isolated. "Walking away" from a limited use of force will convey the impression to adversaries that perseverance and escalation will pay.

The sudden withdrawal of the United States from Beirut in 1984 almost certainly had an impact on Saddam's thinking six years later; events in Somalia affected the calculations of Haiti's military. It is quite possible that Bosnia, Somalia, and Haiti will have an impact on how the Clinton Administration is perceived in other places at other times. On the other hand, Grenada is believed by some observers to have had a sobering effect on then-Marxist Nicaragua and Cuba; although hard to prove, this is consistent with the point that any decision involving the use of force will have repercussions that transcend the immediate circumstances.

AFFECTING INTERNAL POLITICS
THROUGH FORCE IS DIFFICULT

The largest use of force examined here was a traditional one—
the Gulf War. One of the two other major post–World War II engagements, Korea, also was a traditional conflict. The Korean and
Gulf wars may have been the most demanding in a classic military sense, but they were relatively simple in their approaches.
Both involved using force against an adversary, directly and in
the area to be liberated, and both (with the exception of one moment during the Korean War) sought to restore a status quo ante.
The third major U.S. war of the post–World War II era, Vietnam,
was more complicated. It was both a traditional conflict—against
North Vietnam—and a civil conflict in South Vietnam, in which
the United States assisted one side and the North Vietnamese
the other.

Intra-state conflicts are qualitatively different and often pose
more difficult policy questions than inter-state conflicts. Inter-state
conflicts generally have limited aims—involving, for example, a
piece of territory or some policy. By contrast, conflicts that are essentially civil wars, fought along ethnic or sectarian lines, tend to
be more violent, long-lasting, zero-sum struggles (examples include the conflicts in Lebanon, Somalia, Bosnia, and Iraq after the
Gulf War). There is no homeland to return to as is the case when
one is defeated on a foreign battlefield. There are often multiple
protagonists, usually with no clear, authoritative leaders, making
diplomatic efforts that much more difficult. As a result, internal
wars have a way of lingering. Ironically, outside intervention can
reinforce this tendency; as Laurence Martin has observed, "Intervention will produce stalemate rather than solutions—unless, and
it is an immense unless, the interveners are prepared to defeat the
stronger side."[15]

Accomplishing something positive through military intervention
in a civil war is far from simple. Militarily, such wars tend to be
fought along no front—or so many that it is impossible to defend
and advance in an organized, large-scale manner. The absence of

a defined battlefield—relatively open areas where uniformed combatants rather than civilians are found—makes use of force by outsiders extremely difficult. Identifying and destroying appropriate targets, especially concentrations of targets, becomes a major problem, thus minimizing the effectiveness of air power. Collateral damage is an inevitable by-product of substantial use of force, and separating combatant from civilian is difficult, as built-up areas often become battle zones and civilians assume quasi-combatant roles.

The bitterness unleashed by civil wars tends to be hard to overcome, even when one side clearly emerges as a victor. Ending the violence is further complicated by the difficulty of persuading populations to co-exist in shared space; like Humpty Dumpty, putting things back together can prove impossible. Power-sharing may be the ideal solution, but it is rarely an option in the wake of civil war; domination and repression or some form of enforced migration and partition are more common.[16]

By contrast, some situations involving the use of force may be internal, but not ethnic or civil, in nature. For example, Panama, Grenada, and the Philippines were internal struggles, but they were largely free of the widespread violence or deep-seated passion of civil wars. These all proved to be successful interventions. In each case, the opposition, defined by political rather than ethnic or religious or even geographic dimensions, was a distinct minority and could be isolated. It helps, too, if there exists a legitimate authority to back, as in the cases of both the Philippines and Panama.

This situation is in contrast not only to civil conflicts but also to revolutions, where a friendly government is confronted with massive popular opposition, as was the case in Iran in the late 1970s (or as could occur in Algeria or even Egypt). Iran was no Philippines, where the small number of coup-plotters were easily isolated and defeated. Revolutions derive much of their strength from below, unlike coups, which are essentially a top-down phenomenon. It is easier to use force to affect the success of coups or still-modest insurrections—either to support them or oppose them—than it is for revolutions, which by their sheer mass and political character are resistant to interventions by outsiders. For this reason, the Carter Administration was correct to rule out the direct use of military force once the Iranian revolution reached full boil.

One additional point is relevant here. It is difficult to target specific individuals with military force. (This is in addition to the legal prohibition enshrined in an executive order signed into law by President Jimmy Carter that prohibits the assassination of foreign leaders.) U.S. efforts to use force to bring about changes in political leadership failed in the cases of Qaddafi in Libya, Saddam in Iraq, and Aideed in Somalia. Force can create a context in which political change is more likely, but without extraordinary intelligence and more than a little good fortune, force by itself is unlikely to bring about specific political changes. The only way to increase the likelihood of such change is through highly intrusive forms of intervention, such as nation-building, which involves first eliminating all opposition and then engaging in an occupation that allows for substantial engineering of another society. Short of a readiness to assume a commitment of this magnitude, it is wise not to make specific political outcomes part of the mission or purpose of an intervention.

The situation is different in the case of failed states. By definition, a failed state has no local political authority that can act as a national government. Rather, several competing authorities tend to have varying degrees of control in different parts of the country, resulting in chaos, violence, widespread suffering, and the neglect of basic human needs. Somalia in 1992 offers a textbook example.

Two kinds of interventions are possible in such situations. The first is humanitarian, designed to bring relief to some or most of the local population until the political situation sorts itself out. The second kind of intervention can have as its aim nation-building, that is, the fixing of the political situation, which in turn can first require peace-making. Humanitarian interventions are less demanding but offer less and can be open-ended. Interventions aimed at nation-building are potentially more demanding but, if successful, hold out the hope of "fixing" the situation—replacing a failed state with a successful one—and creating circumstances for withdrawal.

In short, internal conflicts can take many forms. They can be civil wars, more narrow struggles for political power, or failed states. There may be humanitarian and/or political grounds for wanting to intervene directly with military force. However, the historical record suggests caution in at least three contexts: civil wars, revolutions, and failed states. It is instructive—and sobering—that nearly two hundred years ago the Swiss strategist Antoine-Henri Jomini described civil wars or "wars of opinion" as "dangerous and deplorable," where traditional principles of war did not apply.[17] If the decision is nonetheless made to proceed, it should only be taken after a careful determination of purpose and with full appreciation of the potential commitment and costs entailed.

MEDIA SHOULD NOT DETERMINE POLICY

The media—above all, televised images, which today can be beamed around the world instantly from almost any location to almost any other location without editing—can have a profound effect on decisions affecting whether to go to war and how to conduct one. Other technologies—fax, telephone, radio—likewise create real-time links that carry raw information and that are often beyond the capacity of local authorities to control or censor. U.S. experience in Lebanon (after the Sabra and Shatila camp massacres in September 1982), northern Iraq (in April 1991), and more recently Somalia, Bosnia, and Rwanda demonstrates that these technologies are contributing to creating a global village that increases awareness of atrocities and hence builds pressure to "do something."

This is not always a good thing. News stories or images, no matter how graphic, should not determine decisions about intervention. If they do, U.S. policy risks being unduly influenced by the domestic and international reactions to words and pictures from those places the cameras and reporters can reach. In both northern Iraq and Somalia, scenes of mass misery helped draw in the United States. It is instructive that images accelerated the U.S. departure from Somalia just months after they had the opposite impact. The United States also risks manipulation in the sense of ignoring those places the cameras cannot go owing to government prohibitions or a lack of order. There is not necessarily a correlation between the most compelling images and important U.S. interests or between those images and the ability of military force to accomplish something useful in a particular setting.

The cases provide numerous examples of presidents either affecting the media or being affected by it. But it is also possible to make decisions either for or against the use of force without media pressure. The Reagan Administration chose to reflag Kuwaiti tankers amidst little or no media coverage. Iraq's invasion of Kuwait was not heavily reported or depicted by the media, which had great difficulty gaining access; nevertheless, the Bush Administration determined that responding with force was in the national interest, and helped create public, congressional, and international support for an interventionist policy. By way of contrast, neither the Bush nor the Clinton administrations made a convincing case for not acting in Bosnia, and both paid a political price for relative inaction. And the Clinton Administration, by failing to explain the potential risks and costs of a more ambitious policy in Somalia, learned it had no reservoir of public support to fall back on.

As a general proposition, policymakers would be wiser to allow media and other communications to affect *how* they use force—for example, deciding to avoid collateral damage and civilian casualties—but not *whether* to intervene.[18] Presidents and administrations that fail to make the case for what they are doing, that do not educate and explain either why the United States ought to intervene or stay out, are far more vulnerable to being buffeted by public passions—passions sometimes created and reinforced by media reports—than are administrations that work diligently at shaping public thinking. The conclusion is much the same in this context as it was for dealing with Congress: there is no substitute for leadership—and where there is a shortage of leadership, the resulting vacuum will be filled by others, including the media.[19]

CHAPTER FIVE

HOW TO INTERVENE

o assessment on whether to use force is complete without examining *how* force is to be used. If a preliminary assessment leads to an inclination or predisposition to use force, the analysis must proceed to examine all aspects of implementation. It makes no sense to use force if it cannot realize its purposes at an acceptable cost; and cost can only be assessed by examining a specific course of action within a specific context and judging likely results.

The purpose here is not to undertake a detailed discussion of tactics. Considerations involving which weapon system or maneuver ought to be employed to fulfill a particular task are better left to the professional military. Rather, this chapter examines lessons derived from previous employments of force, lessons affecting the timing, scale, and intensity of its use; the impact of critical technologies; the political setting; and the relationship between means and ends.

It is important to stress that any use of force or military intervention will be limited for a number of reasons. The United States will not consider using, much less actually use, nuclear or other unconventional weapons in most conceivable instances. It will keep a certain proportion of its forces in reserve for other contingencies. For political reasons, the United States may choose to limit which targets it will attack. In some instances, there may be insufficient time to bring forces to bear on the battlefield. And finally, in the post–Cold War world, wars will be limited geographically; the chance of a local conflict becoming a global one (or a total one) is remote.

But to acknowledge that any use of force must necessarily be limited begs or obscures the critical choices. It does not provide specific guidance about what kinds and amounts of forces are to be used, whether an operation ought to be conducted unilaterally or with others, the targets, the timing of an attack, or the intensity and pace at which it is conducted. Consideration of a potential intervention must address all these questions, not simply to ensure that force used will be used effectively, but to help determine whether force is an attractive option, both on its own terms and compared to other policy instruments.

SOONER TENDS TO BE BETTER THAN LATER

A number of factors—including the "just war" concept that force should only be used as a last resort and the realities of achieving consensus in democracies and coalitions—create a bias against using military force until all other options have failed. There is great pressure to give diplomacy a chance, to try ever more stringent sanctions, even to announce some deadline to allow the other party involved one final opportunity to avoid conflict. The notion of force as a last resort shows up in most lists of guidelines put forth by various practitioners.

This desire to postpone armed conflict is understandable; nonetheless, it can be ill-advised. Waiting until other policies have failed may limit or forfeit the opportunity to use force effectively. The passage of time may mean the loss of surprise and the loss of initiative while giving the adversary opportunity to prepare militarily and politically for the battle to come. Also, waiting for diplomacy or, as is often the case, economic sanctions to work can allow people and other interests to suffer dearly. As David Fisher has written, " . . . it may be morally preferable to use limited military force against carefully targeted military objectives *before* applying such an indiscriminate weapon as general economic sanctions."[1]

The Gulf crisis provides a good example of why waiting can be a costly and dangerous option. In fall 1990, just after Iraq's invasion and occupation of Kuwait, the Bush Administration concluded that with the passage of even a few more months there would be no Kuwait left to save. There was also the risk that there would be no coalition to confront Iraq—the tensions between the Arab states and Israel had the potential to disrupt things at any moment, as they did in October 1990, when Israel used what was widely viewed as excessive force in dealing with Palestinian protestors on the Temple Mount in Jerusalem. The passage of time also posed the risk that U.S. and coalition casualties would be higher if Iraq had more opportunity to ready unconventional military options.

Other cases provide similar evidence. In Grenada, further waiting may have resulted in a hostage situation and the consolidation of a government aligned with Cuba and the Soviet Union. In the Philippines, holding off could have resulted in the government being overthrown. In Panama, postponing action would likely have led to increased attacks on U.S. personnel, on Panamanian moderates, and even on the Canal. In Haiti, the passage of time (and, with it, the effect of sanctions) has increased the misery of the people without necessarily improving the prospects for positive change. In Somalia, an earlier, more assertive use of force might have broken the will and the capacity of Aideed to resist.

Bosnia is a more complex issue. The limited success of the February 1994 initiatives around Sarajevo by the United States and NATO prompted some observers to argue that force should have been introduced earlier by the West against the Serbs, thereby sparing Bosnia's Muslims much of their misery.[2] Clearly, the passage of time increased the amount of territory held by Serbs, the human suffering, and the bitterness that makes any sort of reconciliation highly improbable. Yet it is not clear that intervention would have worked earlier, when the Serbs were determined to increase their territorial control. Coercive force works best when its aims are modest; attempts by the West to prevent Serbian gains would likely have required considerable effort (although less than it would have taken at any point to reverse or roll back Serbian gains). Moreover, gaining early domestic and international political support for intervention is easier said than done; ironically, it often takes a deteriorating situation to make it politically possible to act, which in turn can make a military undertaking even more difficult.

This argument does not necessarily mean that in these cases the United States was right to intervene when it did or wrong not to. Such a conclusion could only be reached after weighing all the factors, not timing alone. Rather, the point here is that the notion of only turning to force as a last resort, after all other options have been tried and shown inadequate, runs the clear risk of missing those moments when force might be used most effectively. At every step of the way, including from the outset of a confrontation, intervening militarily must be weighed against other policy options.

TOO MUCH FORCE IS BETTER THAN TOO LITTLE

Proportionality, not using any more force than is warranted, is a common theme in the writing on intervention and war. It is also a tenet of just war thinking. The notion of proportionality appeals to the American notion of fairness; it has roots in the Old Testament credo of "an eye for an eye," a concept intended as a call not for revenge but for limiting punishment to what was warranted by the crime. The pressure not to use more force than is judged necessary can come from coalition partners and allies (as in the case of some Arab states during the Gulf War) or from domestic political and economic considerations (in order to not appear to be embarking on a major overseas enterprise).

The principle is valid if it means to avoid causing harm to civilians or other innocents or wasting U.S. resources and lives by exposing more people to danger than is warranted. It is not valid, however, to try to accomplish defined objectives with the commitment of as few military resources as possible. To the contrary, it is normally better to go into a hostile or potentially hostile situation with too much rather than too little firepower. This concept is central to the thinking of the classical strategists. More recently, Samuel Huntington has noted that "Bigness not brains is our advantage, and we should exploit it. If we have to intervene, we should intervene with overpowering force."[3]

Having more forces than is thought necessary can compensate for Murphy's law (on the battlefield, everything that can go wrong frequently does) and can add a credible threat of escalation and/or compellence. It also allows for multiple, simultaneous strikes and operations, which can confuse the adversary and shorten the duration and costs of the conflict. This approach can also be less risky; it was clearly used to good effect in Grenada, Panama, and *Desert Storm*.[4]

Contrast these three cases with what took place in Lebanon, Somalia, Iran, Haiti, and Bosnia. In the first two instances, U.S. forces took heavier than expected casualties and failed to achieve their goals. The hostage rescue mission was aborted because of a shortage of helicopters. Similarly, the decision to send a small number of essentially unarmed forces to Haiti may have contributed to the reaction on the docks; a show of substantial force might have had a very different effect. And in Bosnia, the decisions in early 1994 to respond to Serbian violations of both no-fly and exclusion (humanitarian) zones with extremely modest air strikes emptied the NATO/U.N. action of most if not all of its punitive and compellent value. The point is not to use force indiscriminately; rather, it is to err on the side of deploying more rather than less force than is thought necessary.

RELEVANT FORCE MATTERS

The United States may be the world's only superpower, but this counts for little if it is unwilling or unable to act like one. It is relevant force that matters: overall inventories are unimportant if there is little or no likelihood that elements of those inventories will be used. What matters are the forces the United States is willing and able to bring to bear or, in the case of deterrence and compellence, those capabilities the adversary believes it is willing and able to bring to bear. A case in point is Somalia, where the world's only superpower lost eighteen soldiers in a firefight with forces belonging to a local warlord, a tactical setback that within days led to a decision by the United States to withdraw its combat forces from the country.

Having enough forces, much less an overwhelming advantage, is not always possible. It is important to keep in mind that options to use force take time to generate and are rarely available from day one of a crisis. Reserve forces must be called up and trained; active duty forces must be transported and readied. Also, early warning signs that a crisis is brewing or a hostile attack is being readied are often unclear; even when they are clear, the desire to avoid a confrontation often works against deploying forces to the scene. As a result, the United States may be outgunned, particularly in the opening days or even weeks of a crisis. This was precisely what happened in the Gulf; it was only good fortune (and Saddam's mistakes) that gave the United States and its coalition the time necessary to prepare for the confrontation after Iraq occupied Kuwait. Defending Saudi Arabia was far less costly than liberating it would have been if Saddam had continued his offensive south.

DECISIVE EARLY USE OF FORCE IS PREFERABLE TO GRADUALISM

During the Cold War, the theorists of limited war made a strong case on paper for gradual escalation, for beginning modestly and thereafter increasing military force as a military confrontation went on. The logic was to use force as much politically as militarily, both to avoid an unwanted response from the Soviet Union or China and to signal the other side to bargain. The idea was to resolve the immediate, local dispute without the confrontation growing into something larger and more dangerous.

The high-water mark of the application of this thinking came in Vietnam, where the United States engaged in a sustained but limited use of force vis-à-vis North Vietnam (and, indirectly, the Soviet Union and China) in an attempt to balance military requirements, which argued for escalation, and political concerns, which argued for restraint. The political concerns were not just diplomatic; the intended audience was as much domestic as it was foreign. It was deemed essential to signal the limited nature of the conflict to the many at home who feared the United States was already doing too much in a theater of at best modest interests.

The problem is that gradualism, or incrementalism, makes little military sense. It provides the adversary time and opportunity to adjust and adapt, politically, psychologically, and militarily. Gradualism has the effect of diluting the factor of intimidation, or menace, that is inherent in warfare. Thus, much of the residual compellent value of military actions is forfeited. This was the case in Vietnam. Lebanon is another good example; the gradual increase in the force used by the United States, from small arms to the large guns on ships to small numbers of air sorties, had little political or military effect on either Syria or the hostile militias.

The alternative to gradualism is to use force massively from the outset. This guideline is thus a corollary to the first two: military force is best used as something other than a last resort, and when military force is used, it is better to err on the side of using more rather than less. Clausewitz makes the case for concentrated effort: " . . . No conquest can be carried out too quickly, and that to spread it out over a longer period than the minimum needed to complete it makes it not less difficult, but more. . . . "5 Such large-scale uses of force can interrupt an adversary's capacity to orchestrate a response. There is also a valuable psychological factor, in that this approach does not allow the other side to get comfortable with the confrontation. Grenada, Panama, and the Gulf War are all successful examples of leading with the strongest possible punch rather than reserving it for use only if more modest initial attacks fail to achieve desired goals.

Lastly, it has been argued that even if gradualism is not necessary for diplomatic or military reasons, it is necessary for domestic political reasons, that is, to reassure the American people that a foreign involvement is not becoming too great. For example, Robert Osgood argues that, at the time of Vietnam, "Although the critics of gradualism who would opt for sudden escalation may be right on military grounds, they are almost certainly wrong on domestic political grounds."6 This may have been true at that time, given the enormous controversy that surrounded the war effort and the years of involvement that had made the American public and Congress weary of war and fearful that any escalation would only prolong it. But it does not appear to hold as a general proposition. Acting massively at the outset is the best way to shorten a conflict, which in turn tends to increase public support for (or at least decrease public opposition to) military interventions. The result is that what makes the most sense militarily on the scene—acting with maximum effect from the beginning of hostilities—may also make the most sense politically at home.

NEW TECHNOLOGIES INCREASE OPTIONS
BUT ARE RARELY SUFFICIENT

A number of emerging technologies are transforming the battlefield and affecting considerations relating to intervention. Breakthroughs in the realm of communications and intelligence (in particular AWACS and JSTARS,[7] which give an integrated view of air and ground environments) contribute to comprehensive and coordinated offensive and defensive actions. Stealth technologies reduce the vulnerability of selected air platforms; cruise missiles reduce the need to send pilots in harm's way. Precision-guided munitions lessen the need for multiple attacks—a much higher percentage of accurate strikes can be anticipated—and make it possible to use force in a manner that limits unwanted collateral damage and civilian casualties. The Gulf War was testament to all of these.

New technologies also increase certain options for acting unilaterally. Cruise missiles launched from warships are an example; no basing access (and, in some instances, no overflight rights) are involved. The June 1993 Tomahawk cruise missile strike against Iraqi intelligence facilities is a case in point.

Yet there is no technological fix to the myriad problems posed by intervention.[8] Advanced U.S. vessels were vulnerable to primitive mines laid by Iran's relatively simple ships in the Gulf in the late 1980s—just as advanced U.S. helicopters were vulnerable to portable air-defense systems manned by Somali soldiers loyal to Aideed. During the Gulf War, the Patriot missile defense system had at best modest success in intercepting crude Iraqi SCUD missiles.[9] Even smart bombs and the most advanced cruise missiles make mistakes and miss their targets or fail to achieve the desired effect. The efforts during the Gulf War to find and destroy Iraq's SCUD missile launchers mostly failed, despite an extraordinary investment in time and effort; the Pentagon's follow-up study on the war admits that "Locating and destroying mobile missiles proved very difficult and required substantially more resources than planned. This could be a more serious problem in the future against an enemy with more accurate missiles or one who uses weapons of mass destruction."[10]

These examples of the limits of technology are all related to war-fighting, even in fairly ideal battlefield situations. The limits to what technology can accomplish in other contexts, including peacekeeping, peace-making, humanitarian operations, and nation-building, are even greater. Often restraint is called for, distinguishing between friend and foe is impossible, and there is no battlefield per se. The problems encountered in Lebanon, Somalia, and Haiti were not amenable to technical solutions. And no new technology, including an emerging class of non-lethal weapons that can degrade weapons systems and incapacitate individuals, will alter the fact that it is more difficult to apply technology in decisive ways to internal struggles, where many of the traditional laws of war do not apply.

AIR POWER IS USEFUL BUT NO PANACEA

On the modern battlefield, there is no substitute for control of the air. Especially in open areas, it can decisively affect the situation on the ground. In war-fighting, air power has two principal roles. It can be used strategically, to destroy high-value targets and to "prepare the battlefield." Or it can be used tactically, as part of a combined arms operation fully integrated with infantry and armored forces. The long-standing debate over the relative value of these two roles need not be addressed here. What is relevant is that modern air forces can make a major difference in both roles. Again, the Gulf War offers a textbook case; six weeks of U.S. and allied air operations destroyed a large part of the Iraqi army and left what remained demoralized, disorganized, and ineffective. Because of air power, all Iraqi naval vessels were either sunk or neutralized, while Iraq's air force was either destroyed, grounded, or parked in Iran.[11] The air war also confused Iraq's command and control, thwarted its ability to supply troops in the theater, and damaged or destroyed high-value targets central to the functioning of society. This was followed by one hundred hours of fighting in which air power played an integral part in the ground offensive that struck a final and decisive blow.

Air forces have other, more discreet ways to contribute to intervention. A demonstration of air superiority on a much more modest scale, the appearance of two U.S. aircraft in the skies over the Philippines, turned the tide in a scenario where symbols of U.S. policy were uniquely powerful. Air power has also proved extremely useful in establishing and monitoring the no-fly zones over both northern and southern Iraq, deterring Iraq from using its own air platforms in these areas. In all these situations, air power offers a way of affecting internal conflicts while limiting the degree of engagement.

In other situations, though, U.S. advantages in the air were not decisive. In Somalia and Beirut, individual fixed and rotary wing aircraft proved vulnerable to relatively simple ground-based air-defense systems. No-fly zones cannot by themselves stop actions by hostile ground forces that directly or indirectly threaten the well-being of the local inhabitants; they have not, for example, prevented ethnic cleansing in Bosnia or the persecution of the Arabs of southern Iraq. Nor can such zones by themselves assure an environment in which aid can be delivered. Even in the Gulf War, air power had its limits. Iraq's mobile ballistic missiles proved nearly impossible to destroy from the air, while much of its nuclear, biological, and chemical capability survived U.S. and coalition bombing. For all its success, air power could not bring about the withdrawal of Iraq's forces from Kuwait; this required a ground offensive. Nor could it bring about a change in Iraq's government. In all such circumstances, air power remains as much a compellent force as a war-fighting one, and thus requires ground forces to accomplish what air power alone cannot.

IMPOSED HUMANITARIAN INTERVENTIONS OFFER A WAY OUT—AND IN

Much of this chapter has argued for the application of classical or traditional approaches to intervention. This works in battlefield situations, but does not offer much guidance for situations involving failed states or civil conflicts in which there is no defined battle-field or clear adversary. What is needed in these situations is an effective approach to intervention that keeps costs limited and in line with the interests at stake and with what the country will support.

To carry out imposed humanitarian intervention at an acceptable cost, it can be useful to establish geographic zones or safe-havens in which supplies can be introduced and people can be reached—all in an area easily defended. Such safe-havens can be created as a magnet for people or (and this is preferable) they can be established where the endangered people already are if they happen to be concentrated in one or only a few places. Air and a modest number of ground forces are required to protect the humanitarian area or areas—to make a safe-haven safe; in addition, air forces may be called upon to carry out punitive attacks on those who violate its terms.

The early stages of the U.S./U.N. interventions in northern Iraq and Somalia provide a model. (To some extent, the no-fly zone over Bosnia-Herzegovina and the exclusion zone around Sarajevo and other designated cities are additional examples, but their effectiveness was mitigated by the delay in introducing them and by the absence of meaningful punitive threats for violating them.) The basic concept has four parts: 1) protection for people who would otherwise be victims, something not to be confused with becoming a military protagonist or partner in a civil war; 2) physical separation of the warring parties, putting them beyond the range in which their weapons can reach one another; 3) working around any significant resistance, not overcoming it; and 4) requiring that those receiving protection forego using the zones for military purposes lest the forces administering the safe-havens find themselves caught in a cross-fire.

This approach has some obvious costs and drawbacks. Humanitarian zones are open-ended, offering no guaranteed exit date for those who maintain them. Such commitments drain troops and equipment that would otherwise be available for other purposes. There will be casualties. Except in situations where an endangered population already is concentrated in one area, establishing zones can either fail to protect some people or force them to migrate to safety. Most of all, humanitarian zones are limited in what they propose to—and can—accomplish. Humanitarian interventions should not be confused with more ambitious political interventions, especially peace-making and nation-building. They are designed to provide a respite from the problem at an affordable cost, not a solution. They are designed to last until the politics of the situation evolve and the aggressor indicates a willingness to change his ways or the protected party chooses to exchange protection for mounting a counter-attack.

For some, this approach will be inadequate. As Stanley Hoffmann has written, "If the humanitarian crisis is . . . 'structural,' provoked either by the disintegration of a state or by the deliberate evil policies of a government, it becomes extremely difficult for the interveners to remedy the humanitarian disaster without addressing the causes that produced it. If they do not consider the causes, in order to stick to a narrow, humanitarian mandate—helping victims—they may well be doomed to playing Sisyphus . . . If the political causes are not removed, victims will remain in danger and the intervention will risk, at best, being no more than a band-aid, and at worst, becoming part of the problem."[12]

Hoffmann is right to portray the risk of modest efforts, but it is equally important to portray the risks and costs inherent in more ambitious undertakings—risks and costs that are likely to prove difficult to justify in light of limited U.S. interests and the difficulty of peace-making and nation-building. Indeed, Hoffmann himself goes on to offer an effective rebuttal to his own criticism. "Dealing with the humanitarian tip of the iceberg may be frustratingly too little; but dealing with the whole iceberg may be far too much, especially if one wants to move from rescue to prevention."[13]

Ironically, others may consider humanitarian intervention too much involvement. Michael Mandelbaum expresses this view. "Intervention for humanitarian purposes leads inevitably to political tasks, which, although not outside the experience of the United States and its allies, are expensive."[14] But while expanded involvement is a risk, it need not become reality. The U.S. presence in Iraq has remained circumscribed; expanding the mission's objectives in Somalia was not inevitable. Indeed, the essence of the concept of humanitarian intervention is that it does not become "political" unless policymakers consciously decide to make it so and broaden the mission.

SOME PURPOSES FOR USING FORCE CAN BE MUTUALLY EXCLUSIVE

It may not prove sustainable to use force for more than one purpose at the same time. For example, a compellent use of force may make it impossible to carry out peacekeeping and/or consensual humanitarian operations simultaneously, although it may make it possible to do so sequentially. With respect to Bosnia, for example, there has been an ongoing tension between the desire not to jeopardize either the welfare or the efforts of humanitarian troops and the wish to coerce the Serbs into modifying their behavior.

This tension in turn relates back to the importance of clarity of purpose. Before intervening, the United States must determine whether it will conduct itself impartially or as a protagonist. If it is the former (as is normally the case with peacekeeping and humanitarian efforts) and if the United States is to avoid taking sides, then considerable restraint is required in both the means and ends of the intervention. If it is the latter (as is normally the case with both peace-making and war-fighting), then force should be used to dominate the conflict and end it as soon as possible. It is critical that the two must not be allowed to become confused.[15] Again, the questions of whether and how to intervene are inseparable: implementation can only succeed if the nature of the situation and the purpose of the intervention are first clearly defined.

CHAPTER SIX

REVISITING THE PAST

T his study began with short reviews of twelve situations in which the United States used military force on behalf of foreign policy aims. Four of these—Grenada, Panama, the Philippines, and the protection of Gulf shipping—are clear successes by most accounts. Three other interventions—Libya, the Gulf War, and the Gulf War's aftermath—are more controversial. The remaining five cases—the Iran rescue effort, Lebanon, Yugoslavia, Somalia, and Haiti—are widely viewed as failures.

The next chapter attempts to apply the guidelines developed in this study to future interventions. This chapter, however, attempts to apply the guidelines to past interventions; it applies them to the successes, to show why they turned out that way, and to the failures, to illustrate both why they failed and how they could have been more effective. What follows is a discussion of the twelve cases with all the benefits (and limitations) of hindsight.

ATTEMPTED RESCUE OF U.S. HOSTAGES IN IRAN

That the attempt to rescue the American hostages in Iran failed is indisputable. What is less clear is whether it was doomed to fail. The political and military participants involved in planning the rescue attempt were optimistic about their prospects for achieving surprise and overcoming resistance (expected to be minimal) with only modest casualties. The official after-action study concluded that the concept appeared feasible.[1]

It makes little sense to explore what might have happened in Tehran if the rescue mission had proceeded with only five helicopters or if there had been fewer mechanical breakdowns or more helicopters to begin with. There is simply no way of knowing. It is worthwhile, however, to look back at the design of the mission and alternatives available. The abort decision was taken because of the number of remaining helicopters. The need for secrecy and surprise argued for keeping the mission as small as possible in order to reduce chances for leaks and for being sighted. But the small number of helicopters provided little leeway in the event of mechanical or other problems. Because the number of helicopters was central to the operation's potential success, a greater number should have been used; according to the after-action study, as many as eleven could have been used without increasing fuel needs or risking secrecy.[2]

But what about alternatives to a rescue mission? A number of options were in fact explored. Some thought was given at the outset of the crisis to seizing something of value to Iran—say, Kharg Island—and bargaining it in return for the hostages. Similarly, consideration was given to mining, blockade, and compellent bombing. But none of these options offered a direct means of bringing about the release of the hostages; all were premised on an Iranian decision to release them as a result of coercion. If such coercive measures failed, and if the hostages were still alive, the United States would have been faced with the decision to back down—clearly losing face and enhancing the credentials of the new regime—or escalating in ways that failed to help the hostages but threatened to involve the United States in a wider and more costly operation. The options were rejected, in part for the reasons listed above, but also out of concern that Iran might turn to the Soviet Union for help—a real fear since the hostage crisis came just months after the Soviet invasion of Afghanistan.

On balance, a strong case can be made that the Carter Administration was right to try the rescue option even if it was wrong in how it went about it. A rescue mission held out a reasonable chance of freeing the hostages sooner than the diplomatic alternatives and with minimal cost. None of the military alternatives could offer the promise of the release of the hostages; all of the alternatives risked not only harm but a wider confrontation with Iran. Also, a successful rescue mission would have other positive impacts, possibly even weakening the new regime in Iran. The tragedy is that it failed to work.

The other military option that received the most scrutiny was not so much an alternative to a rescue mission as a complement to it—namely, a punitive strike against Iran either in association with a rescue mission or at any time if the hostages were harmed. President Carter reportedly ordered plans to attack economic targets whose loss would have a major impact but would not lead directly to large numbers of civilian casualties. Carter decided against such a course of action at the time of the mission to avoid complicating the military planning and to avoid giving the Soviets an opportunity to exploit. Initiating such a strike after the release of the hostages was not seriously considered by either the Carter or the

Reagan administrations for several reasons: a desire to avoid Soviet involvement; lack of public demand; and concern over where it might lead. Instead, non-military measures were used to penalize Iran for what it had done and for its continuing support of terrorism.[3] A possible negative consequence of this decision not to use force in a punitive fashion was that Iran's leaders may have concluded that the limited price the United States exacted for hostage taking was well worth paying—a judgment that may have contributed to Iran's support of hostage taking in Lebanon over the next decade.

LEBANON

It is difficult to escape the conclusion that military force should not have been used a second time in Lebanon. The initial intervention by the United States and several European governments, a form of peacekeeping designed to provide an escort for departing PLO fighters, succeeded in large part because of the narrow but clear nature of the mission and the desire of all parties to the dispute to see it succeed. The second intervention failed because it lacked these basic requirements. The purposes of the deployment stayed vague, they repeatedly evolved and expanded over time, the context changed and became increasingly hostile to the marines—yet the force used remained modest and was introduced incrementally and never decisively. Indeed, the Lebanon deployment is perhaps most noteworthy in that it violates most of the guidelines put forth here regarding both whether and how to use force. The verdict of the official review commission could hardly have been more damning:

The inability of the Government of Lebanon to develop a political consensus, and the resultant outbreak of hostilities between the LAF [Lebanese Armed Forces] and armed militias supported by Syria, effectively precluded the possibility of a successful peacekeeping mission. It is abundantly clear that by late summer 1983, the environment in Lebanon changed to the extent that the conditions upon which the ... mission was initially premised no longer existed.[4]

The experience in Lebanon underscores a critical point: having foreign policy objectives—in this case, a peaceful and independent Lebanon free of all foreign forces—is not the same as having objectives for a particular use of military force. Lebanon also demonstrates the costs of failed intervention—to those involved, to international perceptions of U.S. staying power, to domestic American willingness to support interventions of any sort. No experience other than Vietnam has had such a profound and discouraging effect on popular, congressional, and uniformed military willingness to use military force on behalf of U.S. interests abroad.

The problems in Lebanon were not simply ones of implementation. There was no sensible way for the United States to use force in Lebanon in the early 1980s. Here, and in sharp contrast to the Iran rescue mission, the real tragedy was that it was tried at all.

GRENADA

Grenada succeeded (despite a surprising number of difficulties encountered and casualties sustained) because of the overwhelming amount of force that was used from the outset relative to the opposition. (One advantage of going in "heavy" is that unexpected setbacks are less likely to upset the larger effort.) That the radical regime was so unpopular and so weak militarily—together with the small size of the country and its population—made it that much easier to isolate and defeat.

The American public was tolerant of costs of the rescue cum war-fighting operation primarily because the conflict was short and succeeded in forestalling what appeared to many to be an imminent hostage situation. Public and congressional support, grudging to begin with, gathered strength as the results of the operation became known. Initial opposition by Britain and some Latin American countries (primarily because of inadequate consultation) was muted, largely because the intervention was short-lived, successful, and had the backing (however artificial) of a local coalition.

LIBYA

The U.S. raid on Libya in April 1986 was designed to punish Libya for its role in supporting the bombing of the La Belle discotheque in Berlin and for sponsoring terrorism more broadly. This punitive action may have accomplished other tasks as well, most importantly compellence. Although the information is sketchy and difficult to interpret, a plausible case can be made that the punitive strike had a sobering (if temporary) effect on Libyan behavior, particularly its support for terrorism.

The alternatives to a punitive action were not attractive. Destroying the means to conduct terror to prevent future terrorism is virtually impossible. Preemption is rarely possible in the absence of detailed, timely intelligence. Doing nothing, on the other hand, would have sent the flawed signal that terrorism could be undertaken without retaliation. Punitive strikes were the best choice regardless of whether they would have an impact on future Libyan behavior.

The principal basis for questioning the U.S. action is that it may have been too modest, violating the guideline to use force heavily and decisively. Certainly, more force could have been used—for example, against Libya's energy industry—with possibly greater effect on future Libyan behavior. But this would have endangered U.S. pilots—avoiding a hostage situation was a priority in this pre-modern-cruise-missile era—and would have risked weakening the international consensus forming behind U.S. diplomacy to isolate Libya economically.

There was, however, no reason the April 1986 strike had to be the last. One of the advantages of punitive strikes is that they can be repeated if there are new transgressions. Libya provided the United States and the world with new grounds to act punitively. If there was a problem with policy toward Libya, it was not so much with the attack that occurred but with follow-up attacks that did not.

PROTECTION OF GULF SHIPPING

The Gulf mission is a good example of a successful limited use of military force. That it succeeded in the face of considerable congressional misgivings only makes it more impressive. The purpose was kept narrow—to protect shipping, not to intervene in the Iran-Iraq war or in the internal affairs of either country. (The use of air and naval forces to carry out the operation contributed to narrowing the involvement.) Substantial forces were sent to carry out the mission, and additional forces were made available and used in a punitive fashion against Iran as required. The mission lasted for a year, but with the considerable interests at stake and its manageable costs, it could have continued for years if necessary. Indeed, the willingness of the United States to undertake an open-ended mission sent a useful signal of commitment and hence deterrence.

PANAMA

The U.S. intervention in Panama succeeded in the short run for many of the same reasons as Grenada—overwhelming force used from the outset against a militarily weak regime unpopular at home and abroad. That it was a unilateral effort helped to simplify the operation. There was domestic political support for the intervention in the United States not just because it was successful, but because there was a widespread perception of real threats to important national interests. The local population welcomed the U.S. action and the seating of the legitimate government.

An assessment of the intervention's long-term impact is somewhat more difficult. Panama is less than a model democracy, and it is still heavily involved in narcotics trafficking.[5] But it is likely that the situation would be worse in Panama—both for its own people and for U.S. personnel and interests—if the intervention had not taken place. Operation *Just Cause* did not solve Panama's problems, but the intervention addressed the most urgent challenges and set Panama on a far more promising path than would have been the case otherwise.

There is a larger point to be made here. No intervention, not even one with a nation-building component, can guarantee long-term, much less permanent, results. By neutralizing an external threat or establishing the prerequisites of domestic order, an effective military intervention can provide a people and their government with an opportunity. But it is largely up to the government and people themselves to maintain democracy and internal stability. Others can assist and indirect forms of military help can make a difference, but basic social reform is largely a task for tools other than force and for a country's citizens rather than outsiders.

PHILIPPINES

Of all the cases examined in this volume, the show of force in the Philippines comes closest to old-fashioned gunboat diplomacy, in which a modest show of force by the United States seemed to turn the tide in a domestic struggle. It is hard to know what lessons to draw from this, because of the special U.S.-Philippine relationship and the ineptitude of the plotters. Two points, though, are worth highlighting: the importance of acting early in a crisis, and the utility of force in affecting coups. A modest U.S. show of force would have proved irrelevant if not counter-productive had the Aquino government faced an imminent challenge not from a handful of disaffected soldiers but from the population at large or from a popular group prepared to use violence on a large scale. The fact that the United States acted quickly may have prevented just such a revolutionary situation from materializing.

THE GULF WAR

The Gulf War is generally and rightfully considered a military success. It is the best example available of the impact of new technologies, of air power, of striking heavily and early with decisive impact. It shows how multilateral coalitions can work together politically, economically, and militarily. The country and the Congress backed an enormous undertaking, in large part because the interests at stake and the nature of the adversary seemed to most to warrant such a response. The purposes were defined and limited, and military force was well-suited to achieve them.[6]

Yet there is lingering controversy surrounding the Gulf conflict, less about what the United States and the coalition did during the war than what they chose not to do. In particular, the Bush Administration has received considerable criticism for stopping the fighting too early and for accepting an outcome that left Saddam Hussein in power and able to crush rebellions in both southern and northern Iraq. Usually, governments come under criticism for "mission creep"; in this instance, the Bush Administration has been attacked for resisting it and not moving beyond the limited purposes of the Gulf intervention.[7]

Clearly, a Gulf War that resulted not only in Kuwait's liberation and Iraq's defeat but also in a democratic (or at least more tolerant and less ruthless) Iraq would have been preferable for all concerned. But using military force—continuing the intervention for these more political ends—brought with it enormous risks and potential costs that persuaded the Bush Administration not to continue the fighting. Allowing the war to go on another 24 or 48 hours, as some critics contend should have taken place, would have resulted in the destruction of several hundred more Iraqi weapons but not enough to prevent Saddam from putting down the rebellions as he did. The real question is whether the war should have been continued until Saddam was overthrown or otherwise removed in favor of a demonstrably better leader or political order.[8]

The answer, in this author's view, is no. Trying to capture individuals, as was learned in Panama and Somalia, is difficult. Trying to overthrow one political system and replacing it with another is even more difficult. The Bush Administration was reluctant to alter war aims and, even more so, to allow U.S. forces to be drawn into an internal situation with the potential to become a multi-front civil war. Doing so would have entailed all sorts of risks. The Administration had no assurance of either external or domestic support if it embarked on a more ambitious policy that was sure to involve considerable additional fighting and costs; to the contrary, the coalition would have unravelled and domestic opponents would have charged that the Administration had gone beyond its authorization.

Months, or more realistically years, of occupation would have been necessary to bring about a basic and potentially enduring change in Iraq's orientation. It is far from clear that this would have been sustainable in the face of modern media coverage, national and religious sentiments in Iraq, and domestic and international perceptions. Equally uncertain is whether even an extended U.S. presence could have ensured the emergence of a more democratic order; open-ended fighting involving Iraq's neighbors and the fragmentation of the country were at least as likely. The only certainty is that the United States would have found itself making the transition from war-fighting, which was clearly to its advantage, to peace-making and nation-building, which were not.

GULF WAR AFTERMATH

The arguments about U.S. policy during the initial period after the war ended are similar to those about how the war ended. Intervening directly or indirectly on behalf of one or both rebellions would have risked getting enmeshed in internal struggles of unknown duration and outcome—including the potential break-up of Iraq, something few in the Bush Administration believed to be in the U.S. national interest. Such involvement would also have raised major problems domestically and internationally, especially if matters did not resolve themselves quickly and relatively painlessly.

There was no way to guarantee or even feel confident about the possibility of a quick resolution. The Bush Administration therefore chose to act conservatively, contenting itself with what had been accomplished and with the hope that this might create a context in which internal political change in Iraq would follow.[9]

Even so, the Administration soon found itself more involved in Iraq's internal developments than it had anticipated. Pursuant to U.N. Security Council Resolutions 687 and 688, and in the face of large-scale Iraqi attacks on its Kurdish and Shia citizens, the United States and other coalition members established a small security zone (safe-haven) in the north and much larger no-fly zones in both the north and south. These are imposed humanitarian missions, whose purpose is not to bring about a change in government (although this would be welcomed) but to limit Iraqi military access to the protected areas with little cost or risk of life to the soldiers involved. They are open-ended missions, but sustainable because of the way in which they are carried out (e.g., armed reconnaissance, highly limited ground presence, and punitive air strikes as warranted against those clearly responsible for illegal behavior). The principal alternative was and remains expanding the size of the security zone in the north and creating one in the south, i.e., complementing the no-fly zones with armed humanitarian zones or safe areas.

SOMALIA

The U.S./U.N. intervention in Somalia provides a clear set of questions and lessons. Some questions pertain to whether it was correct to intervene. Only humanitarian interests were at stake. Hundreds of thousands, possibly millions, of lives were at stake, not because of a deliberate policy of genocide, but because of chaos and violence. The motivation (and rationale) for the intervention thus rested on need—the situation called for it, and only the United States seemed willing and able to do it on short notice—and on an assessment that the costs, like the interests, would be modest and therefore acceptable.

It did not work out that way, and when the costs in terms of American lives and dollars suddenly climbed, domestic public and congressional support for the intervention dissolved. The Clinton Administration concluded that agreeing to an exit by a specific date (March 31, 1994) was the only way to avoid immediate withdrawal. But was this tragic and failed ending inevitable, or could either the Bush or Clinton administrations have pursued different actions with different results?

Even hindsight is less than 20:20, but it is at least plausible and perhaps likely that alternatives would have met with greater success. Once the decision was made to act, the Bush Administration had two options. One was to undertake an imposed humanitarian intervention, the other to pursue peace-making and nation-building.

Providing a humanitarian respite (as was initially done) required making much of Somalia a safe-haven but avoiding Mogadishu, where consent was not forthcoming. Sustaining the effort would have required—perhaps for a period of years, until the internal politics of Somalia sorted themselves out and an authority emerged—at least a limited defense of the safe-haven from internal and external threats. This would have entailed air power and some ground forces from the United States and elsewhere. This approach would have taken time and money but would have incurred few casualties. Ironically, this is essentially what the United States and the United Nations adopted (or returned to) after a more ambitious policy of de facto peace-making and nation-building proved too costly.[10]

The principal alternative to a humanitarian approach was to embark from the outset on a policy of concerted peace-making and nation-building.[11] This would have required aggressively disarming the local factions and arresting those who resisted, setting up a transitional political authority, and creating a professional police and military. It would have meant a greater willingness to accept costs at the beginning of the intervention for which there might not have been much domestic support in the absence of national interests.

The advantage of this approach is that after an initial period of peace-making by U.S. forces, the conditions might have existed for U.N. forces to carry out peacekeeping and nation-building activities.[12]

It was the decision of the Bush Administration to choose the first approach, one of lower risk and lower near-term pay-off. It was the error of the Clinton Administration to move to a policy of de facto peace-making/nation-building in spring 1993 without putting in place the necessary forces or preparing the country for the inevitable costs. Whether U.S. interests (which were limited to the humanitarian) justified a policy of peace-making by either administration is doubtful, in that there appeared to be an alternative and that the limited interests made it difficult to justify the higher costs associated with a more demanding policy.

BOSNIA

The decisions to avoid using significant military force in the former Yugoslavia remain highly controversial. The many debates about *how* force could best be used took place against a backdrop of questions over whether U.S. interests merited any military intervention at all. Some saw considerable interests at stake in addition to humanitarian concerns: the opportunity to define rules of the road for post–Cold War Europe, the risk of a wider war in the Balkans if action was not taken, an unfortunate precedent that would encourage Russian activism immediately beyond its borders in its so-called "near abroad." Others did not accept the presence of these larger stakes and simply saw humanitarian concerns that did not justify the risks associated with intervention. There is no way to resolve this debate to everyone's satisfaction, but the very existence of the debate is a warning about the tenuous nature of domestic support for any expensive undertaking.[13]

Nevertheless, a number of opportunities to use force can be identified and at least partially assessed. (These are in addition to missed opportunities for diplomacy that might have had a constructive impact.) In late 1991 and early 1992, the United States and others (particularly Europeans) could have inserted deterrent forces in Croatia and Bosnia. Although it is possible that Serbia would have held back from attacking for fear of triggering more substantial international intervention, the region's history suggests that it would not have been deterred by a symbolic force. Moreover, a deterrent deployment (or, as Boutros Boutros-Ghali calls it, a "preventive deployment") at that time would have been difficult to build support for. The Yugoslav government, until April 1992 the relevant actor, would not have approved it, and outsiders would have been unlikely to press hard: not only were the consequences of involvement unclear, but most observers at the time did not think that diplomacy had had sufficient opportunity to defuse the situation. Inserting forces for defensive purposes after April 1992, that is, after the recognition of Bosnia's independence, was never seriously entertained largely for fear (reasonably so) that these forces would find themselves caught up in a bitter and messy war.

A second area of controversy in the crisis surrounding former Yugoslavia relates to the decision not to modify the U.N. arms embargo to permit providing indirect help to the Bosnian Muslims. (U.N. Security Council Resolution 713 of September 25, 1991, called for an embargo on the sale of all arms and military equipment to Yugoslavia.) It can be argued that the original decision to treat all protagonists equally was wrong, but it was taken early in the conflict. The real debate came later, when advocates of the "indirect" option made the powerful arguments that the "even-handed" policy worked against the Muslims because of far greater Serbian access to weapons, and that the West had a moral responsibility to arm the Muslims if it was not willing to intervene directly to protect them against Serbian and at times Croat attacks.

Despite these arguments, the embargo was not modified. European countries were concerned that arming the Bosnian Muslims would trigger Serbian retaliation against UNPROFOR II (the U.N. humanitarian mission) and encourage the Bosnians to fight on, thereby undermining chances for a negotiated settlement. The United States was concerned that providing support to Bosnians would have adverse political repercussions for Boris Yeltsin, already struggling at home. With no international consensus to repeal or amend the resolution, the United States would have had to act alone to provide arms to Bosnia—a unilateral act that would have had significant and potentially adverse ramifications for both U.S.-European and U.S.-Russian relations.

Moreover, the indirect strategy of arming the Muslims would not have released the United States and the West from difficult decisions if it proved insufficient. To the contrary, the United States would have felt more rather than less obligated to get involved directly if arming (and possibly training) the Muslims led to a chain of events that on balance worsened their plight in the near term—which was, in fact, likely since Serbia was nearly certain to intensify military operations in the face of a selective lifting of the arms embargo.

These arguments do not necessarily mean that arming the Muslims would have been ill-advised. On reflection, it looks like the least bad of the available military options; it would have provided the Bosnians an opportunity to defend themselves and created an improved basis for negotiating. Nevertheless, it was fraught with problems (diplomatic and otherwise) and would not have insulated the United States and others from choices involving more direct forms of intervention.[14]

A third policy choice made repeatedly was to avoid trying to compel Serbs to moderate their behavior in Bosnia. Debate came to a head in spring, and then in summer 1993, and then again in January and April 1994. The idea most often discussed was to use air power to attack Serbian positions—either in Bosnia or even in Serbia Montenegro itself—in order to persuade Bosnian-Serb and Serbian leaders that their policy of aggression against the Muslims and their interference with relief efforts was not worth the cost. A related and not always differentiated possibility was to use air power to interdict supplies headed toward the conflict areas from Serbia or to strictly enforce the embargo against Serbia. In principle, air strikes could have been used to interfere directly with the war effort or to bring about a change in the political leadership or its behavior, thereby helping to create an acceptable status quo on the ground.[15] In the words of one advocate, "What air power cannot achieve by brute force, it can attain by persistence."[16]

The threat of air strikes seemed to achieve some modest gains; for example, in August 1993, the Serbs partially withdrew their forces from two key mountains near Sarajevo. (The threats failed, however, to affect the basic behavior of Serbian forces, who continued to pressure Sarajevo and other areas of Muslim concentration.) When the issue arose again in early 1994 during the NATO summit, there was no consensus to carry out strikes. There was concern over retribution against humanitarian troops and uncertainty over what would happen if these limited attacks did not have the desired effect. The United States and NATO would have been faced with choices of escalating military involvement, trying a new approach (such as arming the Bosnians), or walking away, with all that would entail for this and other interests around the world.[17]

It is impossible to know what would have transpired if substantial compellent strikes had been carried out against the Serbs at any time beginning with their aggression against Slovenia and Croatia in 1991. But it is important not to lose sight of the special character of wars within (as opposed to between) states. Internal wars tend to be the most bitterly contested, and history suggests the need for skepticism about claims that limited bombing would have turned the tide against a party with a far greater stake in the outcome than the United States and the West—especially if the goal of compellence was to reverse rather than stop or even prevent aggression. The at best partial success of the modest NATO air strikes—triggered by continued Serbian flouting of NATO and U.N. demands—in 1994 tends to bear this out. Again, compellence leaves the initiative in the hands of the target side, which then has the option of retaliating in ways and at times and places of its own choosing.

This does not necessarily mean that air strikes would not have worked or ought not to have been tried. Rather, it is to point out that compellent air strikes constituted a highly uncertain course of action and that significant early use of force would have been required to succeed. However, this would have made it extremely difficult to build domestic and international consensus.

A fourth policy option would have been to give UNPROFOR II a more aggressive mandate (or to have it carry out its mandate more aggressively). This would have required providing more as well as more capable forces. The troops delivering humanitarian aid are at most lightly armed and operate under highly restrictive rules of engagement. When challenged, they do little more than back down and lodge a diplomatic protest. At least in principle, they could have been given a more assertive mission, for example delivering humanitarian aid despite resistance, or even protecting one or more zones outlined in the various plans to cantonize Bosnia-Herzegovina. The ground troops could have been heavily armed for combat. But this would have required transforming their mission into one of peace-making, and would have gradually but inevitably embroiled these troops as full-fledged participants in the civil war. Such a mission would have required large numbers of ground troops and air forces for years. Indeed, the option of military intervention with ground forces to impose or enforce (as opposed to monitor) a partition plan, i.e., peace-making, would likely have proved prohibitively expensive in such an environment.[18] U.S. and Western interests did not justify such a commitment—and even for those who think they do, it is difficult if not impossible to design an operation militarily that promised to be effective.[19]

Yet another approach would have been to take measures to make the "safe areas" safe. On April 17, 1993, the Security Council declared the city of Srebrenica to be a safe area; on May 6, Sarajevo, Tuzla, Zepa, Gorazde, and Bihac were added to the list. At that point, it would have possible not only to create and enforce no-fly zones over these areas (enforcement for such a zone over all of Bosnia was already authorized as of April 7, 1993 by Security Council Resolution 816) but to require that the Serbs and all other parties pull back their artillery and guns.

In effect, six armed humanitarian zones (or even more to cover other cities, such as Mostar) could have been created in predominantly Muslim areas. Costs would have been relatively modest, since the purpose of the forces (mostly air but some ground) would have been to protect the zones; it would not have been to take on the

Serbs or anyone else outside the zones and their immediate vicinity.

This approach would have addressed one of the flaws in the proposals put forward on various occasions by those who wanted air power to be used against the Serbs. These proposals never made clear how such help could be calibrated to be sufficient to coerce the Serbs to desist or even fall back without encouraging the Muslims or the Croats to continue fighting for a settlement resembling the status quo ante. Truly safe "safe-havens" could not be used as a base camp from which to mount operations, while effectively making the surrounding areas arms free would preclude those on the outside shooting in.

In addition, punitive air strikes—designed to inflict substantial pain—could have been threatened and carried out in response to violations of the terms of the zone by those outside—terms to be dictated, not negotiated. If these strikes had the effect of also changing Serbia's leadership or its actions, so much the better. Even if not, sanctions could remain in place to promote reversing Serbia's conquest of territory by force; and those responsible for ethnic cleansing could be tried for war crimes.

There are important drawbacks to making the safe areas safe and turning them into armed humanitarian zones. It would not by itself have reversed the status quo, and it would have offered the Bosnians an uncertain future in non-contiguous safe areas— "reservations" or "Gaza Strips" to their detractors. It would therefore have been rejected by some or many in the Bosnian community. Such a policy would also have been open-ended and required considerable air forces and modest numbers of ground troops. But for all its faults, it might have been preferable both to what transpired and to more ambitious approaches. This approach is related to but not identical to that adopted by the international community in February and then again in April 1994, when the U.N. Security Council, in tandem with the United States and NATO, took limited steps to protect selected Bosnian cities.[20]

Ironically, the initial decision to use force in Bosnia by introducing U.N. forces to the area (UNPROFOR II) for humanitarian purposes may well have been counter-productive. There was little consensus on the ground, which not only limited the effectiveness of the relief operation but also made those involved vulnerable to the Serbs or others willing to threaten them. (It is noteworthy that NATO Secretary General Manfred Woerner cited the need to "avoid situations in which your own troops become hostages" as a lesson of the Yugoslav experience.)[21] This in turn all but ruled out any coercive use of force, whether compellent, indirect, or even punitive. Even if the original decision was not entirely flawed—it did help get aid to people who otherwise would likely have perished—the decision not to withdraw these forces had far-reaching and on balance adverse consequences.[22]

One other aspect of the Bosnian experience is worth highlighting. The Bush Administration received a great deal of criticism for resisting the break-up of Yugoslavia and arguing against recognition of new states. A united Western position that would have made recognition contingent on the republics negotiating with one another and providing for minority rights would have been far preferable to the uncoordinated, unilateral declarations of independence that took place.[23] In retrospect, this series of diplomatic recognitions by the international community, not accompanied by meaningful provisions for security and stability, must bear significant responsibility for setting off the resulting tragedy.[24] Even if one does not fully subscribe to this view—clearly, Serbian nationalism and irresponsible Serbian leadership deserve a major share of the responsibility for events in the former Yugoslavia—it is true that Western diplomacy (in addition to inaction in the face of Serbian aggression) often exacerbated tensions and increased prospects for instability.

Whether more responsible diplomacy might have averted the resulting crisis is a question that can only be debated, not answered. But Yugoslavia's dissolution was clearly not managed with the careful diplomacy it merited. More generally, self-determination cannot be an absolute; to the contrary, ethnically-based polities (as opposed to those that have a territorial and/or political basis) tend to be intolerant and aggressive. Other foreign policy tools, including preventive diplomacy, must be effectively wielded if the tool of military intervention is not to be overwhelmed.

HAITI

As of August 1994, the U.S. approach to Haiti was less an inter-vention than a policy reflecting multiple decisions not to use force. The most dramatic example of this came in October 1993, when the Clinton Administration decided to cancel plans to insert troops sent to provide technical assistance as part of a larger arrangement to transfer power back to ousted President Aristide. When the troops were met by mobs at Port-au-Prince, they sailed back to Guantanamo. Because of the predictable absence of order in Haiti, the sensible choices would have been not to send such troops there at all—much of the work could have been accomplished through training programs located outside Haiti or through civilian con-tractors—or to send troops with greater military capability.

This set of events, coming as it did on the heels of the U.S. de-bacle in Somalia, changed the situation in Haiti dramatically. The military leaders dug in; a consensual transfer of power was no longer possible. The military option at that point became one of war-fighting, which would have required an effort similar in kind to those of the Grenada and Panama operations, that is, defeating and arresting those providing armed resistance, returning right-fully elected political authority to power, and then helping the new government through its transition in a classic nation-building ef-fort. This would have proven extremely difficult given Haiti's his-tory and political culture.

Because of Haitian and hemispheric concerns about U.S. in-tervention, not to mention domestic American concerns about as-suming new burdens, the best approach might have been to as-semble an informal coalition (perhaps including French, Canadian, Venezuelan, and other Latin and Caribbean forces) in which the United States undertook the bulk of the initial inter-vention and the others undertook the task of nation-building. For historical and political reasons, it is unlikely that the Organization of American States would have given formal authorization. On July 31, 1994, the U.N. Security Council passed Resolution 940, authorizing the formation of a multinational force that can "use all necessary means to facilitate the departure from Haiti of the military leadership.[25]

The United States had basically two interests in Haiti: promoting democracy and promoting conditions of stability that would induce Haitians to stay safely at home and not overwhelm U.S. immigration limits.[26] Clearly, these interests were not served by a policy of economic sanctions that increased the misery of the masses (and their desire to flee) but not of the military ruling the country. Easing sanctions (to reduce the need to leave) would not have restored democracy and would have represented a major foreign policy reversal. Tightening sanctions, on the other hand, while possible in principle, was difficult to do in practice and would have hurt rather than helped Haitians; the best way to do it, inserting armed forces along the Haitian-Dominican border, was unacceptable to the Dominican government. Another approach—the indirect option of assembling and training an exile force—would have taken time and ensured considerable violence and led even more Haitians to try to come to the United States. Maintaining an immigration policy that discouraged Haitians from leaving was unpopular with important domestic political constituencies. Diplomatic efforts aimed at dislodging the military leaders appeared unpromising. The result was that by summer 1994, a U.N.-authorized multinational intervention of Haiti designed to minimize the long-term U.S. role appeared to be the most likely course of action to promote order and deal with immigration pressures at a cost the American people and the Congress could be persuaded to support.[27]

CHAPTER SEVEN

CONSIDERING THE FUTURE

I ntervening everywhere is not an option. But how can general guidelines and past lessons be translated into future policies? What should be the criteria for selection? What are American priorities? Which interests lend themselves to being promoted or protected by military force? And what consequences follow for U.S. military forces—and for what we ask of other countries and organizations?

Such questions go to the heart of the foreign policy debate and to the study and practice of international relations. They necessarily raise questions of priorities, of whether emphasis is placed on order *between* states or *within* states, on stability or justice. These are not just matters of intellectual speculation; to the contrary, where one comes out on these matters determines a host of policy considerations.[1]

Traditionally, a foreign policy driven by inter-state relations emphasizes such considerations as the non-use of military force to settle disputes, opposition to the acquisition of territory by force, and respect for state sovereignty. The goal is peace, both for its own sake and because peace is likely to promote the evolution of an international context more supportive of a free flow of goods and services. Moreover, a world at peace with itself and involved in productive commerce is more likely to produce liberal political structures than a world at war militarily and economically.

A foreign policy more attuned to "justice" is less preoccupied with the external behavior of states and more sensitive to their nature—their economic and, above all, their political institutions and practices. Intra-state, not inter-state, considerations dominate. Such an orientation leads to policies designed to promote domestic change—from an American perspective, in the direction of human rights, democracy, and capitalism. The available tools run the gamut, from private and public diplomacy to sanctions and military intervention of one type or another.

It is possible to conclude that there need be no distinction between the two approaches.[2] A foreign policy that concerns itself with security and order alone is likely to have trouble commanding domestic support. It also will find itself unable—or perhaps unwilling—to respond to a host of problems. Perhaps most important, a foreign policy emphasis upon order could be considered short-sighted, because the alternative of promoting justice and democracy is not only inherently desirable for reasons of values, but also beneficial in practice because democracies are more likely to act in an orderly fashion beyond their borders (as good citizens in international society) than are non-democracies.

There is some truth to these criticisms of an emphasis on order, particularly the last one. Liberal democracies are more likely to be less bellicose than totalitarian regimes, especially in their relations with other democracies.[3] But this tendency is not absolute. Democracies have been known to act violently and intolerantly, especially when they are captured by populist and nationalist leaders. Also, because of its diplomatic, economic, and strategic interests, the United States often does not have the luxury of designing and carrying out a foreign policy based upon the domestic nature of states. It needs to work with governments to promote a range of foreign policy interests even if it does not subscribe to all they do or are.

As a result, priority must still be given to the "classic" requirement of foreign policy, that of ensuring the safety and welfare of the state and its citizens. This is especially so when it comes to the military instrument of foreign policy, which is best suited for protecting national interests and curbing the external behavior of others but, as has been shown, is less well-suited for effecting internal change. Indeed, the "order versus justice" debate is less relevant if one considers it not a choice between policy goals so much as a choice between policy instruments. Thus, even if the military instrument is largely (although not exclusively) reserved for more traditional purposes of maintaining international order, there is no a priori reason why other policy instruments must be used in the same way, particularly in trying to influence how governments treat their own people.

The order versus justice debate is rejected by some for yet another reason, namely, that *neither* justifies the costs of involvement in most or all circumstances. Foreign policy "minimalists," for example, argue that the United States has limited foreign policy interests, that little that happens overseas can affect Americans — and that as a result little that happens overseas is worth trying to affect.[4] Closely related are those who believe that what happens domestically is more important and more deserving of resources, and that in most situations the United States simply cannot afford to intervene or maintain the instruments of intervention. These foreign policy "declinists" fear that the costs of activism abroad will undermine the domestic economy and society.[5]

A serious refutation of these ideas is beyond the scope of this study.[6] Suffice to say here that American society and the economy have flourished when there was far higher spending on defense than is the case at present, and that there will continue to be a need for substantial U.S. military strength. Not only does the United States have important national interests to protect (e.g., promoting international order, maintaining access to resources, preventing genocide), but in some circumstances military intervention will be the best way to affect international developments.

Maintaining military strength will be costly, but not as costly as the alternatives in the long run. Neglect will prove to be malign — directly for U.S. overseas interests, indirectly for the quality of life at home. Disorder abroad will disrupt trade and investment, increase immigration pressures, make action against terrorism and narcotics trafficking more difficult, jeopardize access to vital natural resources, stimulate armament by others, and ultimately necessitate more U.S. defense spending and more U.S. military intervention in order to cope with the consequences of international instability that cannot be ignored or avoided.

TRANSLATING INTERESTS INTO INTERVENTIONS: CLASSIC SCENARIOS

How does this line of thinking translate into planning for military intervention and the use of force? The two most demanding scenarios for U.S. use of force in the foreseeable future are also the most straightforward. The first is the need to respond to an imminent or actual North Korean invasion of the Republic of Korea. The second involves responding to an imminent or actual attack by Iran or Iraq upon Kuwait, Saudi Arabia, or several other Gulf states. In both these situations, the decision to respond with force would be almost automatic given the mix of stakes and commitments. Not surprisingly, these are two theaters in which the United States has fought major military engagements in the post–World War II era, in both cases with considerable assistance from others and with explicit, formal international political endorsement.

Interestingly, the U.S. stake in these regions is largely unaffected by the end of the Cold War. North Korea has the potential not only to upset stability on the Korean Peninsula but to disrupt the entire Asia-Pacific theater. The 36,000 U.S. troops in Korea (and a similar number in Japan) add to U.S. concern for what happens in the region, but these forces reflect U.S. interests rather than lead to them. If North Korea dominates the peninsula, perhaps with nuclear weapons, it would trigger regional rearmament and a proliferation of unconventional weapons. In the process, a region that has known considerable stability and unparalleled prosperity for decades and in which four key power centers—China, Japan, Russia, and the United States—have interests would find itself in upheaval. This, in turn, would have a dramatic impact upon the world economy and international relations more broadly.

U.S. involvement in the Gulf is no less significant. U.S. and industrialized world dependence upon Gulf energy resources shows no sign of abating. Moreover, the U.S. commitment to the Middle East, which encompasses the security of Israel, the stability of moderate Arab states, and the continuing peace process, cannot be divorced from developments in the Gulf. Politically, economically, and militarily, developments in the Gulf have a direct and profound impact upon the Middle East and both Central and South Asia. Important and perhaps vital U.S. interests would suffer sharply were the Persian Gulf to fall under the sway of a hostile Iran or Iraq.

A third demanding scenario requiring the potential use of force raises even greater problems: a resurgent Russia bent on reclaiming or reconstructing parts of the former Soviet empire, especially in the Baltics, Eastern Europe, or Ukraine. Such a scenario would raise fundamental concerns over the balance of power and international order.

Because of Russia's political evolution and the deterioration of its armed forces, a scenario involving either the Baltics or Eastern Europe is less likely, at least in the near future, than either the Gulf or Korean scenarios. But if it occurred, a revitalized and expanded NATO would have to deter and if necessary defend against such a classic act of aggression (NATO would have considerable time to prepare for this contingency). If problems with Russia recur, it is better they come on Russia's borders than on Western Europe's. Neither the East European nor the Baltic countries should again come under Moscow's authority.

By contrast, and although it would have major repercussions for the balance of power, a direct military response to Russian use of force against Ukraine would not be advisable. Geography and other factors (including the presence of nuclear weapons on both sides) simply work against U.S. and Western ability to engage on attractive terms; as a result, U.S. policy is best served by making such Russian action less likely. This involves promoting Ukraine's viability, encouraging autonomy for and proper treatment of ethnic Russians in Crimea, and making clear to Russia the price it would pay in its relations with the West if it acted aggressively. Much the same applies to potential Russian uses of force elsewhere in its immediate vicinity (for example, in the Caucasus or Central Asia).

What these potential scenarios have in common is their traditional, inter-state character. At issue are specific interests as well as the basic organizing principle of international society, i.e., defending state sovereignty against external aggression. Each of these cases involves borders, clear divisions between the territory of the attacking state and the attacked. There is a status quo ante that can be restored and maintained. The guidelines suggest that such conflicts can best be fought with massive force used decisively from the outset to destroy the adversary's ability to project military power.

One factor complicating major potential U.S. military interventions is the spread of chemical, biological, and above all nuclear weapons capabilities to states that are likely adversaries. The United States has a compelling interest in keeping regional wars limited to conventional arms. Use of unconventional weapons by adversaries requires U.S. personnel to adapt measures from special equipment to changed tactics that detract significantly from performance. In addition, use of unconventional munitions by foes greatly increases the danger of casualties. The calculus of intervention—the basic assessment of projected costs and benefits—changes if it includes chemical or biological agents or nuclear weapons.

Nevertheless, the United States must prepare for this possibility. In addition to continuing efforts to stop all forms of proliferation, this requires planning for preventive missions against selected targets, ensuring a readiness to carry out preemptive strikes at the outset of any conflict, and placing greater emphasis on deterrence. Deterrence can be enhanced through the private and/or public communication of clear warnings to the adversary of the consequences of using unconventional weapons against U.S. or friendly forces. These consequences include punitive attacks using conventional weapons against valued political and economic targets otherwise safe, possible retaliation in kind, and (in some contexts such as the Korean Peninsula, where South Korean forces provide a natural potential army of occupation) a message that the war will not be terminated until there is a change in regime in the aggressor country.[7] Finally, proliferation requires increased efforts to develop, and when viable build, theater defenses against ballistic missiles carrying unconventional (and especially nuclear) payloads.[8]

The United States must prevent a situation from evolving in which it is deterred from intervening militarily because of the unconventional capabilities of regional adversaries. Nor should it return to the strategy of gradualism and signalling that characterized interventions in the Cold War in order to avoid nuclear use by regional adversaries. Nothing would be more likely to undermine the effectiveness of interventions, stimulate further proliferation, and place U.S. interests and relationships at risk. While an adversary's possession of and willingness to use unconventional weapons must be factors in deciding whether and how to intervene, they should not be decisive.

Another kind of scenario involves more limited potential interventions that are smaller in scope, shorter in duration, but nevertheless have a clear and important purpose. They include hostage rescues, limited punitive reprisals against terrorists or states supporting them, and interdiction on behalf of sanctions, narcotics policy, or immigration regulation. These potential military interventions can be readily defined and can be carried out with high expectations of military success as well as domestic and international support.

The guidelines suggest that such interventions are more likely to prove successful if they are kept narrow in purpose, involve ample force, and are conducted as decisively as possible.

Far more difficult (yet still easy to foresee) are possible calls for military intervention in complex and controversial circumstances. One set of scenarios involves preventive strikes on unconventional military capabilities. A second set of scenarios involves intervening in the internal affairs of others for either humanitarian or political purposes. Both kinds of situations have already been the subject of considerable debate; both are likely to provide the United States with its most difficult foreign policy choices in the years to come.

PREVENTIVE INTERVENTIONS

Preventive uses of force are reactive in the sense that they respond to developments perceived as threats, but they are—and are likely to be viewed as—proactive in every other sense. The temptation to undertake preventive attacks mounts as an emerging threat materializes and as the likelihood of conflict grows. Expressed differently, preventive attacks become more attractive if conflict is seen as increasingly probable on decreasingly favorable terms.

Yet preventive attacks are easier contemplated than carried out. Preventive uses of force will be futile unless the location of sufficiently vulnerable targets is known; in the case of unconventional weapons, those targets must also represent all or most of the relevant capability. In addition, it is important to be prepared to manage any retaliation that might follow.

Preventive strikes are most likely against two types of targets. The first is terrorist capabilities. The problem with these is that they are often "soft" and easily moved or re-created. The second and more likely set of targets are facilities central to the development of unconventional weapons. Here the problems stem from a lack of knowledge—as we learned with Iraq, what we don't know can far exceed what we do—and from inability to destroy the target because of protective measures. Also, preventive attacks can lead to a larger conflict—a limited attack on North Korean nuclear facilities could trigger a massive Korean conflict, possibly including the use by North Korea of unconventional capabilities not eliminated in a preventive strike.

There are also diplomatic problems to consider. The notion of preventive self-defense—"legitimate anticipation" in the words of one legal scholar—is not universally accepted in principle and in any event is difficult to apply in the specific.[9] The international community has long embraced the norm of the right of self-defense, and is beginning to recognize a second norm of humanitarian intervention. It is, however, a long way from accepting a third norm that would legitimize preventive strikes to destroy the nascent unconventional weapons capabilities of states deemed by some to be rogues.

The net result is that preventive uses of force are attractive options only in rare circumstances. Defensive measures and punitive attacks against state sponsors of terror are more effective responses to terrorists, while proliferation concerns can normally be better addressed by a mix of non-proliferation strategies, deterrence, and defensive measures. But preventive attacks may be the best option against the emergence of a militarily significant unconventional capability if diplomacy (or diplomacy buttressed by sanctions) fails to place an acceptable ceiling on the threat, if effective defense is not available, and if war seems likely.

These arguments are sure to be brought up in the context of North Korea.[10] A preventive strike would be a serious option if North Korea was on the verge of developing a significant nuclear weapons capability. Gaining formal international authority for an attack would be impossible; more important would be gaining the support (or at least acquiescence) of those states most likely to be affected adversely by any North Korean response, namely, Japan and especially South Korea. Also, a preventive strike would have to be preceded by conventional military efforts designed to deter or defend against retaliation and, as noted before, by a message to North Korea that war would not be terminated until the peninsula was reunified under the control of the South.

INTERNAL INTERVENTIONS

Direct military involvement in the internal affairs of another state tends to be for one of three purposes: *humanitarian* (providing protection and the basics of life, often through the establishment of safe havens), *nation-building* (recasting the institutions of the society), or *compellence/peace-making* (tilting the balance in favor of a contending individual or group). The question is when to opt for one of the above approaches—as opposed to another or none at all.

HUMANITARIAN INTERVENTIONS

Calls for military intervention for humanitarian purposes are likely to be heard and considered in the context of abusive and failed states and civil unrest that leaves large numbers of people vulnerable. Unfortunately, the list of potential situations in which such interventions may be desired (by a protagonist, an external party, or an observer) is almost unlimited. Indeed, situations potentially meriting humanitarian interventions promise to be a common feature of post–Cold War international relations.

Answering the question of whether to intervene will be extremely difficult because of the need for selectivity. The impossibility of responding to all such situations is not a rationale for inaction—just because we cannot intervene everywhere does not mean we ought not intervene anywhere—but it highlights the need to be able to explain and defend decisions to intervene as well as not to intervene if domestic and international support is to be forthcoming.

Three factors ought to shape the decision to act: a) the actual or potential scale of the problem, b) the existence of non-humanitarian interests, and c) the availability of military options that provide relief at acceptable costs and that promise better results at no greater costs than alternative measures. A decision that ignores any of these factors risks serious problems on the ground as well as at home.

The scale of the problem calls for awkward but necessary judgments. How serious is the situation? Is it life-threatening? If so, to how many people? Repression is not genocide, hunger is not starvation, fifty people getting hurt every day amidst civil violence is not fifty thousand. The greater the scale of the problem—or the greater the likelihood that an even more substantial problem will come about—the greater the weight of the argument on behalf of intervention.

The second consideration is the presence of other interests. Somalia involved only humanitarian interests. In Haiti, immigration concerns had to be factored in; in Bosnia, a number of strategic interests were (and are) involved. If Egypt were threatened with a radical Islamic takeover, it could be argued that vital U.S. interests were in jeopardy. The greater the interest—the closer it comes to being vital—the greater the case for military intervention.

There is, however, an exception to this rule. The presence of additional interests can also inhibit the use of force—for example, if intervention risks complicating relations (or worse) with an important and powerful government; this could include either a government doing the abuse (say, China at the time of Tiananmen Square) or another observer (Russia in the Bosnia situation). We would stay aloof militarily too if humanitarian atrocities were committed on a large scale in China, India, or the former Soviet Union.

The third consideration determining whether the United States intervenes military must be an assessment of the expected benefits and costs in comparison to the alternatives. What will be required? What are the likely economic costs? How dangerous is the operation likely to be? How much does the local political situation and culture provide to work with? What can others be expected to contribute? What will happen in the absence of U.S. military involvement? Are others likely to act if the United States does not? Could other policies (e.g., sanctions) achieve the same or similar ends within an acceptable time frame?

NATION-BUILDING INTERVENTIONS

Similar questions need to be raised before nation-building is undertaken. Like humanitarian intervention, nation-building can be motivated by how a state treats its own people. It can also be motivated by a desire to transform a state's foreign policy so that it does not again resort to force against neighbors. But nation-building is a far more ambitious enterprise. All forms of humanitarian intervention, both consensual and imposed, are limited in means and ends. Their intent and operation is distinctly different from interventions designed to make a country secure and stable—a goal that requires replacing the existing political authority (or creating one where none exists) so that local peoples can lead relatively normal lives. Nation-building requires defeating and disarming any local opposition and establishing a political authority that enjoys a monopoly or near-monopoly of control over the legitimate use of force.

Successful nation-building can involve first going to war, as in the case of both Japan and Germany. In both cases, nation-building required years of occupation. To succeed, nation-building sometimes must seek to do nothing less than to remake a political culture. It is more demanding in the near term than humanitarian interventions, but potentially less so over the very long term. It is highly intrusive, as even the limited nation-building efforts in Panama, Grenada, and Somalia all demonstrate.

When should the choice be nation-building rather than doing nothing or simply undertaking a humanitarian intervention? The calculation involves assessing *cause* (How damaging or threatening is the offending state, both to its own people and its neighbors?); *opportunity* (Does the society or culture lend itself to remaking?); *costs* (What will it take and are others willing to share the burden?); and *alternatives* (What other ways are available to affect the target entity or to cope with it?).

Humanitarian intervention (building safe-havens) can be the best response in countries torn by ethnic conflict, such as Bosnia. By contrast, nation-building can be the most appropriate option when a weak government is the principal source of the problem and the entire population and/or its neighbors are at risk. Either provides a possible course of action vis-à-vis failed states; the choice should hinge primarily on willingness to commit the greater resources necessitated by nation-building and a judgment of whether the country is a good political and cultural candidate for a "remaking."

Opportunities for successful nation-building will be rare—certainly less common than for humanitarian interventions. Few regimes are that dangerous, and even when they are, not many outsiders will want to pay the price. As one analyst has noted, "The task is of imperial proportions and possibly of endless duration."[11] Also, it is impossible to be confident that the values the United States seeks to promote will take root. Neither the United States nor the world would likely stand for the sort of methods—and the time they require—imposed on Germany and Japan after World War II. North Korea appears to be a prime exception because of its demonstrated aggression and the availability of South Koreans to undertake an occupation.

Recent experience suggests the need for caution. The United States shied away from attempting nation-building in Iraq out of concern that it would take years, be opposed by the American people and the Arab members of the coalition, result in many casualties, lead to Iraq's break-up, and in the end fail anyway because of nationalist and Islamic traditions in Iraq. In Somalia, nation-building was not given a fair chance; it was never preceded by the necessary (and expensive) peace-making. But even if those measures had been taken, there is no guarantee that nation-building would have worked or would have been worth the cost since a humanitarian alternative existed. Where it did work somewhat, in Grenada and Panama, the United States enjoyed conditions not easily replicated. Grenada proved receptive in part because it was so modest in size and population. Panama was accustomed to an intrusive U.S. presence and already had a democratically-elected government supported by the majority of the people (although it was prevented from taking office).

PEACE-MAKING AND COMPELLENT INTERVENTIONS

Opportunities for successful peace-making and compellent interventions are also likely to be rare. Vietnam and Lebanon demonstrated that peace-making is extremely demanding militarily and difficult to sustain politically, both at home (because of the high costs and uncertain prospects for success) and in the target country (where nationalist pressures, the difficulties of working with disorganized internal forces, and the need to act with great restraint in order not to alienate neutrals must be considered). Compellent actions are easier to mount; the problem is what to do if they do not succeed. As in Bosnia, the choice then tends to be between escalating to peacemaking or backing away from direct military intervention.

Recent and current examples illustrate how these considerations can be applied in practice. In Rwanda's civil war in spring 1994, the United States did not intervene despite the scale of the disaster—in which hundreds of thousands lost their lives and many more became refugees. This decision is understandable given the absence of non-humanitarian interests and the difficulty of accomplishing anything useful because of the speed with which the problem developed, its horrendous size, and the lack of ready coalition partners. Indeed, the same considerations that argue for intervention also weigh against it by making the requirements for successful involvement so great. The only viable approach in Rwanda would have been a purely humanitarian undertaking in which Africans assumed the lion's share of the burden over time; this would have involved imposing humanitarian zones or safe-havens to protect those whose lives were in danger. This was the sort of intervention undertaken by France beginning in late June 1994—something not to be confused with the relief effort mounted by the United States a month later to assist Rwandan refugees once the civil war had largely run its course.[12]

In Haiti, the scale of the problem is considerably less than in Rwanda but the argument for U.S. intervention is stronger. Why? First, the humanitarian situation, while not genocide, is still sufficiently bad to make intervention a legitimate option. Second, U.S. interests go beyond the humanitarian; they include a desire to support democracy and to end a refugee flow into the United States. Third, the weakness of the ruling military and the absence of civil strife mean that an intervention could gain control of the country with relative ease; the major challenge would come in nation-building, a task that could be shared with others. A key consideration thus becomes the willingness of others to participate in the nation-building phase of the operation, which will be difficult and take years.

Iraq provides another example. The central government is gradually intensifying its war on the people of the south and could with little warning resume a major assault on the Kurds of the north. Creating a humanitarian zone would appear to be the proper response to the situation in the south; if either that zone or the zone in the north is challenged, an appropriate action would be to retaliate massively with air power against military targets throughout the country and targets of value in Baghdad in an effort to compel Iraq to act in an acceptable manner.

Another illustrative case is Algeria, which is in the throes of incipient civil war as radical Islamic forces battle a military government that took power in January 1992 after an initial round of elections revealed unexpected strength on the part of extremist religious elements. The United States has economic, humanitarian, and especially political interests in the outcome; it has a stake in Egyptian stability, the Middle East peace process, and Gulf security. Nevertheless, there is no appropriate role for military intervention. Just as in Iran in the late 1970s, direct military intervention is virtually irrelevant when it comes to affecting the course of internal political situations once they reach the revolutionary stage. Although the situation has humanitarian consequences, it does not (at least not yet) call for a humanitarian intervention.

A similar situation could arise in Egypt. If it did, the appropriate response might be massive indirect aid for government forces coupled with selective compellent actions against rebels. But the time to consider acting is when coups or insurrections are still in an early phase. If the situation in Egypt deteriorated into a revolutionary one, as was the case in Iran in the late 1970s, and as is increasingly the case in Algeria, options for direct military intervention would fade, U.S. vital interests notwithstanding.

The dangers of a more interventionist bias are manifest. Using military force to intervene on behalf of a people against their government or nongovernmental forces is a complicated undertaking that can place the intervening party squarely in the middle of another nation's politics. As Michael Walzer has pointed out, "The burden of proof falls on any political leader who tries to shape the domestic arrangements or alters the conditions of life in a foreign country."[13] Moreover, a norm tolerant of intervention can easily be abused by others looking for a pretext to intervene. And even if there is a real reason to intervene, it can quickly lead to counter-interventions by additional outside parties. Indeed, it is precisely these concerns that helped create the norm in favor of state sovereignty and against outside intervention.

Obviously, policy must and will differ from case to case. This selectivity or inconsistency will cause problems for some and some problems for everyone—as Pierre Hassner has noted, " . . . to find legitimacy, military intervention must be based on universal principles, while its implementation depends on a particular constellation of power and interest"[14]—but it is unavoidable. No two situations are alike, either in degree or in their susceptibility to being fixed with outside military force.

MAKING INTERVENTION POSSIBLE

A wide range of situations will call for a military response or at least demand consideration of one. But such considerations will count for little if adequate forces are not available, if policymakers lack adequate intelligence or political support, or if these forces are overwhelmed by a range of crises that might have been avoided or better dealt with by other actors or instruments. But the most basic requirement for successful military intervention necessarily concerns the forces themselves.

The future requirements for U.S. military forces promise to be demanding. Potential scenarios requiring U.S. forces include as many as two major regional conflicts (the Persian Gulf and the Korean Peninsula)—so-called half wars—and possibly (although less likely) an even larger war involving a resurgent Russia moving against Eastern Europe. Requirements also include several smaller contingencies (hostage rescue, punitive attacks, preventive attacks, interdiction efforts, and so on) as well as the need to contribute to both peacekeeping (in the Middle East and possibly elsewhere) and selected peace-making and humanitarian operations. Clearly, all of these situations occurring at once would overtax any conceivable level of U.S. capabilities—and require a higher level of forces than existed at any time during the entire Cold War.

Indeed, the most critical question affecting force sizing is the assumption about the need for simultaneity. Some argue that planning for one "half war" and several smaller demands is adequate; others disagree, and argue that planning must assume the possibility of two half wars occurring at the same time.[15] The Clinton Administration initially tried to compromise with a proposed "win-hold-win" strategy, in which the United States would fight one half war, conduct a holding action in a second if it erupted, and then initiate offensive actions in the second theater once the first was secured.[16] The proposal was still-born when critics pointed out that "holding" provided precious little comfort for friends and allies in the second theater but more than a little incentive for adversaries to initiate hostilities in that theater. Moreover, a great deal of damage could be done to U.S. interests during the hold phase even if it were successful, which could not be assured.[17]

Like many debates, this one involves its share of theology. The United States has not had the ability to fight two half wars at full tilt in two theaters simultaneously for some time. A number of critical U.S. capabilities were stretched to the limit by the single half war in the Gulf. Nevertheless, given U.S. interests in both the Persian Gulf and the Korean peninsula as well as the existing and potential threats to them, planning for the capability to wage two half wars appears to be the best choice. This force sizing also makes forces available for lesser but still demanding contingencies elsewhere and provides a foundation for a capability in Europe should a Russian threat to Central or Eastern Europe re-emerge.

In either a Persian Gulf or Korean half war, the United States would need to respond with major forces—say six army/marine divisions together with aircraft and cruise missiles. It would need to be able to attack a wide range of targets on the battlefield as well as inside the territory of the attacking country from the onset of hostilities. Planning can also safely assume that the United States would operate in either theater with significant direct and indirect help from the states directly involved and from allies near and far.

Current defense budget projections resulting from the Clinton Administration's 1993 "bottom-up review" call for a force consisting of ten active army divisions, twenty active and reserve air wings, and some 365 naval ships. (This is slightly lower than the final "base force" plan developed by the Bush Administration and is less than a force designed to fight two half wars.) There is no way to answer definitively in the abstract whether this is enough—it depends upon an assessment of likely threat scenarios, assumptions about assistance from friends and allies, and tolerance for risk—although it is arguably too little and certainly not too much given the potential range of contingencies.[18]

Moreover, almost always more significant than "how much" is "how" defense monies are spent. Thus, equally if not more important than overall force structure will be maintaining adequate stocks of key munitions—there is almost always a tendency to underestimate the intensity of conflicts—spare parts, logistics-related equipment, and peacetime training.[19] Prepositioning and forward deployment in the Gulf and Northeast Asia become critical; so too does a pool of U.S.-based forces that can be moved quickly to trouble spots. Warning time needs to be exploited to get forces in place, either to deter or provide an initial response should deterrence fail. Specific funds need to be set aside for humanitarian and related operations so that overall military readiness does not suffer.

One other aspect of U.S. forces needs to be addressed: personnel. There is a fundamental difference between combat and non-combat operations. The most recent edition of the U.S. Army's basic field manual devotes a separate chapter to operations other than war; within that chapter, it provides principles to guide U.S. personnel, several of which contradict or at least depart from the basic principles meant to guide combat operations. Most interesting among these is the call for perseverance and restraint. "In operations other than war, victory comes far more subtly than in war. Disciplined forces, measured responses, and patience are essential to successful outcomes."[20]

This difference in approach argues for utilizing either separate ("dedicated") troops or troops that have received special training for different missions. The problem with the first of these approaches is that U.S. force levels are already barely adequate—or perhaps even inadequate—relative to existing requirements. Setting aside a significant number of troops for peacekeeping, peace-making, and nation-building purposes would only exacerbate this. Separate troops would also limit U.S. deployment flexibility. And having separate forces probably exaggerates the difference between peace-making and war-fighting. Better would be an approach along the lines of current policy, i.e., one army prepared to undertake a range of missions, with personnel receiving special mission-specific training just prior to departure.[21]

A second personnel-related issue concerns the source of U.S. manpower. A strong argument can be made for the continuation of a volunteer military. The All Volunteer Force (AVF) can be justified on grounds of quality. But it is also important for political reasons. It is more difficult to justify conscription when U.S. forces may find themselves used for ends unrelated to vital or even important national interests. Moreover, public support for interventions would be even more sensitive to costs if the personnel involved were conscripts. These same considerations suggest that the increased reliance of the U.S. military on reserves—especially for skills such as civil affairs critical for non-war-fighting tasks—should be rethought.

Intelligence is yet another national capability that must be considered as part of preparedness. Good intelligence is essential to any military intervention. Only with such knowledge is it possible to contemplate preventive or preemptive strikes with any confidence. But intelligence is also necessary for more than targeting or planning for war-fighting; it is critical to assessing accurately the staying power of adversaries, government control of groups within its territory, and other factors that can spell the difference between failure and success in interventions short of all-out combat. Intelligence made possible the Iran hostage rescue attempt and contributed significantly during the Gulf War; a lack of intelligence led to a decision to avoid getting involved in Panama in October 1989, while its existence proved crucial to the successful U.S. intervention that followed.

SHARING THE BURDENS

A good deal of debate has focused on the choice between "unilateralism" and "multilateralism," between going it alone and acting with others. In reality, the choice is less stark, as the opportunities for purely unilateral action will be few. In most situations, interventions will be partly multilateral, involving other countries in addition to the United States. The United States will need from others one or more forms of assistance: base rights, overflight, intelligence, combat forces, economic help, political support. The questions worth asking, though, are in which situations the United States will want to marginalize or even eliminate the involvement of others, and, in those situations where such involvement is deemed either necessary or desirable, in what form should it come.

These are difficult questions to answer, for multilateralism brings with it both attractions and problems. On the positive side, multilateralism is closely tied to international legitimacy. Arab force contributions in the Gulf War were critical, albeit for political more than military reasons, just as the support of the Organization of Eastern Caribbean States was useful during the Grenada action. Foreign involvement also helps at home, where resentment is all but certain to undermine support for a costly and extended intervention if the United States bears most or all the economic, military, and human burdens of that commitment. The involvement of other countries is no guarantee of domestic support—approval evaporated for the U.S. presence in Beirut after the October 1983 bombing of the marine barracks despite the presence of European troops—but it can be crucial where the human costs are not so high as to overwhelm all other considerations.

But multilateralism is not cost-free. Such costs transcend the economic price of the United States assuming its share (nearly one-third, scheduled to decline to one-fourth) of U.N. operations. Keeping the Gulf coalition intact necessitated going to the United Nations, which in turn slowed down the use of force, most notably early in the crisis when ships with goods intended for or leaving Iraq were interdicted. Multilateralism can translate into a loss of control over the situation on the ground. A good example is Somalia, where the United States encountered problems over both strategy and operations because it shared responsibility with the United Nations and other countries contributing troops. Bosnia is another example, as humanitarian operations involving European troops were cited by European governments as justification for opposing the more aggressive policies suggested by the United States in early 1993. Bosnia also illustrates the problems that can stem from a cumbersome chain of command, which in Bosnia involved political and military officials, both on site and at headquarters, representing the United States, the coalition (in this case, NATO), and the United Nations.

Generalization is impossible. Instead, it is more useful to assess potential approaches to multilateralism.

COLLABORATION AMONG CONCERNED NATIONS

Gathering those countries most affected by a situation, or those most inclined to do something, and acting with a degree of coordination, is the least confining form of multilateralism. The U.S.-French-British-Italian effort in Lebanon is a model; failure cannot be attributed to the way it was organized. The advantage of this approach is that it includes only those disposed to act and avoids cumbersome political and military arrangements that can inhibit actions and take time and money. The disadvantage is that the partnership does not exist until after a crisis materializes, and even then it is an ad hoc arrangement that can suffer from poor planning and coordination. This approach also lacks the international legitimacy of more formal regional or U.N.-sanctioned undertakings.[22]

INFORMAL COALITIONS

In the coalition or "posse" approach, a single country, say the United States, becomes the de facto sheriff and enlists others to participate in bringing about a defined outcome. The classic example here is the Gulf War, in which the United States took the lead and dozens of other countries contributed militarily in the form of troops, overflight rights, bases, and equipment, or economically by providing support for the military effort or sanctions enforcement. The Gulf War model is important in another way, in that the U.S.-led posse acted pursuant to various Security Council resolutions, which cast the United Nations in the role of legitimizer.

The attraction of the "sheriff and posse" approach is that it complements more than constrains U.S. leadership. Like the concerned nations approach, it avoids standing bureaucracies and those who are uninterested or opposed; it differs from the concerned nations approach, however, in that it is more coordinated and has a clear leader. The drawbacks are the time it takes to put together such an effort and the often tenuous ties that bind the participants, which can hinder agreement on both means and objectives. This approach also places most of the responsibility on the "sheriff," that is, the United States. It may not enjoy widespread legitimacy if it does not have a blessing from the United Nations or the relevant regional organization.[23]

REGIONAL ORGANIZATIONS

Standing regional entities can take the lead in a crisis, such as NATO has done (or at times failed to do) in Bosnia. At least in principle, various regional organizations—NATO, the Organization of American States (OAS), the Organization of African Unity (OAU)—could undertake peacekeeping, selective peace-making, and nation-building operations. The obvious advantages include proximity, knowledge of language and culture, a stake in success if only to avoid refugee flows and a wider war, a sharing of burdens, and increased political legitimacy for the intervention. The disadvantage is that regional organizations, lacking the military capability and the political consensus to intervene in most situations, are likely to prove undependable. This is especially true for the OAU and OAS, which do not possess significant means and rarely enjoy consensus. NATO has the means, but gaining support from all sixteen members, especially in a timely manner, is difficult if not impossible in most instances, especially when it involves matters where national interests outweigh collective, alliance-wide concerns. This is likely to become more frequent in the post–Cold War world.

THE UNITED NATIONS AS ORGANIZER

In the Gulf crisis, the United Nations provided the U.S.-led coalition substantial political support; this was important to Congress and the American people, as well as to several of the participants. But throughout the Gulf crisis, the U.N. role was political, not military. A very different role can be envisioned in which member states make forces available to the United Nations, which would then assume operational control or authorize one country to take on that role.

This process was anticipated by Article 43 of the U.N. Charter, which obligates all members of the organization to make available to the Security Council " . . . armed forces, assistance, and facilities . . . necessary for the purpose of maintaining international peace and security." Agreements are to be negotiated between members and the Security Council covering "numbers and types of forces, their degree of readiness and general location, and the nature of the facilities and assistance to be provided."

This approach would create a pool of potential forces that could be trained and equipped and then utilized in a range of scenarios; at other times, these forces would remain available to (and the responsibility of) their own governments. At least in principle, this is a desirable objective; it would provide resources for a broad range of military-related tasks, especially those that are manpower-intensive, thereby reducing the burden on the United

States. Designating selected units or force levels to participate in joint uses of force does not necessarily guarantee their availability in a particular instance, which would need to be decided on a case-by-case basis.[24]

A force composed of Article 43 contributions would have a number of disadvantages. It would be primarily for enforcement actions, which by definition are more demanding militarily and could quickly overtax its capacity. Moreover, a combined force would prove slow to assemble and would be of uneven ability. Since no state can be required to make any particular level of forces available, it might never materialize. Moreover, a U.N. Security Council in which Russia and China enjoy vetoes could not be counted on to support interventions the United States views as desirable. Trying to build consensus not only takes time, but would make it more difficult for the United States to act in the event of diplomatic failure.

Indeed, strengthening the norm that intervention must be approved (much less conducted) by the Security Council is more likely to affect the United States than other countries less concerned about public opinion and international law. The fact that Article 43 remains unused a half century after the United Nations' founding is relevant. Placing too much stock in a combined U.N. force is almost certain to disappoint, putting the United States in difficult situations. It might be more realistic to designate pools of forces that would be available in principle for traditional (consensual, Chapter 6) peacekeeping and for consensual humanitarian operations rather than for more demanding enforcement actions.[25]

U.N. STANDING ARMY

This last approach is different from both the United Nations as legitimizer (where it provides only political cover for the actions of individual states or groups of states) and organizer (where it would bring together and lead the forces of contributors in peacekeeping and, under Article 43, in enforcement actions). A U.N. standing army—say, on the order of several brigades—would report to the Secretary General and be available for whatever mission the

Security Council supported or directed. Troops could be volunteers. Command would be in the hands of the United Nations.[26]

A standing force would be available on short notice. At least in principle, it could be used for missions of tactical deterrence, that is, it could be sent to border areas or other enclaves where clashes appear imminent. It could also take on small peacekeeping and limited peace-making missions. The drawbacks, however, would be considerable. In addition to matters of expense (salaries, training, logistics, and so on), questions include availability (far from assured since both Russia and China wield a veto in the Security Council) and military capability. Such a small force could easily be overwhelmed. Member states, particularly the United States, would then come under pressure to act, not simply to deal with the situation at hand, but to save the credibility of the United Nations. A final danger is that a U.N. force would probably be seen as an alternative to U.S. forces—and a competitor for resources—even though the potential of a U.N. force to take on the same tasks would be negligible in most instances.

FORGING A COMPREHENSIVE APPROACH

How, then, does the United States choose? How does the United States utilize the advantages of multilateralism while minimizing its drawbacks? The above considerations argue for a policy based on unilateralism combined with modest forms of multilateralism, namely, collaboration among concerned nations and informal coalitions. Strengthening regional organizations ought to be a goal, but it will require years, if it comes to fruition at all. The United Nations appears most attractive as a legitimizer for war-fighting and as a major organizer of consensual humanitarian undertakings and peacekeeping. In addition, the United States may want to turn to the United Nations to organize selective peace-making and nation-building efforts under Article 43. Even to do this, however, the United Nations would need to modernize and expand its capacity to prepare for and coordinate multinational field operations.[27]

The United States needs to maintain a unilateral military option. It cannot plan its forces on the assumption that others, including the United Nations, will be willing or able to bear the burdens of major military undertakings. Nor does the United States want to give others a veto when it decides to intervene with force. Indeed, in some cases, such as large-scale combat or war-fighting, multilateralism will be mostly supportive of the United States. In other cases, particularly preventive and punitive actions, rescue efforts, or intervention in places where there are special interests or a special role (such as Panama, the Philippines, or the Middle East), U.S. leaders may want or need to act alone.

As a rule, interventions calculated to be modest and short-term lend themselves to unilateralism (or at most modest forms of multilateralism). Unilateral uses of force maximize speed and secrecy of decision-making and implementation and enhance political and military freedom of action. This was the case in both the Philippines and Panama, as well as with the Iran hostage rescue effort and Libya. It was also the case in June 1993 when the United States launched cruise missile strikes on Iraq. Unilateralism can also be helpful when deterrence or compellence are called for; it avoids the often time-consuming debates of joint efforts and does not require building a broad consensus.

But acting alone has its costs and drawbacks. As already noted, it is hard to execute most interventions without some form of help from others. Also, acting unilaterally can be expensive; it risks domestic support as Congress and the American people ask why the United States is bearing burdens no one else is. It can also be controversial internationally, as questions of legality and legitimacy inevitably arise.

U.S. unilateralism also runs the risk of stimulating unilateral actions by others. In any event, the United States will simply not have adequate forces to come close to meeting all the claims on it. It will have to do some things with others or delegate them entirely. Unilateralism can become unsustainable over time if costs begin to mount.

For those tasks that place a premium on war-fighting, which can only succeed with the whole-hearted involvement of the United States or other large powers, the United Nations and the major regional organizations are best limited to legitimizing actions; concerned nations or informal coalitions provide the best operational approach. In principle, the larger the U.S. stake and the larger (and more demanding) the U.S. contribution, the more the United States should limit the formal multilateral dimension of an undertaking. Direct military contributions from others can complicate military operations if the degree of interdependence is too high. The Gulf War, in which countries were assigned specified tasks in specified sectors, proved far more successful than Somalia, where individual U.S. units to some extent depended upon the responses of individual units from other contributors.

There is little reason for U.S. involvement in peacekeeping, a mission that can be readily undertaken by the forces of many countries, unless it is expressly sought by the protagonists and where U.S. interests justify the contribution, as in the Middle East. U.S. peacekeeping forces have added to the stability of Israel's relationship with Egypt and could do the same for Israel and Syria if a treaty is reached. The case for Bosnia, however, is less clear-cut. Pressure will inevitably emerge for the United States to commit ground as well as air forces to participate in a multinational "peacekeeping" force for Bosnia if an agreement is signed by the parties to the conflict.[28] The danger is that what appears to be peacekeeping could quickly evolve into peace-making if, as seems likely, local commitment to a political settlement is not both widespread and deep. As a result, the United States would be wise not to undertake such role until a settlement becomes clearly durable.

In general, the United States should stay outside of, or minimize its role in, peace-making and nation-building. These missions do not exploit the unique capabilities of U.S. forces for high-intensity combat. They are time consuming and tie down U.S. troops which could be used elsewhere. They are inherently costly, whether measured in terms of dollars or casualties and lives. Where appropriate, the United States would be wise to advocate establishing humanitarian zones as an alternative. If, however, peace-making or nation-building are deemed desirable and feasible, such missions should almost always be undertaken by coalitions, either formal regional organizations or something more informal. And the United States should insist that in return for its support the mission is designed with an adequate appreciation of the risks and costs. The same guidelines that determine whether the United States intervenes militarily should be applied to multilateral operations for which the United States is considering providing support.

U.S. participation in multinational peace-making and nation-building raises special questions. Lebanon, Somalia, and Haiti all suggest that direct U.S. involvement can be counter-productive as it can stimulate opposition and aggressive action against the effort; in many settings, taking on the United States and demonstrating an ability to kill or capture soldiers of the world's only superpower has political value. The comparative advantage of the United States in such situations is in the realms of intelligence, transportation, and logistics support. This said, it can be difficult to lead if the United States is unwilling to share the risks; as a result, in situations that meet U.S. criteria, some combat participation (air if not always ground) may be required if others are to be persuaded to join in. In these cases, the United States must be mindful of the risks and use sufficient force.[29]

U.S. willingness to operate under the command of others should depend upon the circumstances. As a rule of thumb, the greater the stakes and the greater the U.S. role, the more U.S. forces should act under U.S. commanders. But where U.S. forces are but a small part of an overall effort, there is no reason to preclude non-American command, particularly if the operation is designed so that U.S. forces enjoy considerable autonomy within the area or mission they are assigned. Here, the NATO parallel comes to mind: essential self-command of U.S. forces in the field even if over-all direction of the operation is shared or held by others.

Some would claim that the mix of unilateralism and resistance to more formal forms of multilateralism presented here lacks legitimacy. Instead, they would require some regional or U.N. Security

Council mandate pursuant to which the United States would act. One observer argues that "[T]he United States should explicitly surrender the right to intervene unilaterally in the internal affairs of other countries by overt military means or by covert operations."[30] But this approach is overly legal in principle and impractical in practice. It would require frequent recourse to organizations that might well prove unable or unwilling to provide timely and unconditional approval. In the final analysis, *legitimacy must reside in the policy and derive from the ends and means of the intervention, not from some external organization or international court of law.*[31]

Multilateralism can be a useful or necessary military and/or political precondition to U.S. intervention; at the same time, it can prove cumbersome or an obstacle. It is not, however, an alternative to U.S. leadership. Multilateralism is most likely to be effective (and something other than an obstacle) if the United States takes the lead in making the case for a collective response and in contributing to the common effort. The more ambitious the undertaking, the more U.S. leadership and contribution will be necessary and the more likely the United States will want to act in a loosely structured fashion. The more uncertain the stakes, or the greater the gap between stakes and likely costs, the more careful the United States ought to be about lending its support, much less participation, to any effort.

CHAPTER EIGHT

CONCLUSION

D etermining whether to intervene militarily, and then carrying it out so that objectives are met, is an extraordinarily difficult undertaking. Even so, such determinations can be made less difficult for the United States as it navigates the post–Cold War world if certain considerations are kept firmly in mind and applied no less firmly in the field.

There is no need to repeat all the guidelines here. It is worth stating, however, that the prospects for the United States intervening effectively in certain circumstances—principally those involving real or imminent aggression by states against their neighbors—have improved. A number of factors—the emergence of a new generation of advanced conventional weapons, the end of the Cold War risk of escalation to global war, the fact that many adversaries may find themselves lacking great power support—all support the ability of the United States to use military force effectively on the battlefield. This potential will only be realized, however, if undertakings use ample force early and decisively.

Three other developments, however, are less encouraging. First, the United States will be challenged more often in the future. Second, some of these challenges will probably include unconventional weaponry; if the United States is not to be deterred from acting for fear of large-scale casualties, it must develop strategies and weapons that will reduce the likelihood and costs of other countries escalating to chemical, biological, and/or nuclear arms. Third, there is declining popular and congressional support for military interventions. The proper response is not to bow to this mood, but to take it into account. Sustaining interventions will require substantial political effort from the most senior levels of government. The greater the costs, the greater the effort that will be required.

The potential for intervening effectively with military means for other purposes, particularly internal conflicts, is less clear cut. The advantages of modern technology that are useful on the open battlefield often are irrelevant in civil conflicts that take place in heavily congested areas where friend cannot be distinguished from foe. Television pictures may increase our desire to act when we see innocent people suffer as a consequence of governmental policy or inaction, and new ways of thinking may provide a legal basis for intervention. But intervening in internal situations can prove difficult and dangerous for an outsider—even one who possesses great power— if the local protagonists are prepared to fight to the end.

This does not argue for always staying out of such situations. Military force cannot substitute for political and economic efforts, but it can provide a context in which they are more likely to succeed. Sometimes it is necessary to act—when the need is great and it is possible to use force to improve matters at a cost that is commensurate with the stakes. In such cases, the United States may want to consider options that create safe-havens providing long-term relief at a cost it and others can sustain rather than take on the more ambitious enterprises of peace-making or nation-building.

The United States will also want to consider what is a desirable and sustainable division of labor between itself, regional organizations, and the United Nations. Here, though, the presumption should be in favor of continued U.S. leadership, at times alone, more often in informal coalitions. There is a real question about how much the United States can and should seek to devolve formal responsibility to other organizations and the United Nations in particular.

The United States should not delude itself; the effectiveness of regional groupings or the United Nations will be influenced considerably by the level of U.S. involvement. Moreover, peace-making and nation-building are no less demanding when undertaken by regional or international organizations. They, too, ought to approach such missions with great caution, and U.S. support for or participation in such missions should be decided by a process as rigorous as that which is used for unilateral or less formal collective efforts.

Whether the United States uses force alone or with others, there must be consistency, or better yet a match, among key factors. It is critical to introduce rigor into the equation: clarity of purpose, a consistency of means and ends, use of adequate forces given objectives and the threats or impediments. The survey of cases in this volume showed that success tends to follow when there is consistency among these factors; failure results when one or more factors are out of synch. The greatest failures come from approaching a mission as one of peacekeeping when in fact it is much more. There is little that can be done (short of using force) to affect an existing threat; as a result, planners of any military intervention need to adjust either their objectives downward or their forces upward (regarding both the level and how they are used) if there is any doubt as to whether what is planned is likely to be adequate.

If the question of military intervention remains terribly difficult, it is nevertheless terribly important to get it right. A great deal is at stake. A failed intervention will undermine the well-being of the particular interests at stake and endanger the particular forces involved. A pattern of failed interventionism for the United States could result in a policy of isolationism, with all its attendant costs.

A similar pattern for the United Nations risks undermining the organization's utility and potential.

But getting it right will be difficult. Policymakers must always exercise judgement. Guidelines are just that; they are not rules, much less absolutes. Interests alone do not provide answers or dictate choices. One must begin with an assessment of whether intervention is desirable, then address its feasibility, and then return to the question of desirability. Intervening must pass muster both on its own terms and compared to the alternatives. One should never forget that military intervention is but one instrument in the tool-chest available to policymakers. It may or may not be the most appropriate for a given situation, depending upon how it is used and what other tools are available and with what prospects. Making policy is always about choosing; deciding whether to intervene with military force is no exception. It is only that the stakes are greater.

AFTERWORD:
SUMMER 1994 TO SUMMER 1999

Military intervention continues to be a central feature of post–Cold War American foreign policy and international relations. In a period spanning only a little more than five years, that is, since the first edition of this volume appeared in the summer of 1994, the United States dispatched air and naval forces to the Taiwan Straits in order to signal to China its commitment to Taiwan; bombed Iraq, Bosnia's Serbs, an Afghan terrorist camp, and a pharmaceutical facility in Sudan; occupied Haiti; kept the peace in Bosnia in the aftermath of the Dayton peace accords; and went to war with Serbia over Kosovo. During this same period—the second half of the first post–Cold War decade—the United States determined not to intervene to stop genocide in Rwanda and on several occasions decided not to use force against Iraq when its government violated one or more of the obligations spelled out in relevant U.N. Security Council resolutions.

As is clear from this summary, military force was either used or contemplated in a host of settings and for a host of ends. Actual or would-be interventions occurred in the Caribbean, Africa, the Persian Gulf, Europe, and the Asia-Pacific region, and included punitive raids, coercive (compellent) attacks, deterrence, preventive and preemptive strikes, peacekeeping, peace-making, and nation-building. In this chapter I summarize these interventions, assesses their effectiveness, and close with a consideration of the consequences of this recent set of experiences for the use of military force by the United States in the post–Cold War world.

HAITI

By the summer of 1994, the situation in Haiti had deteriorated markedly. Sanctions and internal violence had turned Haiti into a failing, if not failed, state. Substantial numbers of people—measured in the tens of thousands—were willing to risk their lives to take boats or rafts to reach safety in Florida. In the aftermath of the October 1993 Harlan County fiasco, when an organized mob of protesters prompted the Clinton Administration to withdraw a ship carrying 200 U.S. and Canadian soldiers to Haiti to provide training and engineering assistance, U.S. diplomacy and U.S. military preparations became increasingly active and visible in an effort to intimidate Haiti's military rulers and persuade them to leave office. These efforts came to a head with the passage on July 31, 1994, of U.N. Security Council Resolution 940, which authorized the use of all necessary means to facilitate the departure of the military leadership from Haiti, the prompt return of the elected president, the installation of the rightful government, and the creation of a secure and stable environment.

After months of waiting, the United States finally decided to launch Operation *Uphold Democracy* and invade Haiti to Bimplement the Security Council resolution—but as it did, Haiti's leaders decided not to resist. An eleventh-hour diplomatic initiative led by former President Jimmy Carter, carried out against the dramatic backdrop of visible preparations for an invasion, proved to be a successful exercise in coercive diplomacy. As a result, a large and capable multinational force—in reality, a 20,000 person American force—arrived in Haiti on September 19, 1994, and landed without opposition. A week later, a fire-fight in Cap-Haïtien between U.S. and Haitian forces loyal to the already ousted military *junta* left ten Haitians dead and ended effective resistance, thereby paving the way for a peacekeeping mission. A month later, the democratically elected government of Jean-Bertrand Aristide was restored to power.

There then ensued a long period of nation-building. In March 1995, the multinational force was disestablished, replaced by the U.N. Mission in Haiti (UNMIH), a 6,000 person military force (and a nearly 1,000 person civil police force) that in reality was composed mostly of troops who had been in the multinational force, including 2,400 Americans. Its purpose was to maintain order, carry out limited disarmament of unauthorized Haitian forces, and train Haitians so that they could assume the burden of national defense and policing. Presidential elections were held in December 1995, and in February 1996, René Preval assumed office. For many in the U.S. Congress, this peaceful political transition brought to an end the rationale for a significant American military presence in Haiti; partly as a result, the UNMIH gave way in mid-1996 to the U.N. Support Mission in Haiti, a much smaller force of mostly Canadian and Pakistani soldiers whose priorities were policing and training. Just under 500 U.S. troops—a mix of engineers, medical personnel, and a few combat forces—also remained on the island but outside the formal U.N. structure.

By mid-1999, there were reports that even this small American contingent was to be withdrawn, leaving only a few hundred U.N. peacekeepers advising Haitian police stationed on the island. At the same time, it appeared that the international effort had not had the desired effect. Haiti's economy was not recovering. Political violence mounted, as did the number of people leaving the island illegally by sea. The U.S. invasion and subsequent international occupation was able to diffuse the crisis but not to address the underlying problems of Haiti's political, economic, and social malaise. The occupation had created an opportunity for Haiti to right itself, but the evidence suggests that this opportunity was not exploited by Haiti's leaders. As a result, the potential exists for another crisis—which would once again raise the question of whether the United States should act with military force to prevent humanitarian suffering and mass migration.

BOSNIA

By the summer of 1994, the situation in Bosnia had reached something of an impasse. The international Contact Group (France, Germany, Russia, the United Kingdom, and the United States) presented the parties with a map that essentially divided Bosnia in half, with the Bosnian-Croat side getting 51 percent and the Bosnian Serbs getting 49 percent. Diplomacy focused on persuading the Bosnian Serbs to accept this division, which would require them to give up some but far from all of what they had gained on the ground by military means. Meanwhile, fighting continued. America's hands were largely tied: the use of U.S. ground forces was ruled out for domestic political reasons; the launch of a massive aerial campaign was ruled out by the allies, who feared for the safety of their humanitarian forces (UNPROFOR) on the scene; and the arms embargo prevented the strengthening of the Bosnian side, a situation that was not materially affected that autumn when Congress passed legislation ending American enforcement of (but not compliance with) the arms ban.

A four-month cease-fire negotiated by former President Jimmy Carter, along with winter weather, limited fighting until the spring of 1995, but a Bosnian Croat offensive broke the relative calm. On several occasions NATO bombed Bosnian Serb ammunition sites when heavy weapons were not kept in assigned depots. The principal effect of this punitive action was to prompt the Bosnian Serbs to take hostage several hundred European peacekeepers serving in UNPROFOR. This humiliation confronted the United States, Europeans and the United Nations with a stark choice. They could either withdraw UNPROFOR, given the fact that the environment had deteriorated to the point that it made no sense to maintain peacekeeping forces—a step that would have required the deployment of a heavily armed NATO extraction force to escort UNPROFOR out of Bosnia. Or they could beef up UNPROFOR into a peace-making force that would then enter the conflict on behalf of the weaker Bosnian side. There were also variations on the first option, including ending the embargo and arming the Bosnians and/or attacking Bosnian Serb forces from the air in an effort to weaken them, so that the Bosnian Croat forces could prevail, or to induce the Bosnian Serbs to accept a lasting cease-fire.

What effectively settled the debate in favor of withdrawing UNPROFOR and attacking the Bosnian Serb forces and equipment from the air were mounting Bosnian Serb attacks on so-called Bosnian safe areas. Shells fell on Sarajevo on May 7; two months later an all-out assault was launched against Srebrenica, resulting in mass executions, deportations, and ultimately the fall of the city on July 16. Then on August 28, 1995, the Serbs shelled Sarajevo marketplace, killing nearly forty people. Two days later, NATO initiated Operation *Deliberate Force*, a large-scale air campaign that was designed to target Bosnian Serb forces, shift the military balance in the direction of the Bosnian Croat Federation, and induce the Bosnian Serbs to settle. Weeks before, in early August, the Croat army had begun an offensive that expelled ethnic Serbs from the disputed Krajina area of Croatia. Operation *Deliberate Force*—consisting of some 3,500 sorties over the course of two weeks—helped the Bosnian Croat forces regain some of the land they had lost; indeed, by the time a cease-fire was established, the situation on the ground closely approximated the nearly equal division of Bosnia envisioned in the draft peace accord and ultimately agreed to at Dayton that November and signed in Paris in December.

The diplomacy that led to the Dayton agreement is beyond the scope of this book and has been written about elsewhere; suffice to say that two military interventions (the Croatian one that cleared out the Krajina region and the NATO air campaign) coupled with Slobodan Milosevic's decision to abandon the Bosnian Serbs, stemming from his desire to be free of sanctions and to avoid having to absorb additional refugees, made the dispute ripe for resolution. The success at Dayton, however, led to new decisions involving military force, in this instance, what to do to keep the peace. Here again there was a fundamental choice between narrowly construed peacekeeping (supervising a cease-fire, manning de facto borders, monitoring troop withdrawals, and redeploying weapons) and a more expansive mission that would include significant involvement in such activities as the arrest of indicted war criminals, the return of people forced to leave their homes, and supervision of elections. Although the Dayton agreement contained the more expansive set of objectives, it was the more narrow interpretation that in the end won out in practice; a fairly large implementation force (IFOR) of some 60,000 peacekeepers, including some 20,000 combat-ready Americans, began entering Bosnia as soon as the agreement was signed.

The initial U.S. deployment was for a period of one year, until mid-December 1996. Driving this arbitrary time limit was a desire to avoid a long-term commitment that would tie down U.S. troops and provoke opposition in Congress. This anxiety to limit the duration of any military presence was buttressed by confidence that the conditions of stability—a local military balance brought about by arming the Bosnian Croat Federation, arms control, or both—could be brought about in a year. The reality, however, proved to be very different, in that in the months after Dayton analysts concluded that the withdrawal of international forces would precipitate the breakdown of the Dayton accords and the resumption of widespread fighting. The Clinton Administration was thus forced to ask for an eighteen-month extension as December 1996 approached, and then for another extension a year later. Not until December 1997 did the Administration finally admit that it could not predict how long U.S. troops would be required to contribute to SFOR, the Bosnian stabilization force that succeeded IFOR. By mid-1999, just over 6,000 U.S. soldiers were serving in Bosnia as part of a total force of some 30,000; announcements made in July 1999 indicated that the U.S. total would be reduced further to 4,000, thereby confirming the decision to interpret the mission as a narrow peacekeeping intervention, rather than as something more ambitious in the nation-building realm.

TAIWAN STRAITS

The U.S. decision to dispatch naval and air forces to Northeast Asia in 1996 also warrants examination. The Chinese provocatively initiated missile tests in late July 1995, largely in response to the visit of Taiwan's President Lee Teng-hui to the United States the previous month. Ostensibly a private trip to receive an honorary degree from Cornell University, his alma mater, Lee's trip nonetheless marked a departure in U.S.-Taiwanese relations, certainly as seen by Beijing. The missile tests were followed by a steady build-up of Chinese forces deployed in Fujian Province, opposite Taiwan. All this took place against a backdrop of preparations for presidential elections in Taiwan, scheduled for March 23, 1996, and mounting calls by some politicians for Taiwan's independence—unacceptable to Beijing, which continues to believe that there is only one China and that Taiwan is a part of China. Early in March 1996, the Chinese government took a number of additional military actions—live weapons firing in the Straits of Taiwan, additional troop deployments to Fujian, and exercises of operations that would be central to any invasion of Taiwan—meant as a signal to Taiwan that a declaration of independence risked a conflict that could threaten the island's prosperity. The Chinese also declared that they were temporarily closing three areas, where they intended to test M-9 nuclear-capable ballistic missiles. In contrast to the 1995 test sites, the closed areas extended to within fifteen to twenty miles from the coast of Taiwan and lay close to two of Taiwan's major commercial ports.

Although the size and mix of the forces involved in the exercises made it virtually certain that China was not preparing to attack, much less to invade Taiwan at that moment, the Chinese signaling—in particular, the intimidation intended by the missile tests—put the United States in a difficult position. Washington had no desire to encourage Taiwanese moves toward independence that might spark a major crisis and possibly a conflict with the mainland; yet at the same time, the United

States opposed any use of force by the mainland against Taiwan to reunify China. A central consideration in this latter regard was the 1979 Taiwan Relations Act, under which the United States is committed to helping Taiwan maintain self-defense capabilities, through the provision of defense articles and services, and to undertaking other "appropriate action" in response to threats.

In an effort to balance these considerations and remind both parties that further escalation of tensions in the region was contrary to American desires and interests, the Clinton Administration decided to reposition and augment U.S. forces in the region. The USS *Independence* carrier battle group, normally home-ported in Japan, was dispatched to a location off the east coast of Taiwan, while a second carrier battle group built around the USS *Nimitz* was ordered to the region from the Persian Gulf, arriving in late March. The U.S. deployment was a classic case of signaling and tactical deterrence, intended to underscore the U.S. commitment to Taiwan, to express concern over Chinese coercive measures, and to discourage any possible use of force (however unlikely) by China against Taiwan. The American action also constituted a form of reassurance to Taiwan and other countries in the region, including Japan and South Korea, that depended on the United States for their security. The intervention appeared to do all these things and set the stage for the resumption of dialogue between China and Taiwan over their relationship. In the long run, however, the U.S. intervention also may have had some less constructive consequences, including increasing Taiwan's propensity to take risks vis-à-vis Beijing, stimulating an extant regional arms race, and accelerating Chinese defense modernization efforts designed to counter the conventional military presence of the United States in the region.

KOSOVO

A thorough history of Kosovo runs the risk of covering hundreds of years and almost as many pages. Even a truncated history would have to go back to the late 1980s, when Serbia's Slobodan Milosevic first discovered the full appeal of nationalism and rode it to power. In subsequent years, Milosevic focused his attention on the sovereign units of the former Yugolaslavia—Slovenia, Croatia, and especially Bosnia—fighting wars with each at one time or another.

Kosovo itself is (or was) a small province with nearly 2 million inhabitants, mostly ethnic Albanians, located in southern Serbia and bordering on Macedonia and Albania. In 1989, Milosevic revoked Kosovo's autonomy. There ensued mounting clashes between government forces and those of a pro-independence insurgent group, the Kosovo Liberation Army (KLA). Fearing that the Serbian government was about to launch a major offensive against the people of Kosovo, in December 1992 the lame-duck Bush Administration issued the so-called Christmas warning, informing the Yugoslav government and President Milosevic that the United States was prepared to use force on behalf of the people of Kosovo in the event of such a conflict. This warning was later reiterated on several occasions by the Clinton Administration. Nevertheless, the situation in Kosovo gradually deteriorated; political and personal freedom became increasingly limited and violence escalated.

In an effort to bring the mounting cycle of violence to an end, the United States initiated a diplomatic effort led by special envoy Richard Holbrooke, the architect of the Dayton accords that resolved the Bosnian crisis. Against a backdrop of threatened air strikes, in October Holbrooke appeared to succeed in persuading Milosevic to halt all repression of the Kosovars, to withdraw some Serbian troops from Kosovo, and to allow unarmed international monitors to oversee the cease-fire. Over time, however, this agreement proved a mirage, as fighting resumed, atrocities mounted, and concern grew for the safety of the vulnerable monitors. Once again, the United States and NATO attempted to marry diplomacy and threats of air power. This renewed effort came to a head in February 1999 at Rambouillet in France. The proposed agreement presented by

U.S. Secretary of State Madeleine Albright had several components: a reduction to 5,000 in the number of Serbian military and paramilitary forces allowed to remain in Kosovo; the restoration of considerable political autonomy for the people of the province; a three-year transition period, after which an international meeting would be convened to determine Kosovo's political status; the disarmament of the KLA; and the deployment of an armed NATO peacekeeping force to the province during the transitional period. At first, the government in Belgrade and the representatives of the people of Kosovo (dominated by militant KLA leaders) resisted signing on to the proposed accord, which was presented in a "take it or leave it" fashion to both sides. NATO was not prepared to use air power against both parties to coerce acceptance, and the only leverage vis-à-vis the KLA was its fear of being left without outside support. Only when the KLA accepted the agreement and Serbia still refused to sign was the stage set for NATO military action.

In contrast to October 1998, when the threat of bombing may have had a role in influencing Milosevic to accept an agreement (although it is quite possible that his acceptance had more to do with the fact that he had no intention of abiding by the agrement), U.S. and NATO threats in early 1999 had no discernible impact on Serbian behavior. NATO initiated its military response on March 24, 1999. The attack was an air-only operation, using cruise missiles and both land- and sea-based aircraft. Initial targets were limited in number and in kind, and included a range of military sites in and around Belgrade as well as in Kosovo. The air campaign was linked to an explicit set of political demands; once Milosevic met these, the bombing would come to an end.

But NATO airstrikes failed to stop Serbian aggression. To the contrary, the initiation of the air campaign coincided with an intensification of military pressure by Serbian ground forces against the people of Kosovo. In a matter of weeks, hundreds of thousands of Kosovars became refugees, crossing over into Macedonia and Albania. An unknown number were internally displaced, homeless but trapped inside Kosovo. An estimated 5,000 to 10,000 Kosovars—mostly men—were slaughtered.

Over time, the air campaign became more intense and less discriminating. After eleven weeks of increasingly severe pounding, Milosevic, who by this point had been indicted by the International War Crimes Tribunal, capitulated and accepted NATO demands that he stop all repression; withdraw nearly all Serbian military and paramilitary forces from Kosovo; allow a large international, NATO-dominated peacekeeping force in the province; and allow the restoration of political autonomy in Kosovo. (There was no mention, however, of the three-year transition period proposed at Rambouillet.) His reasons for giving way at that juncture remain murky. Contributing factors may have included loss of any hope of Russian support, an increasingly effective KLA ground capability, and signals that the United States and NATO might reconsider their aversion to using ground forces, combined with the cumulative effect of a bombing campaign that increased markedly both in intensity and in the number of civilian targets.

The "success" of the air war paved the way for another intervention: the deployment of an international peacekeeping force (KFOR) of over 55,000 troops, essentially provided by European members of NATO but also including approximately 7,000 U.S. soldiers. Unlike the air campaign, the peacekeeping effort is buttressed by a U.N. Security Council resolution. The duration of the intervention was left open-ended; its mission is to ensure Serb compliance with NATO demands, thereby creating and maintaining a safe environment in which the people of Kosovo can return to their homes and live free of fear. More difficult to realize are the related objectives, including bringing about the demilitarization of the KLA; preventing revenge attacks by ethnic Albanians against Serbs, and more generally making Kosovo safe for the Serbian minority; and helping the Kosovars rebuild their society and economy, a task complicated by unclear lines of authority among NATO peacekeepers, nongovernmental organizations, the United Nations, and the Kosovars themselves.

IRAQ

In the period under consideration, Iraq provides not just one example of intervention but in reality many. Moreover, it provides examples of situations in which force was used and others in which force was eschewed.

The first incident occurred in September 1994, when Iraq moved more than a division of ground troops near its border with Kuwait. The United States responded by dispatching a carrier battle group to the Persian Gulf, airlifting a marine expeditionary brigade to augment other marine forces already in the area, and sending both mechanized armed forces and tactical air forces. Many of these forces married up quickly with equipment already positioned in the region. Iraq's forces quickly pulled back. This appears to have been a successful instance of tactical deterrence, although even in retrospect it is impossible to divine Iraq's intentions. It is also worth pointing out that Iraq paid no real price for its action, as no punitive strike was launched.

A second major incident took place two years later, when Iraqi armed forces moved into northern Iraq. Although Iraqi forces acted with great violence against various Kurdish groups and individuals, the United States was handicapped given that the Iraqis were invited into the area by one of the two principal Kurdish factions and because Iraq did not violate the northern no-fly zone. Nevertheless, the United States responded in a manner that was modest, punitive, and above all indirect, launching cruise missile strikes against selected military targets in the south of Iraq and extending the no-fly zone in the south by one degree.

On several occasions in 1998, Iraq challenged the ability of the inspectors of the U.N. Special Commission (UNSCOM) to ensure that Iraq maintained no weapons of mass destruction or production capabilities for such weapons. A standoff in February 1998 ended when U.N. Secretary-General Kofi Annan negotiated new rules of the road for UNSCOM. Iraq violated these in August by terminating all special or challenge inspections of suspected production or storage sites. Iraq further upped the ante in mid-November by declaring that it would no longer permit passive monitoring of sites already determined to be clear of weapons of mass destruction. U.S.-led military attacks were cancelled at the eleventh hour when Iraq again capitulated—but they were reinstated as the seventy-hour Operation *Desert Fox* in mid-December, after the head of UNSCOM reported that Iraqi interference made it impossible for him to fulfill his mandate.

These attacks were punitive. They succeeded in modestly "degrading" Iraqi missile and conventional military capabilities. They had no appreciable impact on Iraq's unconventional weapon capabilities, which were at the core of the confrontation. The limited duration of Operation *Desert Fox* was determined arbitrarily, apparently out of concern that regional and international opposition to prolonged or open-ended air strikes would threaten what was left of the U.N. sanctions regime. The attacks were not linked to any clear purpose, such as persuading Iraqi officials to grant U.N. weapons inspectors unconditional access to suspected sites. The attacks thus ended with no clear result, as Iraq continued to defy U.S. and international calls for renewed cooperation with weapons inspectors and compliance with U.N. resolutions. Subsequent aerial attacks, carried out intermittently in response to Iraqi violation of either of the two no-fly zones maintained over large portions of the country, likewise had little discernible effect.

AFGHANISTAN AND SUDAN

Several motives were reflected in the U.S. decision in August 1998 to dispatch cruise missiles to attack terrorist training facilities in Afghanistan and a pharmaceutical plant in Sudan suspected of producing ingredients for chemical weapons. The attacks were at once punitive—a response to the August bombings of U.S. embassies in Kenya and Tanzania by persons associated with Osama Bin Laden, which killed several hundred persons, including a dozen Americans—and both preemptive and preventive—to interfere with preparations for new terrorist attacks and to disrupt the potential for chemical weapons production. They may also have contained a deterrent dimension, in that it was hoped that strikes would discourage further acts of terrorism by Bin Laden (a wealthy, Saudi-born individual who had fought alongside the anti-Soviet resistance in Afghanistan and later emerged as a leading sponsor of international terror) as well as by others.

How effective or warranted the attacks were remains an open question. Terrorist training camps lack much in the way of infrastructure; the Zhawar Kili Al-Badr complex in eastern Afghanistan (near the border with Pakistan) was composed of little more than tents, obstacle courses, firing ranges, and an ammunition depot. The five dozen cruise missiles sent to Afghanistan surely cost more than anything that was destroyed. Moreover, the fact that most of the persons who were meant to be in the camp at that time were missed also points out the difficulty of using long-range systems such as cruise missiles for anything so time sensitive. Still, the strike may have disrupted plans for specific operations and seems to have had a moderating effect on long-term behavior.

The attacks on the Al-Shifa pharmaceutical facility in Khartoum raised the different question of whether the intelligence that led to the attack was sufficiently strong to justify the action. There is controversy over whether a precursor chemical for VX-nerve gas was in fact produced or stored at the targeted factory and whether Bin Laden had a tie to the factory. Such lingering doubts highlight the political and diplomatic questions that inevitably surround any preventive use of military force. The lack of a clear case in this instance may also make it more difficult to build domestic and international support for preventive strikes in the future.

RWANDA

Just as significant as any intervention discussed above is one instance in which the United States largely avoided the use of force: Rwanda. The complicated story begins in August 1993 with the Arusha peace accords, designed to end a civil war that had been going on for several years between Rwanda's majority Hutu population and the minority Tutsis. Signed by Rwandan President Juvenal Habyarimana and representatives of the Rwandan Patriotic Front (RPF), a rebel force dominated by Tutsi exiles, the accords laid out a new and more democratic political order that better took into account the legitimate interests of the Tutsis.

Implementation was never completed, however, in large part due to the resistance of militant Hutus, who opposed any such power-sharing. The result was a peace accord that did not deliver peace. This situation called for peace-making and a force capable of defeating armed Hutu resistance. But in the aftermath of the failed peace-making effort in Somalia, there was little stomach in the Clinton Administration or at the United Nations for such an undertaking. Instead, in Resolution 872 of October 1993, the Security Council created the U.N. Assistance Mission for Rwanda (UNAMIR) for an initial six-month period. UNAMIR proved to be a weak multinational peacekeeping force whose mission was to monitor the cease-fire and refugee repatriation, assist with mine clearance, and investigate alleged non-compliance with the Arusha accords. At its peak, in the spring of 1994, UNAMIR numbered 2,500 soldiers.

UNAMIR might have proved adequate had the situation called for peacekeeping. The moment of truth was not long in coming, however. In January 1994, UNAMIR's commander, General Romeo Dallaire of Canada, cabled U.N. headquarters with information about extremist Hutu hit squads targeting Hutu moderates, Tutsi leaders, and U.N. peacekeepers. Dallaire estimated that he could restore order and provide an environment in which the Arusha accords could be implemented with five infantry battalions and associated support, something on the scale of a 5,000 person augmented "division-ready brigade" of a U.S. air assault division. But his request for a more capable force and a more assertive mission that would seize illegal arms and challenge those threatening the cease-fire—in short, for peace-making—was never approved. Safe havens were never established. Subsequent radio broadcasts by Hutu extremist leaders in Rwanda encouraging what amounted to acts of genocide against the Tutsis did not alter the calculus in either New York or Washington.

In April the Rwandan president was assassinated by the downing of his airplane as he was returning from Dar es Salaam, where the Organization for African Unity and the president of Tanzania had called a summit to revive the Arusha pact. In a separate action, Rwanda's prime minister was killed, along with ten Belgian peacekeepers who were protecting her. A full-fledged genocide of Tutsis and Hutu moderates erupted in early April in the aftermath of these events. The international reaction was merely to reduce the number of international peacekeepers to under 500 and call on the parties to stop the killing. The Clinton Administration's reluctance—based on the fear of public and congressional opposition to "another Somalia" and the ongoing U.S. involvement in Bosnia—was a principal reason that the United Nations did not do more. It is estimated that between half a million and one million people lost their lives; millions more became refugees.

Gradually, anti-government RPF forces gained the upper hand on the battlefield. But violence against unarmed civilians continued, as did massive refugee flows. Faced with this reality, the U.N. Security Council authorized a follow-on force, UNAMIR II, to help protect civilians. This second force was hobbled by the absence of a clear or strong mandate and by its lack of troops. France moved belatedly to fill part of this vacuum, launching Operation *Turquoise* in June 1994. The two-month French operation involved 2,500 heavily-armed combat troops, who established a large humanitarian zone throughout southwestern Rwanda and dealt decisively with any resistance. During the same period the United States confined itself to a limited humanitarian operation that provided food and medical relief. The French effort had but a modest effect, and much of this was ultimately undermined by the arbitrary French withdrawal in late August and the inability of UNAMIR II to maintain stability throughout the country.

LEARNING FROM RECENT EXPERIENCE

The recent interventions discussed in this chapter suggest a number of lessons that should inform the use of military force by the United States in the post–Cold War world. These lessons are for the most part consistent with those drawn from the earlier episodes, although several new insights emerge.

Air power can accomplish many things but not everything. This is perhaps the cardinal lesson of Kosovo, the largest intervention examined here. Air power did, over the course of some eleven weeks, help persuade Slobodan Milosevic agree to NATO terms. But terrible things happened during that period. Thousands of innocent people lost their lives and hundreds of thousands lost their homes and were internally displaced or made refugees. In the end, Kosovo was not one but two wars: a ground war dominated by Serbian military and paramilitary forces and an air war dominated by NATO.

Air power might have accomplished more in Kosovo if NATO and the Clinton Administration had observed various guidelines for the effective use of military force. Delay was (as often is the case) costly. Use of air power immediately after the wholesale violation of the October 1998 agreement and before so many additional Serbian troops had been deployed to Kosovo would certainly have proven more successful. In addition, decisiveness is almost always preferable to gradualism. In the case of Kosovo, starting at a relatively modest pace diluted the psychological and political impact of the NATO action; it also gave Serbia an almost free hand to pursue its objectives using ground forces. Further, operations were inhibited by the requirement that they avoid collateral damage, insisted on by European members of NATO. It did not help that U.S. and NATO officials misjudged the likely Serbian response to either the threat or the limited application of NATO air power. Indeed, the Kosovo bombing highlights the necessity of preparing from the outset for follow-on interventions in the event that the adversary does not respond or the situation does not unfold as anticipated.

Some of these shortcomings stemmed directly from the decision to use air power alone rather than in conjunction with ground forces. This decision was based on political and not strategic grounds. More than anything else, the exclusion of ground forces derived from the view that Congress and the American people would not support the human costs of such a commitment. It is true that American interests in Kosovo were less than vital and that persuading the American people and their elected representatives of the need to make large sacrifices, including casualties, would not have been easy. But the Administration never tried to do so. As a result, the intervention failed to achieve one of the principal goals that the United States and NATO set for themselves, namely, the protection of the people of Kosovo. Protecting the forces and avoiding casualties can and should be considerations in determining the form of an intervention—but not the only ones.

Still, it is important to distinguish between what proved in the end to be a successful application of coercive force in Kosovo and the failure in Iraq. In the former, air power was deployed in significant amounts and in an open-ended fashion. The condition for stopping the attacks was clear: Milosevic had to meet a specified set of demands. NATO, meanwhile, had to be prepared to stay the course until those demands were met. Compellence is a risky form of intervention because it cedes the initiative to the target, who has to decide whether to hold out or to compromise. Before initiating a compellent intervention, it is therefore imperative to be confident that the intervention can be sustained politically and militarily. But compellence does have the advantage of clarity, in that it links the intervention with a particular goal.

Punitive interventions are in many ways the opposite: they lack any such clear purpose or linkage and their principal advantage is that the initiative is retained by the attacking side, which alone decides when it is satisfied. Operation *Desert Fox* employed a modest amount of air power for a short and arbitrary period of time and with no goal other than to weaken the adversary's strength to some vague and unspecified degree. In this instance, however, rather than a punitive attack it would have been far better to have conducted a compellent attack that was both massive in scope and open-ended in application, tied to Iraq agreeing to accept unconditional international inspections of suspect facilities for weapons of mass destruction. To be sure, this course of action would have been more costly and would have provoked significant international opposition. Yet it would have had the potential to achieve the important goal of reinstating inspections and humiliating Saddam Hussein in the process, two outcomes that arguably would have justified the diplomatic costs.

The cases discussed in this chapter indicate that deterrence can work on occasion. Dispatching a carrier task force to the Taiwan Straits was a classic example of gunboat diplomacy. A long-term strategic commitment was backed up by a sizable show of force. Whether it actually deterred any action by China is less clear, because it is difficult to discern China's intentions. Regardless, the U.S. deployment may have had an impact on subsequent Chinese behavior by signaling that any military move against Taiwan would likely be contested by the United States. By contrast, the threats against Serbia over Kosovo failed, suggesting that deterrence requires credibility—markedly absent in this context, given the history of threats that were not backed up with action.

As suggested earlier in the book, carrying out more than one kind of intervention in the same place at the same time can invite trouble. This was the case both in Bosnia, where the presence of UNPROFOR made the use of air power risky, and again in Kosovo, where the presence of unarmed monitors undermined the credibility of threats of attack. The problem goes beyond the all too real danger of hostage-taking. It is difficult, if not impossible, to carry out an operation that requires consent at the same time as threatening or actually carrying out an operation that is compellent or otherwise hostile. The consensual operation needs to be brought to an end before the aggressive effort can be credibly and safely undertaken.

New technology is no panacea. To begin with, no system is invulnerable. Even a stealth aircraft can be shot down. Smart bombs go astray from time to time, missing their intended targets and possibly causing unintended damage and destruction. Bombs and missiles can be fooled by decoys and frustrated by mobility and masking. Also, no system is better than the intelligence provided. Accuracy is no virtue if the target is misidentified, as was the case with the Chinese embassy bombed by mistake in Belgrade, or if the intelligence is in itself flawed, as may have been the case in the attack on the alleged chemical plant in Sudan. The Sudanese episode, along with the raid on suspected terrorist installations in Afghanistan, underscore the uncertainty of preventive and preemptive interventions when critical information is difficult to attain or time sensitive.

Several of the cases examined in this chapter highlight the reality that it is difficult to affect the internal politics or political culture of a target using the military instrument. The experiences in both Iraq and Kosovo suggest that, short of occupation, military force is not a good tool for changing a regime, although a successful military intervention that weakens or humiliates an adversary can help bring about a political environment that encourages domestic opponents of the regime to act. Moreover, as shown in the case of Haiti, even prolonged occupation is no guarantee of favorable results. Here, though, the prospects for success are clearly affected by the ways in which other foreign policy tools (such as economic assistance) are employed. Again, military force is good at creating contexts, but what happens within those contexts is more a matter for other instruments and policies.

The cases also furnish additional evidence that exit dates ought not to be confused with exit strategies. Bosnia reveals that arbitrary deadlines are more likely to cause political problems than to provide guidance. The notion that an intervention will provide a fixed amount of breathing room, after which the local people and governments will be on their own—an argument advanced in a March 1996 speech by then National Security Advisor Anthony Lake (see Appendix I)—is unsustainable. The United States cannot turn its back on a humanitarian problem if it deteriorates beyond certain limits or if U.S. interests are adversely affected. This lesson seems to have been learned, for the Clinton Administration eschewed any talk of specific withdrawal dates when it inserted peacekeeping forces into Kosovo. Moreover, the lesson of several interventions, including those in Somalia, Haiti, and Bosnia, seems to be that prolonged commitments are not controversial at home so long as casualties are kept to a minimum—which is more likely to be the case if the scope of the intervention is kept modest.

What also emerges from recent history is a new appreciation of the impact of a decision not to use force. The clearest example is Rwanda, where non-intervention almost surely forfeited an opportunity to accomplish much good at limited cost. In the case of Iraq, decisions not to use force (or to place sharp limits on how much force would be used) have provided Saddam the time and the opportunity to defy U.N. demands and reconstitute weapons of mass destruction. In Kosovo, the refusal to commit ground forces likely increased the vulnerability of local people. In other instances—Bosnia comes to mind—limits on the peacekeepers' mission kept costs down but also placed a ceiling on what they were likely to accomplish. The same can be said for the nation-building exercise in Haiti, which reduced the risk to U.S. forces by limiting efforts to disarm locals. One can debate the trade-off in each case—in my view, more ambitious interventions in Bosnia or Haiti would not have been justified by the likely costs and results—but there is no doubting that there is a trade-off. The good news is that where interests do not warrant costly (in both financial and human terms) peace-making or nation-building operations, there may be narrower and less expensive options for doing good, such as establishing one or more safe havens in an affected country or designing operations to keep hostile factions apart. Indeed, the current enthusiasm for encouraging multi-ethnic arrangements (along with an equal hostility toward partition schemes) in dealing with divided societies such as exist in Bosnia and Kosovo ought to be rethought.

Taken as a whole, what is most noteworthy about the principal American military interventions over the past five years is their number and range. Military force continues to be relevant for a wide range of tasks. One conclusion that follows from this judgment is the continuing need for a large, flexible U.S. military. Other governments and organizations are not in a position to provide more than limited assistance; the lion's share of any demanding military operation will have to be borne by the United States. This said, the United States does not have the luxury of maintaining a military that is tailored only to traditional battlefields. The dismal showing of the Apache helicopters in Kosovo—the problems of getting them there and their operational diffculties—is a strong warning that the U.S. military needs great flexibility, a force that is easily moved and capable of coping with a wide range of missions and environments. At present the U.S. military (notably the Army) is too heavy and is organized in units that are often too large. The American military is also short on sea and air lift that can use the majority of the world's airfields and ports, has inadequate stores of advanced munitions, and lacks the specialized command, control, and intelligence assets and platforms needed for modern combat operations.

Still, even an ideal military cannot succeed if it is undermined by either of two constraints. The first is an unwillingness to commit—to allow the military to operate—when it is judged that interests warrant some action and that the military tool is the most appropriate. Recent experience reveals a pattern of holding back until the situation on the ground has deteriorated to the point where any intervention is likely to be more difficult and expensive. Such delay is understandable—it is more difficult to marshal domestic and international support for intervening in the absence of overwhelming cause—but nonetheless costly, as the opportunity to act preventively and with lesser amounts of resources is often squandered.

A different form of reluctance to commit is that involving ground troops. Analysis shows that there are clear limits in what air power can be expected to accomplish. In some instances, such as where high-value targets are rare and hard to locate or the adversary is exploiting its advantage in ground forces, only ground forces will be able to protect the interests involved. Domestic opposition to such a commitment can be reduced and overcome by concerted presidential effort and by designing interventions in which the level of casualties can be justified and explained by the interests at stake. This requires an expense of time and political capital, but they are well spent. Interventions shaped more by politics than by strategy are unlikely to succeed.

The second constraint is in some ways the opposite of the first: over-reliance on the military instrument. The United States cannot commit its military might everywhere, all the time. It needs to be discriminating lest it exhaust its resources and be left unable to cope with situations in which vital interests are at stake. When it comes to humanitarian interventions, military force must be reserved for those situations in which it is likely to accomplish good, and also for those rare situations that are truly dire, those in which other countries and organizations are likely to share the burden, and those in which more important interests would not be adversely affected. Moreover, poor application of other foreign policy tools can create pressures to respond militarily to deteriorating circumstances. For example, better use of sanctions in Haiti and of diplomacy in Bosnia and Kosovo might have prevented such deterioration and the necessity to intervene with military force. Military force is but one form of intervention; it cannot be expected to bear the full burden of the foreign policy of the United States or of any other nation.

APPENDICES

CHARTER OF THE UNITED NATIONS*

CHAPTER I: PURPOSES AND PRINCIPLES

Article 1

The Purposes of the United Nations are:

1. To maintain international peace and security, and to that end: to take effective collective measures for the prevention and removal of threats to the peace, and for the suppression of acts of aggression or other breaches of the peace, and to bring about by peaceful means, and in conformity with the principles of justice and international law, adjustment or settlement of international disputes or situations which might lead to a breach of the peace;

2. To develop friendly relations among nations based on respect for the principle of equal rights and self-determination of peoples, and to take other appropriate measures to strengthen universal peace;

3. To achieve international co-operation in solving international problems of an economic, social, cultural, or humanitarian character, and in promoting and encouraging respect for human rights and for fundamental freedoms for all without distinction as to race, sex, language, or religion; and

4. To be a centre for harmonizing the actions of nations in the attainment of these common ends.

Article 2

The Organization and its Members, in pursuit of the Purposes stated in Article 1, shall act in accordance with the following Principles.

Selected excerpts, June 16, 1945.

1. The Organization is based on the principle of the sovereign equality of all its Members.

2. All Members, in order to ensure to all of them the rights and benefits resulting from membership, shall fulfil in good faith the obligations assumed by them in accordance with the present Charter.

3. All Members shall settle their international disputes by peaceful means in such a manner that international peace and security, and justice, are not endangered.

4. All Members shall refrain in their international relations from the threat or use of force against the territorial integrity or political independence of any state, or in any other manner inconsistent with the Purposes of the United Nations.

5. All Members shall give the United Nations every assistance in any action it takes in accordance with the present Charter, and shall refrain from giving assistance to any state against which the United Nations is taking preventive or enforcement action.

6. The Organization shall ensure that states which are not Members of the United Nations act in accordance with these Principles so far as may be necessary for the maintenance of international peace and security.

7. Nothing contained in the present Charter shall authorize the United Nations to intervene in matters which are essentially within the domestic jurisdiction of any state or shall require the Members to submit such matters to settlement under the present Charter; but this principle shall not prejudice the application of enforcement measures under Chapter VII. . . .

CHAPTER VI:
PACIFIC SETTLEMENT OF DISPUTES

Article 33

1. The parties to any dispute, the continuance of which is likely to endanger the maintenance of international peace and security, shall,

first of all, seek a solution by negotiations, enquiry, mediation, conciliation, arbitration, judicial settlement, resort to regional agencies or arrangements, or other peaceful means of their own choice.

2. The Security Council shall, when it deems necessary, call upon the parties to settle their dispute by such means.

Article 34

The Security Council may investigate any dispute, or any situation which might lead to international friction or give rise to a dispute, in order to determine whether the continuance of the dispute or situation is likely to endanger the maintenance of international peace and security.

Article 35

1. Any Member of the United Nations may bring any dispute, or any situation of the nature referred to in Article 34, to the attention of the Security Council or of the General Assembly.

2. A state which is not a Member of the United Nations may bring to the attention of the Security Council or of the General Assembly any dispute to which it is a party if it accepts in advance, for the purposes of the dispute, the obligations of pacific settlement provided in the present Charter.

3. The proceedings of the General Assembly in respect of matters brought to its attention under this Article will be subject to the provisions of Articles 11 and 12.

Article 36

1. The Security Council may, at any stage of a dispute of the nature referred to in Article 33 or of a situation of like nature, recommend appropriate procedures or methods of adjustment.

2. The Security Council should take into consideration any procedures for the settlement of the dispute which have already been adopted by the parties.

3. In making recommendations under this Article the Security Council should also take into consideration that legal disputes should as a general rule be referred by the parties to the

International Court of Justice in accordance with the provisions of the Statute of the Court.

Article 37

1. Should the parties to a dispute of the nature referred to in Article 33 fail to settle it by the means indicated in that Article, they shall refer it to the Security Council.

2. If the Security Council deems that the continuance of the dispute is in fact likely to endanger the maintenance of international peace and security, it shall decide whether to take action under Article 36 or to recommend such terms of settlement as it may consider appropriate.

Article 38

Without prejudice to the provisions of Articles 33 to 37, the Security Council may, if all the parties to any dispute so request, make recommendations to the parties with a view to a pacific settlement of the dispute.

CHAPTER VII: ACTION WITH RESPECT TO THREATS TO THE PEACE, BREACHES OF THE PEACE, AND ACTS OF AGGRESSION

Article 39

The Security Council shall determine the existence of any threat to the peace, breach of the peace, or act of aggression and shall make recommendations, or decide what measures shall be taken in accordance with Articles 41 and 42, to maintain or restore international peace and security.

Article 40

In order to prevent an aggravation of the situation, the Security Council may, before making the recommendations or deciding upon the measures provided for in Article 39, call upon the parties concerned to comply with such provisional measures as it deems necessary or desirable. Such provisional measures shall be without prejudice to the rights, claims, or position of the parties concerned. The Security Council shall duly take account of failure to comply with such provisional measures.

Article 41

The Security Council may decide what measures not involving the use of armed force are to be employed to give effect to its decisions, and it may call upon the Members of the United Nations to apply such measures. These may include complete or partial interruption of economic relations and of rail, sea, air, postal, telegraphic, radio, and other means of communication, and the severance of diplomatic relations.

Article 42

Should the Security Council consider that measures provided for in Article 41 would be inadequate or have proved to be inadequate, it may take such action by air, sea, or land forces as may be necessary to maintain or restore international peace and security. Such action may include demonstrations, blockade, and other operations by air, sea, or land forces of Members of the United Nations.

Article 43

1. All Members of the United Nations, in order to contribute to the maintenance of international peace and security, undertake to make available to the Security Council, on its call and in accordance with a special agreement or agreements, armed forces, assistance, and facilities, including rights of passage, necessary for the purpose of maintaining international peace and security.

2. Such agreement or agreements shall govern the numbers and types of forces, their degree of readiness and general location, and the nature of the facilities and assistance to be provided.

3. The agreement or agreements shall be negotiated as soon as possible on the initiative of the Security Council. They shall be concluded between the Security Council and Members or between

the Security Council and groups of Members and shall be subject to ratification by the signatory states in accordance with their respective constitutional processes.

Article 44

When the Security Council has decided to use force it shall, before calling upon a Member not represented on it to provide armed forces in fulfillment of the obligations assumed under Article 43, invite that Member, if the Member so desires, to participate in the decisions of the Security Council concerning the employment of contingents of that Member's armed forces.

Article 45

In order to enable the United Nations to take urgent military measures, Members shall hold immediately available national air-force contingents for combined international enforcement action. The strength and degree of readiness of these contingents and plans for their combined action shall be determined, within the limits laid down in the special agreement or agreements referred to in Article 43, by the Security Council with the assistance of the Military Staff Committee.

Article 46

Plans for the application of armed force shall be made by the Security Council with the assistance of the Military Staff Committee.

Article 47

1. There shall be established a Military Staff Committee to advise and assist the Security Council on all questions relating to the Security Council's military requirements for the maintenance of international peace and security, the employment and command of forces placed at its disposal, the regulation of armaments, and possible disarmament.

2. The Military Staff Committee shall consist of the Chiefs of Staff of the permanent members of the Security Council or their representatives. Any Member of the United Nations not permanently

represented on the Committee shall be invited by the Committee to be associated with it when the efficient discharge of the Committee's responsibilities requires the participation of that Member in its work.

3. The Military Staff Committee shall be responsible under the Security Council for the strategic direction of any armed forces placed at the disposal of the Security Council. Questions relating to the command of such forces shall be worked out subsequently.

4. The Military Staff Committee, with the authorization of the Security Council and after consultation with appropriate regional agencies, may establish regional sub-committees.

Article 48

1. The action required to carry out the decisions of the Security Council for the maintenance of international peace and security shall be taken by all the Members of the United Nations or by some of them, as the Security Council may determine.

2. Such decisions shall be carried out by the Members of the United Nations directly and through their action in the appropriate international agencies of which they are members.

Article 49

The Members of the United Nations shall join in affording mutual assistance in carrying out the measures decided upon by the Security Council.

Article 50

If preventive or enforcement measures against any state are taken by the Security Council, any other state, whether a Member of the United Nations or not, which finds itself confronted with special economic problems arising from the carrying out of those measures shall have the right to consult the Security Council with regard to a solution of those problems.

Article 51

Nothing in the present Charter shall impair the inherent right of individual or collective self-defence if an armed attack occurs against a Member of the United Nations, until the Security Council has taken measures necessary to maintain international peace and security. Measures taken by Members in the exercise of this right of self-defence shall be immediately reported to the Security Council and shall not in any way affect the authority and responsibility of the Security Council under the present Charter to take at any time such action as it deems necessary in order to maintain or restore international peace and security.

CHAPTER VIII: REGIONAL ARRANGEMENTS

Article 52

1. Nothing in the present Charter precludes the existence of regional arrangements or agencies for dealing with such matters relating to the maintenance of international peace and security as are appropriate for regional action, provided that such arrangements or agencies and their activities are consistent with the Purposes and Principles of the United Nations.

2. The Members of the United Nations entering into such arrangements or constituting such agencies shall make every effort to achieve pacific settlement of local disputes through such regional arrangements or by such regional agencies before referring them to the Security Council.

3. The Security Council shall encourage the development of pacific settlement of local disputes through such regional arrangements or by such regional agencies either on the initiative of the states concerned or by reference from the Security Council.

4. This Article in no way impairs the application of Articles 34 and 35.

APPENDIX B

WAR POWERS RESOLUTION*

Joint Resolution
Concerning the war powers of Congress and the President

Resolved by the Senate and House of Representatives of the United States of America in Congress assembled,

SHORT TITLE

SECTION 1 This joint resolution may be cited as the "War Powers Resolution".

PURPOSE AND POLICY

SEC. 2 (a) It is the purpose of this joint resolution to fulfill the intent of the framers of the Constitution of the United States and insure that the collective judgment of both the Congress and the President will apply to the introduction of United States Armed Forces into hostilities, or into situations where imminent involve-

* Public Law 93–148. Passed by the 93rd Congress, Joint Resolution 542, November 7, 1973.

ment in hostilities is clearly indicated by the circumstances, and to the continued use of such forces in hostilities or in such situations.

(b) Under article I, section 8, of the Constitution, it is specifically provided that the Congress shall have the power to make all laws necessary and proper for carrying into execution, not only its own powers but also all other powers vested by the Constitution in the Government of the United States, or in any department or officer thereof.

(c) The constitutional powers of the President as Commander-in-Chief to introduce United States Armed Forces into hostilities, or into situations where imminent involvement in hostilities is clearly indicated by the circumstances, are exercised only pursuant to (1) a declaration of war, (2) specific statutory authorization, or (3) a national emergency created by attack upon the United States, its territories or possessions, or its armed forces.

CONSULTATION

SEC. 3 The President in every possible instance shall consult with Congress before introducing United States Armed Forces into hostilities or into situations where imminent involvement in hostilities is clearly indicated by the circumstances, and after every such introduction shall consult regularly with the Congress until United States Armed Forces are no longer engaged in hostilities or have been removed from such situations.

REPORTING

SEC. 4 (a) In the absence of a declaration of war, in any case in which United States Armed Forces are introduced—

(1) into hostilities or into situations where imminent involvement in hostilities is clearly indicated by the circumstances;

(2) into the territory, airspace or waters of a foreign nation, while

equipped for combat, except for deployments which relate solely to supply, replacement, repair, or training of such forces; or

(3) in numbers which substantially enlarge United States Armed Forces equipped for combat already located in a foreign nation;

the President shall submit within 48 hours to the Speaker of the House of Representatives and to the President pro tempore of the Senate a report, in writing, setting forth—

(A) the circumstances necessitating the introduction of United States Armed Forces;

(B) the constitutional and legislative authority under which such introduction took place; and

(C) the estimated scope and duration of the hostilities or involvement.

(b) The President shall provide such other information as the Congress may request in the fulfillment of its constitutional responsibilities with respect to committing the Nation to war and to the use of United States Armed Forces abroad.

(c) Whenever United States Armed Forces are introduced into hostilities or into any situation described in subsection (a) of this section, the President shall, so long as such armed forces continue to be engaged in such hostilities or situation, report to the Congress periodically on the status of such hostilities or situation as well as on the scope and duration of such hostilities or situation, but in no event shall he report to the Congress less often than once every six months.

CONGRESSIONAL ACTION

SEC. 5 (a) Each report submitted pursuant to section 4(a)(1) shall be transmitted to the Speaker of the House of Representatives and to the President pro tempore of the Senate on the same calendar day. Each report so transmitted shall be referred to the Committee on Foreign Affairs of the House of Representatives and to the Committee on Foreign Relations of the Senate for appropriate action. If, when the report is transmitted, the Congress has adjourned sine die or has adjourned for any period in excess of three calendar days, the Speaker of the House of Representatives and the President pro tempore of the Senate, if they deem it advisable (or if petitioned by at least 30 percent of the membership of their respective Houses) shall jointly request the President to convene Congress in order that it may consider the report and take appropriate action pursuant to this section.

(b) Within sixty calendar days after a report is submitted or is required to be submitted pursuant to section 4(a)(1), whichever is earlier, the President shall terminate any use of United States Armed Forces with respect to which such report was submitted (or required to be submitted), unless the Congress (1) has declared war or has enacted a specific authorization for such use of United States Armed Forces, (2) has extended by law such sixty-day period, or (3) is physically unable to meet as a result of an armed attack upon the United States. Such sixty-day period shall be extended for not more than an additional thirty days if the President determines and certifies to the Congress in writing that unavoidable military necessity respecting the safety of United States Armed Forces requires the continued use of such armed forces in the course of bringing about a prompt removal of such forces.

(c) Notwithstanding subsection (b), at any time that United States Armed Forces are engaged in hostilities outside the territory of the United States, its possessions and territories without a declaration of war or specific statutory authorization, such forces shall be removed by the President if the Congress so directs by concurrent resolution. . . .

INTERPRETATION OF JOINT RESOLUTION

SEC. 8 (a) Authority to introduce United States Armed Forces into hostilities or into situations wherein involvement in hostilities is clearly indicated by the circumstances shall not be inferred—

(1) from any provision of law (whether or not in effect before the date of the enactment of this joint resolution), including any provision contained in any appropriation Act, unless such provision specifically authorizes the introduction of United States Armed Forces into hostilities or into such situations and states that it is intended to constitute specific statutory authorization within the meaning of this joint resolution; or

(2) from any treaty heretofore or hereafter ratified unless such treaty is implemented by legislation specifically authorizing the introduction of United States Armed Forces into hostilities or into such situations and stating that it is intended to constitute specific statutory authorization within the meaning of this joint resolution.

(b) Nothing in this joint resolution shall be construed to require any further specific statutory authorization to permit members of United States Armed Forces to participate jointly with members of the armed forces of one or more foreign countries in the headquarters operations of high-level military commands which were established prior to the date of enactment of this joint resolution and pursuant to the United Nations Charter or any treaty ratified by the United States prior to such date.

(c) For purposes of this joint resolution, the term "introduction of United States Armed Forces" includes the assignment of members of such armed forces to command, coordinate, participate in the movement of, or accompany the regular or irregular military forces of any foreign country or government when such military forces are engaged, or there exists an imminent threat that such forces will become engaged, in hostilities.

(d) Nothing in this joint resolution—

(1) is intended to alter the constitutional authority of the Congress or of the President, or the provisions of existing treaties; or

(2) shall be construed as granting any authority to the President with respect to the introduction of United States Armed Forces into hostilities or into situations wherein involvement in hostilities is clearly indicated by the circumstances which authority he would not have had in the absence of this joint resolution.

SEPARABILITY CLAUSE

SEC. 9 If any provision of this joint resolution or the application thereof to any person or circumstance is held invalid, the remainder of the joint resolution and the application of such provision to any other person or circumstance shall not be affected thereby.

EFFECTIVE DATE

SEC. 10 This joint resolution shall take effect on the date of its enactment.

APPENDIX C

THE USES OF MILITARY POWER

BY CASPAR W. WEINBERGER*

... Of all the many policies our citizens deserve—and need—to understand, none is so important as those related to our topic to-day—the uses of military power. Deterrence will work only if the Soviets understand our firm commitment to keeping the peace, ... and only from a well-informed public can we expect to have that national will and commitment.

So today, I want to discuss with you perhaps the most important question concerning keeping the peace. Under what circumstances, and by what means, does a great democracy such as ours reach the painful decision that the use of military force is necessary to protect our interests or to carry out our national policy?

National power has many components, some tangible—like economic wealth, technical pre-eminence. Other components are intangible—such as moral force, or strong national will. Military forces, when they are strong and ready and modern, are a credible—and tangible—addition to a nation's power. When both the intangible national will and those forces are forged into one instrument, national power becomes effective. ...

Aware of the consequences of any misstep, yet convinced of the precious worth of the freedom we enjoy, we seek to avoid conflict, while maintaining strong defenses. Our policy has always been to work hard for peace, but to be prepared if war comes. Yet, so blurred

* Excerpts from Remarks by Secretary of Defense Caspar W. Weinberger to the National Press Club, Washington, D.C., November 28, 1984.

have the lines become between open conflict and half-hidden hostile acts that we cannot confidently predict where, or when, or how, or from what direction aggression may arrive. We must be prepared, at any moment, to meet threats ranging in intensity from isolated terrorist acts, to guerilla action, to full-scale military confrontation.

Alexander Hamilton, writing in the *Federalist Papers,* said that "it is impossible to foresee or define the extent and variety of national exigencies, or the correspondent extent and variety of the means which may be necessary to satisfy them." If it was true then, how much more true it is today, when we must remain ready to consider the means to meet such serious indirect challenges to the peace as proxy wars and individual terrorist action. And how much more important is it now, considering the consequences of failing to deter conflict at the lowest level possible. While the use of military force to defend territory has never been questioned when a democracy has been attacked and its very survival threatened, most democracies have rejected the unilateral aggressive use of force to invade, conquer or subjugate other nations. The extent to which the use of force *is* acceptable remains unresolved for the host of other situations which fall between these extremes of defensive and aggressive use of force.

We find ourselves, then, face to face with a modern paradox: The most likely challenge to the peace—the gray area conflicts— are precisely the most difficult challenges to which a democracy must respond. Yet, while the source and nature of today's challenges are uncertain, our response must be clear and understandable. Unless we are certain that force is essential, we run the risk of inadequate national will to apply the resources needed.

Because we face a spectrum of threats—from covert aggression, terrorism, and subversion, to overt intimidation, to use of brute force—choosing the appropriate level of our response is difficult. Flexible response does not mean just any response is appropriate. But once a decision to employ some degree of force has been made, and the purpose clarified, our government must have the clear mandate to carry out, and continue to carry out, that decision until the purpose has been achieved. That, too, has been difficult to accomplish.

The issue of which branch of government has authority to define that mandate and make decisions on using force is now being strongly contended. Beginning in the 1970s Congress demanded, and assumed, a far more active role in the making of foreign policy and in the decision-making process for the employment of military forces abroad than had been thought appropriate and practical before. As a result, the centrality of decision-making authority in the executive branch has been compromised by the legislative branch to an extent that actively interferes with that process. At the same time, there has not been a corresponding acceptance of responsibility by Congress for the outcome of decisions concerning the employment of military forces.

Yet the outcome of decisions on whether—and when—and to what degree—to use combat forces abroad has never been more *important* than it is today. While we do not seek to deter or settle all the world's conflicts, we must recognize that, as a major power, our responsibilities and interests are now of such scope that there are few troubled areas we can afford to ignore. So we must be prepared to deal with a range of possibilities, a spectrum of crises, from local insurgency to global conflict. We prefer, of course, to *limit* any conflict in its early stages, to contain and control it—but to do that our military forces must be deployed in a *timely* manner, and be fully supported and prepared *before* they are engaged, because many of those difficult decisions must be made extremely quickly.

Some on the national scene think they can always avoid making tough decisions. Some reject entirely the question of whether any force can ever be used abroad. They want to avoid grappling with a complex issue because, despite clever rhetoric disguising their purpose, these people are in fact advocating a return to post–World War I isolationism. While they may maintain in principle that military force has a role in foreign policy, they are never willing to name the circumstance or the place where it would apply.

On the other side, some theorists argue that military force can be brought to bear in any crisis. Some of these proponents of force are eager to advocate its use even in limited amounts simply because they believe that if there are American forces of *any* size present they will somehow solve the problem.

Neither of these two extremes offers us any lasting or satisfying factory solutions. The first—undue reserve—would lead us ultimately to withdraw from international events that require free nations to defend their interests from the aggressive use of force. We would be abdicating our responsibilities as the leader of the free world—responsibilities more or less thrust upon us in the aftermath of World War II—a war incidentally that isolationism did nothing to deter. These are responsibilities we must fulfill unless we desire the Soviet Union to keep expanding its influence unchecked throughout the world. In an international system based on mutual interdependence among nations, and alliances between friends, stark isolationism quickly would lead to a far more dangerous situation for the United States: We would be without allies and faced by many hostile or indifferent nations.

The second alternative—employing our forces almost indiscriminately and as a regular and customary part of our diplomatic efforts—would surely plunge us headlong into the sort of domestic turmoil we experienced during the Vietnam War, without accomplishing the goal for which we committed our forces. Such policies might very well tear at the fabric of our society, endangering the *single*-most critical element of a successful democracy: *a strong consensus of support and agreement for our basic purposes.*

Policies formed without a clear understanding of what we hope to achieve would also earn us the scorn of our troops, who would have an understandable opposition to being *used*—in every sense of the word—casually and without intent to support them fully. Ultimately this course would reduce their morale and their effectiveness for engagements we *must* win. And if the military were to distrust its civilian leadership, recruitment would fall off and I fear an end to the all-volunteer system would be upon us, requiring a return to a draft, sowing the seeds of riot and discontent that so wracked the country in the '60s. . . .

In today's world where minutes count, such decisive leadership is more important than ever before. Regardless of whether conflicts are limited, or threats are ill-defined, we *must* be capable of quickly determining that the threats and conflicts either *do* or *do not* affect the vital interests of the United States and our allies . . . and then responding appropriately.

Those threats may not entail an immediate, direct attack on our territory, and our response may not necessarily require the immediate or direct defense of our homeland. But when our vital national interests and those of our allies *are* at stake, we cannot ignore our safety, or forsake our allies.

At the same time, recent history has proven that we cannot assume unilaterally the role of the world's defender. We have learned that there are limits to how much of our spirit and blood and treasure we can afford to forfeit in meeting our responsibility to keep peace and freedom. So while we may and should offer substantial amounts of economic and military assistance to our allies in their time of need, and help them maintain forces to deter attacks against them—usually we cannot substitute our troops or our will for theirs.

We should only engage *our* troops if we must do so as a matter of our *own* vital national interest. We cannot assume for other sovereign nations the responsibility to defend *their* territory—without their strong invitation—when our own freedom is not threatened.

On the other hand, there have been recent cases where the United States has seen the need to join forces with other nations to try to preserve the peace by helping with negotiations, and by separating warring parties, and thus enabling those warring nations to withdraw from hostilities safely. In the Middle East, which has been torn by conflict for millennia, we have sent our troops in recent years both to the Sinai and to Lebanon, for just such a peacekeeping mission. But we did not configure or equip those forces for combat—they were armed only for their self-defense. Their mission required them to be—and to be recognized as—peacekeepers. We knew that if conditions deteriorated so they were in danger, or if because of the actions of the warring nations, their peacekeeping mission could not be realized, then it would be necessary either to add sufficiently to the number and arms of our troops—in short to equip them for combat, . . . or to withdraw them. And so in Lebanon, when we faced just such a choice, because the warring nations did not enter into withdrawal or peace agreements, the President properly withdrew forces equipped only for peacekeeping.

In those cases where our national interests require us to commit combat forces, we must never let there be doubt of our resolution. When it is necessary for our troops to be committed to combat, we *must* commit them, in sufficient numbers and we *must* support them, as effectively and resolutely as our strength permits. When we commit our troops to combat we must do so with the sole object of winning.

Once it is clear our troops are required, because our vital interests are at stake, then we must have the firm national resolve to commit every ounce of strength necessary to win the fight to achieve our objectives. In Grenada we did just that.

Just as clearly, there are other situations where United States combat forces should *not* be used. I believe the postwar period has taught us several lessons, and from them I have developed *six* major tests to be applied when we are weighing the use of U.S. combat forces abroad. Let me now share them with you:

(1) *First,* the United States should not commit forces to *combat* overseas unless the particular engagement or occasion is deemed vital to our national interest or that of our allies. That emphatically does not mean that we should *declare* beforehand, as we did with Korea in 1950, that a particular area is outside our strategic perimeter.

(2) *Second,* if we decide it *is* necessary to put *combat* troops into a given situation, we should do so wholeheartedly, and with the clear intention of winning. If we are *un*willing to commit the forces or resources necessary to achieve our objectives, we should not commit them at all. Of course if the particular situation requires only limited force to win our objectives, then we should not hesitate to commit forces sized accordingly. When Hitler broke treaties and remilitarized the Rhineland, small combat forces then could perhaps have prevented the holocaust of World War II.

(3) *Third,* if we *do* decide to commit forces to combat overseas,

we should have clearly defined political and military objectives. And we should know precisely how our forces can accomplish those clearly defined objectives. And we should have and send the forces needed to do just that. As Clausewitz wrote, "No one starts a war—or rather, no one in his senses ought to do so—without first being clear in his mind what he intends to achieve by that war, and how he intends to conduct it."

War may be different today than in Clausewitz's time, but the need for well-defined objectives and a consistent strategy is still essential. If we determine that a combat mission has become necessary for our vital national interests, then we must send forces capable to do the job—and not assign a combat mission to a force configured for peacekeeping.

(4) *Fourth*, the relationship between our objectives and the forces we have committed—their size, composition and disposition—must be continually reassessed and adjusted if necessary. Conditions and objectives invariably change during the course of a conflict. When they do change, then so must our combat requirements. We must continuously keep as a beacon light before us the basic questions: *"Is this conflict in our national interest?"* "Does our national interest require us to fight, to use force of arms?" If the answers are "yes", then we *must* win. If the answers are "no", then we should not be in combat.

(5) *Fifth*, before the U.S. commits combat forces abroad, there must be some reasonable assurance we will have the support of the American people and their elected representatives in Congress. This support cannot be achieved unless we are candid in making clear the threats we face; the support cannot be sustained without continuing and close consultation. We cannot fight a battle with the Congress at home while asking our troops to win a war overseas or, as in the case of Vietnam, in effect asking our troops *not* to win, but just to be there.

(6) *Finally*, the commitment of U.S. forces to combat should be a last resort.

I believe that these tests can be helpful in deciding whether or not we should commit our troops to combat in the months and years ahead. The point we must all keep uppermost in our minds is that if we ever decide to commit forces to combat, we must support those forces to the *fullest* extent of our national will for as long as it takes to win. So we must have in mind objectives that are clearly defined and understood and supported by the widest possible number of our citizens. And those objectives must be vital to our survival as a free nation and to the fulfillment of our responsibilities as a world power. We must also be farsighted enough to sense when immediate and strong reactions to apparently small events can prevent lion-like responses that may be required later. We must never forget those isolationists in Europe who shrugged that "Danzig is not worth a war," and "why should we fight to keep the Rhineland demilitarized?"

These tests I have just mentioned have been phrased negatively for a purpose—they are intended to sound a note of caution—caution that we must observe prior to committing forces to combat overseas. When we ask our military forces to risk their very lives in such situations, a note of caution is not only prudent, it is morally required.

In many situations we may apply these tests and conclude that a combatant role is not appropriate. Yet no one should interpret what I am saying here today as an abdication of America's responsibilities—either to its own citizens or to its allies. Nor should these remarks be misread as a signal that this country, or this Administration, is unwilling to commit forces to combat overseas.

We have demonstrated in the past that, when our vital interests or those of our allies are threatened, we are ready to use force, and use it decisively, to protect those interests. Let no one entertain any illusions—if our vital interests are involved, we are prepared to fight. And we are resolved that if we *must* fight, we *must* win.

So, while these tests are drawn from lessons we have learned from the past, they also can—and should—be applied to the future. For example, the problems confronting us in Central America today are difficult. The possibility of more extensive Soviet and Soviet-proxy penetration into this hemisphere in months ahead is something we should recognize. If this happens we will clearly need more economic and military assistance and training to help those who want democracy.

The President will not allow our military forces to creep—or be drawn gradually—into a combat role in Central America or any other place in the world. And indeed our policy is designed to prevent the need for direct American involvement. This means we will need sustained congressional support to back and give confidence to our friends in the region.

I believe that the tests I have enunciated here today can, if applied carefully, avoid the danger of this gradualist incremental approach which almost always means the use of insufficient force. These tests can help us to avoid being drawn inexorably into an endless morass, where it is not vital to our national interest to fight. . . .

THE USE AND USEFULNESS
OF MILITARY FORCES IN THE
POST-COLD WAR, POST-SOVIET
WORLD

BY LES ASPIN*

. . . I'd like to take just a few minutes to discuss with you a question that I think will be central to our national defense in the new post-Soviet, post–Cold War world. The question is, how are our military forces going to be used in the future? Now, we have, of course, had debates about the use of military force by the United States before. In particular, we had a debate after the bombing of the Marine barracks in Beirut in the middle eighties. Where is this debate going in the new era? I think there are going to be a few new twists, but at the moment we have more questions than answers. I think now is the time to start asking those questions and I think this is the right kind of informed, interested citizens group that should be considering this issue.

The debate on the use of force has been fueled by what many say were ill-considered military ventures. Following those events, a number of people tried to design a set of rules of thumb by which we could judge ahead of time whether the use of military force would be a good idea. Kind of a check-list, if you will.

Senator Gary Hart attempted such a list, as did Secretary of Defense Caspar Weinberger. On November 2, 1984, Secretary Weinberger outlined a six-point check-list to govern the decision on the use of force. Three of those tests concerned when to use force. He

---

* Excerpts from an address by the Chairman of the House Armed Services Committee to the Jewish Institute for National Security Affairs, Washington, D.C., September 21, 1992.

argued that one, force should only be used in the defense of our vital interests; two, only with the support of the American people and Congress; and three, only as a last resort. The other three Weinberger tests dealt with how force ought to be used: first, with the clear intent of winning; second, when military objectives can be clearly defined; and third, only so long as the objectives were worth the risk.

There was a lot of discussion not only about the points, but about whether such a check-list helped or simply raised more questions. One particularly troublesome point was the question of public support. Some said that it was not known whether there would be support beforehand, and besides, the purpose of leadership was to create support. In fact, most wars start out to be popular and may become unpopular if they drag on. Ultimately, there is no guarantee that the American people simply won't change their minds.

Weinberger was not the last word. Similar sentiments about the need for a high threshold for the use of force have been heard very recently. President Bush stated before the Gulf War that, and I quote, "I will not as Commander-in-Chief ever put somebody into a military assessed situation that we do not win . . . there is not going to be any drawn out agony like Vietnam." This debate was not only conducted among civilian officials, defense analysts, columnists and editorial writers alone. There was another level of debate, one that was very important. That debate was in the officer corps of the U.S. military. The men who carried the burden of battle developed their own views of when military force should be used.

They spent more time thinking about it and they gradually developed—and recently honed—the concept. By the beginning of this decade, 1990 I would say, the view of the U.S. military came down to four propositions on when it is appropriate to use force.

NUMBER ONE Force should only be used as a last resort. Diplomatic and economic solutions should be tried first.

NUMBER TWO Military force should only be used when there is a clear-cut military objective. We should not send military forces to achieve vague political goals.

NUMBER THREE Military forces should be used only when we can measure that the military objective has been achieved. In other words, we need to know when we can bring the troops back home.

NUMBER FOUR Probably the most important. Military force should be used only in an overwhelming fashion. We should get it done quickly and with little loss of life, and therefore, with overwhelming force.

What all this reveals is that there is a substantial block of very expert opinion that says this is the way to go. This camp says that if we ignore these prescriptions we are likely to end with another Vietnam or another Beirut. We have learned through bitter experience, they say, and we should not make the same mistakes again. We can call this the "all-or-nothing" school. If you want a name associated with it, it would be Colin Powell . . . he is a believer in this. This school says if you aren't willing to put the pedal to the floor, don't start the engine.

This school would also say that this checklist avoids the problem of maintaining public support. It allows the troops to go in, get the job done and get out quickly. And because it is done with overwhelming force you don't run into the problem of public support. All wars are popular at the beginning and all wars are popular if they don't result in a lot of American lives lost. Gets around the problem very nicely.

And, in fact, these criteria—although only recently fully formulated—have served us extraordinarily well. The two most recent examples of the use of force followed this formula almost exactly—Operation Just Cause and Operation Desert Storm. The formula worked in both cases. And with those successes a lot of people believe that the thorny problem of the use of American military force has been finally solved. Just follow the formula, this four-part formula, and we will avoid Vietnams and Beiruts, and we will only have Operation Just Causes and Operation Desert Storms.

But just when we might think we've got the problem solved, it becomes clear that this brand new world of ours is a world of turmoil and agitation. And that agitation has provoked calls for the use of military force in a whole range of circumstances that don't fit the old I've just described.

Right now the U.S. military is either already involved in or may soon be involved in the following: One, enforcing a no-fly zone in southern Iraq. Two, helping deliver humanitarian aid to Bosnia and/or pressuring Serbia to leave its neighbors alone. Three, delivering humanitarian aid to Somalia in the face of roving gangs that want to steal and sell the aid. And four, providing emergency relief for the victims of hurricanes in Florida, Louisiana and Hawaii. None of these situations fall within the "Colin Powell" categories I've just outlined.

So there we are. Just when we thought we had the problem solved. Just when we thought we had a check-list that would tell us when to use military force and military assets and when not to use them, we enter into a world where there is serious public opinion in favor of using the military in situations when the categories don't apply.

Now some would say, as Yogi Berra has, "it's just deja vu all over again." If the categories don't fit, military force and military assets should not be used. Acting Secretary of State Larry Eagleburger said in late August that he was, "horrified" by what he called the "arm chair strategists and generals" calling for U.S. military involvement in the Yugoslavian conflict.

Eagleburger has said he was not prepared to accept the argument that there was a level of successful involvement somewhere between that which we had in Vietnam and doing nothing. He asserted that when there is no clear purpose and no clear end, the result can be a situation like Vietnam. He claims there is no middle ground. Here are his words: "It's again what has got us into Vietnam. You do a little bit and it doesn't work, what do you do next?" End quote.

But those who disagree with the all-or-nothing school are unwilling to accept the notion that military force can't be used prudently short of all-out war. They go further to suggest this new world we live in is going to demand it. We can call this camp the opposite camp, the limited objectives school. The argument made by this school has two main parts, one dealing with results, the other with process. The name that goes with this school is Mrs. Thatcher.

The limited objectives school wants the kind of results that often require military action or at least the credible threat of military action. Today, the examples are Iraq and Bosnia. This school says we should use military force if necessary to enforce U.N. resolutions against Iraq, particularly those to get rid of Iraq's weapons of mass destruction. Otherwise, they argue, Operation Desert Storm will become a hollow victory and Saddam will continue his nuclear, chemical and biological weapons programs. This school also wants to do something to stop the ethnic cleansing in Bosnia. If we do not, they say, others may follow these horrific practices. And there is no scarcity of candidates.

The debates over Iraq and Bosnia, incidentally, have scrambled the political spectrum in this country pretty well and jumbled the views of both isolationists and internationalists. Many of our citizens are clearly upset that Saddam Hussein is thumbing his nose at U.N. resolutions after Operation Desert Storm; others are upset with what they see going on in Bosnia. Some people wanted to use force in Iraq and Bosnia, some in neither, some in Iraq but not Bosnia, some in Bosnia and not Iraq.

So, we can see the break up of the Eastern Bloc has opened up the possibility of ethnic or nationalist conflicts in many parts of the world. Therefore, a signal should be sent to deter such behavior. Contrary to the all-or-nothing school, the U.S. military is likely to be used very, very rarely. The limited objectives camp says the military will become, in fact, very much like the nuclear weapons during the Cold War—important, expensive but not useful. It will not be a useful tool for achieving the objectives if it's only going to be used in the extreme cases. And therefore, this argument goes, support for it will diminish and it will become basically irrelevant to the problems that the United States faces on a day-to-day basis in the post–Cold War world.

There is a related argument that can be made here. It concerns the willingness of the American people to pay $250 billion or even

$200 billion a year for a military that is not very useful. It may be that to maintain a military for the extreme contingencies, it will be necessary to show that it is useful in lesser contingencies, too.

What with the existence of these conflicting camp means, I think, is that we will face a debate over the use of force every time fate sends a recalcitrant Iraq or a Bosnia our way.

The debate in each case will hinge on two questions—one, something called escalation, and, two, something called compellence.

First escalation. Is escalation inevitable? In other words, is every military action with a limited objective a potential quagmire? The all-or-nothing school would answer yes. Escalation is the central fear of this school. As Larry Eagleburger said, and again I'm quoting, "You do a little bit and it doesn't work. What do you do next?" End quote. They would cite Vietnam as the prime example of escalation gone wrong.

But there has been one very big development since Vietnam—the Soviet Union has dissolved. The superpower rivalry is no more. The stakes do not automatically go up every time the United States decides to use force. In Vietnam, American policy makers kept escalating our involvement because they were afraid of what our allies and adversaries would think—and do—if we withdrew. If we failed to keep our commitment, we would embolden our adversaries and cause our allies to question our commitment to them. During the Cold War you could not just walk away.

That's not to say we don't have to worry about signals and outcomes today. There are still aggressors out there and we don't want them to get any wrong ideas. And U.S. presidents have to worry about winning and losing. The American electorate does not like anything that looks like a lost war.

But on the whole, the escalation argument has been affected by the collapse of the Soviet Union. So, escalation is the first question in the debate. The second question is about something called "compellence." Compellence is the use of military force against an adversary to influence his behavior elsewhere.

The issue of compellence is at the heart of the argument made by the limited objectives camp. What we are really talking about here is striking military targets or assets to influence behavior elsewhere, most often air strikes in one place to convince someone to change their behavior in another place. Airpower is the heart of this limited objectives argument.

Let's look at the record, which has been mixed. Compellence did not work very well in Vietnam. Earlier, the bombing of cities in Britain and Germany during World War II seemed to strengthen rather than weaken resolve. On the other side, the bombing of Libya worked. Quadafi cut back his export of terrorism.

But World War II, Vietnam, even Libya, are old news. The most important question we can ask today is what has happened that bears on use of compellence, as a policy objective of the U.S. military. There are two sets of developments to look at here. One concerns sophisticated technology and the other sophisticated targeting.

As far as technology goes, we are living in a different world than we did even as we bombed the targets in Libya. We have stealthy aircraft and we have stealthy planes and precision guided munitions, some provided by Israel. Let's look at some Air Force figures to see how much has changed. In World War II, if we wanted to have a 90 percent chance of knocking out a medium-sized target, we had to plan to drop 9,000 bombs on it. In Vietnam, the figure was about 175 bombs. In Operation Desert Storm, we are talking about numbers in the single digits.

What this means is that we have technology which has improved our ability to make air strikes with little, if any, loss of U.S. lives and with a minimum of collateral damage and loss of civilian lives on the other side. This is a big, big change.

But we've also become more sophisticated about targeting at a time when our adversaries have become more dependent on the kinds of things we can target. We can target communications nodes, power grids, and command and control assets. These things are the kinds of targets that national leadership and military commands hold dear.

So what do all these developments mean for the use of military force in the future?

I think we are still going to have to decide the question of the use of force case by case. Nothing has happened that would lead us to say on the one hand that we're never going to use force short of the all-out war, as in the case of Desert Storm, or on the other hand, that we're going to be the cop on the beat for the whole world.

I do think one thing has happened to weaken the all-or-nothing or Colin Powell school and one thing has happened to strengthen the limited objectives or Maggie Thatcher school. The all-or-nothing school was weakened when the collapse of the Soviet Union removed some—not all—but some of the pressure for escalation that accompanied any limited military venture.

The limited objectives school has been strengthened as technological developments have improved our ability to achieve compellence.

I think these things are going to tilt future debates somewhat in the direction of the limited objectives school or Mrs. Thatcher's point of view, but it has by no means been decided. Stay tuned for the case-by-case debates.

I also think these developments send a signal here at home. It's a signal that we'd better be careful how we structure our military in the future. We have to make sure that our forces are flexible enough to do a number of simultaneous, smaller contingencies. We want these case-by-case debates settled on the merits, not predetermined because our forces lack flexibility. . . .

APPENDIX E

U.S. FORCES: CHALLENGES AHEAD

BY COLIN L. POWELL*

... The new national military strategy is an unclassified document. Anyone can read it. It is short, to the point and unambiguous. The central idea in the strategy is the change from a focus on global war-fighting to a focus on regional contingencies. No communist hordes threaten western Europe today and, by extension, the rest of the free world. So our new strategy emphasizes being able to deal with individual crises without their escalating to global or thermonuclear war.

Two and a half years ago, as we developed the new strategy, we saw the possibility of a major regional conflict in the Persian Gulf—and it turned out we were right—and a major regional conflict in the Pacific, perhaps on the Korean peninsula, where the Cold War lingers on. We knew then, and we know now, that prudent planning requires that we be able to deal simultaneously with two major crises of this type, however unlikely that might be. In our judgment, the best way to make sure their coincidence remained unlikely was to be ready to react to both, so that if we were involved in one, no one would tempt us into the other.

Moreover we can see more clearly today that danger has not disappeared from the world. All along the southeastern and southern borders of the old Soviet empire, from Moldova to Tajikistan, smoldering disputes and ethnic hatreds disrupt our post–Cold War

* Reprinted, by permission, from Foreign Affairs, Vol. 71, No. 5 (Winter 1992/93). Copyright (1992) by the Council on Foreign Relations, Inc.

reverie. In the Balkans such hatreds and centuries-old antagonisms have burst forth into a heart-wrenching civil war. The scenes from Sarajevo defy our idea of justice and human rights and give new meaning to the word "senseless." In Somalia, relief operations are underway amid the chaos and anarchy of another civil war that wracks our idea of justice, human rights and the rule of law. Ruthless warlords make money from donated food and medical supplies. Relief workers are threatened if they do not comply with a local dictator's whims.

We cannot tell where or when the next crisis will appear that will demand the use of our troops. But we can say that in the last three years, our troops have acted in the Philippines (twice), Panama (three times), El Salvador, Liberia, Iraq (three times), Somalia (twice), Bangladesh, Zaire, Cuba, the former Soviet Union, Angola and Yugoslavia. We could also mention our troops' involvement in U.N. actions from western Sahara, Cambodia and Bosnia-Herzegovina, and in disaster relief actions in our own territory from southern Florida to Guam. Truly it has been a busy season for America's men and women in uniform.

These crises have spanned the range of extremes. They have included humanitarian actions in response to natural disasters and emergency evacuation of American citizens from war zones. They have included the use of very limited force and the use of massive force. For example, a pair of Phantom fighter jets was all that was needed in the Philippines in December 1989; while 540,000 troops and a large part of our arsenal were needed in the Persian Gulf in 1990–91. To deal with such a wide range of possibilities, our armed forces must be capable of accomplishing a wide range of missions.

FUTURE MISSIONS AND CLEAR OBJECTIVES

What sorts of missions can we envision? I believe peacekeeping and humanitarian operations are a given. Likewise our forward presence is a given—to signal our commitment to our allies and to give second thoughts to any disturber of peace. It is in the category of the use of "violent" force that views begin to differ.

Occasionally these differences in view have been categorized quite starkly as the "limited war" school and the "all-out war" school. For the man or woman in combat, however, such academic niceties are moot. I am reminded of the famous Bill Mauldin cartoon that shows two GIs—Willie and Joe—flat on the ground while machine-gun tracers lick overhead and exploding artillery rounds light up the night sky. Joe says to Willie, "I can't git no lower, Willie. Me buttons is in th' way." But while such distinctions as limited and all-out war mean little to a soldier who is clutching the ground while bullets whiz by his ears, they do serve to illuminate our debate.

All wars are limited. As Carl von Clausewitz was careful to point out, there has never been a state of absolute war. Such a state would mean total annihilation. The Athenians at Melos, Attila the Hun, Tamerlane, the Romans salting the fields of the Carthaginians may have come close, but even their incredible ruthlessness gave way to pragmatism before a state of absolute war was achieved.

Wars are limited by three means: by the territory on which they are fought (as in Korea or Vietnam); by the means used to fight them (no nuclear weapons in Korea; no massive mobilization for Vietnam); or by the objectives for which they are fought—the most significant limitation in political terms and therefore the limitation that is most often discussed and debated.

Objectives for which we use "violent" force can range from hurting an enemy enough so that he or she ceases to do the thing that is endangering our interests (air strikes against Libya in 1986 to prevent further Libyan-sponsored terrorism), to unseating the enemy's government and altering fundamentally his or her way of life (World War II).

The Gulf War was a limited-objective war. If it had not been, we would be ruling Baghdad today—at unpardonable expense in terms of money, lives lost and ruined regional relationships. The

Gulf War was also a limited-means war—we did not use every means at our disposal to eject the Iraqi Army from Kuwait. But we did use overwhelming force quickly and decisively. This, I believe, is why some have characterized that war as an "all-out" war. It was strictly speaking no such thing.

To help with the complex issue of the use of "violent" force, some have turned to a set of principles or a when-to-go-to-war doctrine. "Follow these directions and you can't go wrong." There is, however, no fixed set of rules for the use of military force. To set one up is dangerous. First, it destroys the ambiguity we might want to exist in our enemy's mind regarding our intentions. Unless part of our strategy is to destroy that ambiguity, it is usually helpful to keep it intact.

Second, having a fixed set of rules for how you will go to war is like saying you are always going to use the elevator in the event of fire in you apartment building. Surely enough, when the fire comes the elevator will be engulfed in flames or, worse, it will look good when you get in it only to fill with smoke and flames and crash a few minutes later. But do you stay in your apartment and burn to death because your plan calls for using the elevator to escape and the elevator is untenable? No, you run to the stairs, an outside fire escape or a window. In short, your plans to escape should be governed by the circumstances of the fire when it starts.

When a "fire" starts that might require committing armed forces, we need to evaluate the circumstances. Relevant questions include: Is the political objective we seek to achieve important, clearly defined and understood? Have all other nonviolent policy means failed? Will military force achieve the objective? At what cost? Have the gains and risks been analyzed? How might the situation that we seek to alter, once it is altered by force, develop further and what might be the consequences?

As an example of this logical process, we can examine the assertions of those who have asked why President Bush did not order our forces on to Baghdad after we had driven the Iraqi army out of Kuwait. We must assume that the political objective of such an order would have been capturing Saddam Hussein. Even if Hussein had waited for us to enter Baghdad, and even if we had been able to capture him, what purpose would it have served? And would serving that purpose have been worth the many more casualties that would have occurred? Would it have been worth the inevitable follow-up: major occupation forces in Iraq for years to come and a very expensive and complex American procunsulship in Baghdad? Fortunately for America, reasonable people at the time thought not. They still do.

When the political objective is important, clearly defined and understood, when the risks are acceptable, and when the use of force can be effectively combined with diplomatic and economic policies, then clear and unambiguous objectives must be given to the armed forces. These objectives must be firmly linked with the political objectives. We must not, for example, send military forces into a crisis with an unclear mission they cannot accomplish—such as we did when we sent the U.S. Marines into Lebanon in 1983. We inserted those proud warriors into the middle of a five-faction civil war complete with terrorists, hostage-takers and a dozen spies in every camp, and said, "Gentlemen, be a buffer." The results were 241 dead Marines and Navy personnel and a U.S. withdrawal from the troubled area.

When force is used deftly—in smooth coordination with diplomatic and economic policy—bullets may never have to fly. Pulling triggers should always be toward the end of the plan, and when those triggers are pulled all of the sound analysis I have just described should back them up.

Over the past three years the U.S. armed forces have been used repeatedly to defend our interests and to achieve our political objectives. In Panama a dictator was removed from power. In the Philippines the use of limited force helped save a democracy. In Somalia a daring night raid rescued our embassy. In Liberia we rescued stranded international citizens and protected our embassy. In the Persian Gulf a nation was liberated. Moreover we have used our forces for humanitarian relief operations in Iraq, Somalia, Bangladesh, Russia and Bosnia.

All of these operations had one thing in common: they were successful. There have been no Bay of Pigs, failed desert raids, Beirut bombings or Vietnams. Today American troops around the world are protecting the peace in Europe, the Persian Gulf, Korea, Cambodia, the Sinai and western Sahara. They have brought relief to Americans at home here in Florida, Hawaii and Guam. Ironically enough, the American people are getting a solid return on their defense investment even as from all corners of the nation come shouts for imprudent reductions that would gut their armed forces.

The reason for our success is that in every instance we have carefully matched the use of military force to our political objectives. We owe it to the men and women who go in harm's way to make sure that this is always the case and that their lives are not squandered for unclear purposes.

Military men and women recognize more than most people that not every situation will be crystal clear. We can and do operate in murky, unpredictable circumstances. But we also recognize that military force is not always the right answer. If force is used imprecisely or out of frustration rather than clear analysis, the situation can be made worse.

Decisive means and results are always to be preferred, even if they are not always possible. We should always be skeptical when so-called experts suggest that all a particular crisis calls for is a little surgical bombing or a limited attack. When the "surgery" is over and the desired result is not obtained, a new set of experts then comes forward with talk of just a little escalation—more bombs, more men and women, more force. History has not been kind to this approach to war-making. In fact this approach has been tragic—both for the men and women who are called upon to implement it and for the nation. This is not to argue that the use of force is restricted to only those occasions where the victory of American arms will be resounding, swift and overwhelming. It is simply to argue that the use of force should be restricted to occasions where it can do some good and where the good will outweigh the loss of lives and other costs that will surely ensue. Wars kill people. That is what makes them different from all other forms of human enterprise.

When President Lincoln gave his second inaugural address he compared the Civil War to the scourge of God, visited upon the nation to compensate for what the nation had visited upon its slaves. Lincoln perceived war correctly. It is the scourge of God. We should be very careful how we use it. When we do use it, we should not be equivocal: we should win and win decisively. If our objective is something short of winning—as in our air strikes into Libya in 1986—we should see our objective clearly, then achieve it swiftly and efficiently. . . .

APPENDIX F

REMARKS AT THE UNITED STATES
MILITARY ACADEMY

BY PRESIDENT GEORGE BUSH*

. . . Any President has several functions. He speaks for and to the Nation. He must faithfully execute the law. And he must lead. But no function, none of the President's hats, in my view, is more important than his role as Commander in Chief. For it is as Commander in Chief that the President confronts and makes decisions that one way or another affects the lives of everyone in this country as well as many others around the world.

I have had many occasions to don this most important of hats. Over the past 4 years, the men and women who proudly and bravely wear the uniforms of the U.S. armed services have been called upon to go in harm's way and have discharged their duty with honor and professionalism.

I wish I could say that such demands were a thing of the past, that with the end of the cold war the calls upon the United States would diminish. I cannot. Yes, the end of the cold war, we would all concede, is a blessing. It is a time of great promise. Democratic governments have never been so numerous. What happened 2 or 3 days ago in Moscow would not have been possible in the cold war days. Thanks to historic treaties such as that START II pact just reached with Russia, the likelihood of nuclear holocaust is vastly diminished.

But this does not mean that there is no specter of war, no threats to be reckoned with. And already, we see disturbing signs of what

* *Delivered at the U.S. Military Academy, West Point, January 5, 1993.*

this new world could become if we are passive and aloof. We would risk the emergence of a world characterized by violence, characterized by chaos, one in which dictators and tyrants threaten their neighbors, build arsenals brimming with weapons of mass destruction, and ignore the welfare of their own men, women, and children. And we could see a horrible increase in international terrorism, with American citizens more at risk than ever before.

We cannot and we need not allow this to happen. Our objective must be to exploit the unparalleled opportunity presented by the cold war's end to work toward transforming this new world into a new world order, one of governments that are democratic, tolerant and economically free at home and committed abroad to settling inevitable differences peacefully, without the threat or use of force.

Unfortunately, not everyone subscribes to these principles. We continue to see leaders bent on denying fundamental human rights and seizing territory regardless of the human cost. No, an international society, one more attuned to the enduring principles that have made this country a beacon of hope for so many for so long, will not just emerge on its own. It's got to be built.

Two hundred years ago, another departing President warned of the dangers of what he described as "entangling alliances." His was the right course for a new nation at that point in history. But what was "entangling" in Washington's day is now essential. This is why, at Texas A&M a few weeks ago, I spoke of the folly of isolationism and of the importance, morally, economically, and strategically, of the United States remaining involved in world affairs. We must engage ourselves if a new world order, one more compatible with our values and congenial to our interest, is to emerge. But even more, we must lead.

Leadership, well, it takes many forms. It can be political or diplomatic. It can be economic or military. It can be moral or spiritual leadership. Leadership can take any one of these forms, or it can be a combination of them.

Leadership should not be confused with either unilateralism or universalism. We need not respond by ourselves to each and every outrage of violence. The fact that America can act does not mean that it must. A nation's sense of idealism need not be at odds with its interests, nor does principle displace prudence.

No, the United States should not seek to be the world's policeman. There is no support abroad or at home for us to play this role, nor should there be. We would exhaust ourselves, in the process wasting precious resources needed to address those problems at home and abroad that we cannot afford to ignore.

But in the wake of the cold war, in a world where we are the only remaining superpower, it is the role of the United States to marshal its moral and material resources to promote a democratic peace. It is our responsibility, it is our opportunity to lead. There is no one else.

Leadership cannot be simply asserted or demanded. It must be demonstrated. Leadership requires formulating worthy goals, persuading others of their virtue, and contributing one's share of the common effort and then some. Leadership takes time. It takes patience. It takes work.

Some of this work must take place here at home. Congress does have a constitutional role to play. Leadership therefore also involves working with the Congress and the American people to provide the essential domestic underpinning if U.S. military commitments are to be sustainable.

This is what our administration, the Bush administration, has tried to do. When Saddam Hussein invaded Kuwait, it was the United States that galvanized the U.N. Security Council to act and then mobilized the successful coalition on the battlefield. The pattern not exactly the same but similar in Somalia: First the United States underscored the importance of alleviating the growing tragedy, and then we organized humanitarian efforts designed to bring hope, food, and peace.

At times, real leadership requires a willingness to use military force. And force can be a useful backdrop to diplomacy, a complement to it, or, if need be, a temporary alternative.

As Commander in Chief, I have made the difficult choice to use military force. I determined we could not allow Saddam's forces to ravage Kuwait and hold this critical region at gunpoint. I thought then, and I think now, that using military force to implement the resolutions of the U.N. Security Council was in the interest of the United States and the world community. The need to use force arose as well in the wake of the Gulf war, when we came to the aid of the peoples of both northern and southern Iraq. And more recently, as I'm sure you know, I determined that only the use of force could stem this human tragedy of Somalia.

The United States should not stand by with so many lives at stake and when a limited deployment of U.S. forces, buttressed by the forces of other countries and acting under the full authority of the United Nations, could make an immediate and dramatic difference, and do so without excessive levels of risk and cost. Operations Provide Comfort and Southern Watch in Iraq and then Operation Restore Hope in Somalia all bear witness to the wisdom of selected use of force for selective purposes.

Sometimes the decision not to use force, to stay our hand, I can tell you, it's just as difficult as the decision to send our soldiers into battle. The former Yugoslavia, well, it's been such a situation. There are, we all know, important humanitarian and strategic interests at stake there. But up to now it's not been clear that the application of limited amounts of force by the United States and its traditional friends and allies would have had the desired effect given the nature and complexity of that situation.

Our assessment of the situation in the former Yugoslavia could well change if and as the situation changes. The stakes could grow; the conflict could threaten to spread. Indeed, we are constantly reassessing our options and are actively consulting with others about steps that might be taken to contain the fighting, protect the humanitarian effort, and deny Serbia the fruits of aggression.

Military force is never a tool to be used lightly or universally. In some circumstances it may be essential, in others counter-productive. I know that many people would like to find some formula, some easy formula to apply, to tell us with precision when and where to intervene with force. Anyone looking for scientific certitude is in for a disappointment. In the complex new world we are entering, there can be no single or simple set of fixed rules for using force. Inevitably, the question of military intervention requires judgment. Each and every case is unique. To adopt rigid criteria would guarantee mistakes involving American interests and American lives. And it would give would-be trouble-makers a blueprint for determining their own actions. It could signal U.S. friends and allies that our support was not to be counted on.

Similarly, we cannot always decide in advance which interests will require our using military force to protect them. The relative importance of an interest is not a guide: Military force may not be the best way of safeguarding something vital, while using force might be the best way to protect an interest that qualifies as important but less than vital.

But to warn against a futile quest for a set of hard-and-fast rules to govern the use of military force is not to say there cannot be some principles to inform our decisions. Such guidelines can prove useful in sizing and, indeed, shaping our forces and in helping us to think our way through this key question.

Using military force makes sense as a policy where the stakes warrant, where and when force can be effective, where no other policies are likely to prove effective, where its application can be limited in scope and time, and where the potential benefits justify the potential costs and sacrifice.

Once we are satisfied that force makes sense, we must act with the maximum possible support. The United States can and should lead, but we will want to act in concert, where possible involving the United Nations or other multinational grouping. The United States can and should contribute to the common undertaking in a manner commensurate with our wealth, with our strength. But others should also contribute militarily, be it by providing combat or support forces, access to facilities or bases, or overflight rights. And similarly, others should contribute economically. It is unreasonable to expect the United States to bear the full financial burden of intervention when other nations have a stake in the outcome.

A desire for international support must not become a prerequisite for acting, though. Sometimes a great power has to act alone. I made a tough decision—I might say, on advice of our outstanding military leaders who are so well known to everybody here—to use military force in Panama when American lives and the security of the Canal appeared to be threatened by outlaws who stole power in the face of free elections. And similarly, we moved swiftly to safeguard democracy in the Philippines.

But in every case involving the use of force, it will be essential to have a clear and achievable mission, a realistic plan for accomplishing the mission, and criteria no less realistic for withdrawing U.S. forces once the mission is complete. Only if we keep these principles in mind will the potential sacrifice be one that can be explained and justified. We must never forget that using force is not some political abstraction but a real commitment of our fathers and mothers and sons and daughters, brothers and sisters, friends and neighbors. You've got to look at it in human terms.

In order even to have the choice, we must have available adequate military forces tailored for a wide range of contingencies, including peacekeeping. Indeed, leading the effort toward a new world order will require a modern, capable military, in some areas necessitating more rather than less defense spending. As President, I have said that my ability to deploy force on behalf of U.S. interests abroad was made possible because past Presidents, and I would single out in particular my predecessor, Ronald Reagan, and past Secretaries of Defense sustained a strong military. Consistent with this sacred trust, I am proud to pass on the my successor, President-elect Clinton, a military second to none. We have the very best.

Yet, it is essential to recognize that as important as such factors are, any military is more than simply the sum of its weapons or the state of its technology. What makes any armed force truly effective is the quality of its leadership, the quality of its training, the quality of its people. . . .

CONFRONTING THE CHALLENGES OF A BROADER WORLD

BY PRESIDENT BILL CLINTON *

As we work to keep the world's most destructive weapons out of conflict, we must also strengthen the international community's ability to address those conflicts themselves. For as we all now know so painfully, the end of the Cold War did not bring us to the millennium of peace. Indeed, it simply removed the lid from many cauldrons of ethnic, religious, and territorial animosity.

The philosopher Isaiah Berlin has said that a wounded nationalism is like a bent twig forced down so severely that when released it lashes back with fury. The world today is thick with both bent and recoiling twigs of wounded communal identities.

This scourge of bitter conflict has placed high demands on United Nations peace-keeping forces. Frequently the blue helmets have worked wonders. In Namibia, El Salvador, the Golan Heights, and elsewhere, UN peace-keepers have helped to stop the fighting, restore civil authority, and enable free elections.

In Bosnia, UN peace-keepers, against the danger and frustration of that continuing tragedy, have maintained a valiant humanitarian effort. And if the parties of that conflict take the hard steps needed to make a real peace, the international community, including the United States, must be ready to help in its effective implementation.

In Somalia, the United States and the United Nations have worked together to achieve a stunning humanitarian rescue, saving literally hundreds of thousands of lives and restoring the con-

* *Address to the U.N. General Assembly, New York, September 27, 1993.*

ditions of security for almost the entire country. UN peace-keepers from over two dozen nations remain in Somalia today. And some, including brave Americans, have lost their lives to ensure that we complete our mission and to ensure that anarchy and starvation do not return just as quickly as they were abolished.

Many still criticize UN peace-keeping, but those who do should talk to the people of Cambodia, where the UN's operations have helped to turn the killing fields into fertile soil through reconciliation. Last May's elections in Cambodia marked a proud accomplishment for that war-weary nation and for the United Nations. And I am pleased to announce that the United States has recognized Cambodia's new government.

UN peace-keeping holds the promise to resolve many of this era's conflicts. The reason we have supported such missions is not, as some critics in the United States have charged, to subcontract American foreign policy but to strengthen our security, to protect our interests, and to share among nations the costs and effort of pursuing peace. Peace-keeping cannot be a substitute for our own national defense efforts, but it can strongly supplement them.

Today, there is wide recognition that the UN peace-keeping ability has not kept pace with the rising responsibilities and challenges. Just 6 years ago, about 10,000 UN peace-keepers were stationed around the world. Today, the UN has some 80,000 deployed in 17 operations on 4 continents. Yet until recently, if a peace-keeping commander called in from across the globe when it was nighttime here in New York, there was no one in the peace-keeping office even to answer the call. When lives are on the line, you cannot let the reach of the UN exceed its grasp.

As the Secretary General and others have argued, if UN peace-keeping is to be a sound security investment for our nation and for other UN members, it must adapt to new times. Together we must prepare UN peace-keeping for the 21st century. We need to begin by bringing the rigors of military and political analysis to every UN peace mission.

In recent weeks in the Security Council, our nation has begun asking harder questions about proposals for new peace-keeping missions: Is there a real threat to international peace? Does the proposed mission have clear objectives? Can an end point be identified for those who will be asked to participate? How much will the mission cost? From now on, the United Nations should address these and other hard questions for every proposed mission before we vote and before the mission begins.

The United Nations simply cannot become engaged in every one of the world's conflicts. If the American people are to say yes to UN peace-keeping, the United Nations must know when to say no. The United Nations must also have the technical means to run a modern, world-class peace-keeping operation. We support the creation of a genuine UN peace-keeping headquarters with a planning staff, with access to timely intelligence, with a logistics unit that can be deployed on a moment's notice, and with a modern operations center with global communications.

And the UN's operations must not only be adequately funded but also fairly funded. Within the next few weeks, the United States will be current in our peace-keeping bills. I have worked hard with the Congress to get this done. I believe the United States should lead the way in being timely in its payments, and I will work to continue to see that we pay our bills in full. But I am also committed to work with the United Nations to reduce our nation's assessment for these missions.

The assessment system has not been changed since 1973. And everyone in our country knows that our percentage of the world's economic pie is not as great as it was then. Therefore, I believe our rates should be reduced to reflect the rise of other nations that can now bear more of the financial burden. That will make it easier for me as President to make sure we pay in a timely and full fashion.

Changes in the UN's peace-keeping operations must be part of an even broader program of United Nations reform. I say that, again, not to criticize the United Nations but to help to improve it. As our ambassador, Madeleine Albright, has suggested, the United States has always played a twin role to the UN—first friend and first critic. . . .

APPENDIX H

THE CLINTON ADMINISTRATION'S POLICY ON REFORMING MULTILATERAL PEACE OPERATIONS*

INTRODUCTION
THE ROLE OF PEACE OPERATIONS IN U.S. FOREIGN POLICY [1]

Serious threats to the security of the United States still exist in the post–Cold War era. New threats will emerge. The United States remains committed to meeting such threats.

When our interests dictate, the U.S. must be willing and able to fight and win wars, unilaterally whenever necessary. To do so, we must create the required capabilities and maintain them ready to use. UN peace operations cannot substitute for this requirement.

Circumstances will arise, however, when multilateral action best serves U.S. interests in preserving or restoring peace. In such cases, the UN can be an important instrument for collective action. UN peace operations can also provide a "force multiplier" in our efforts to promote peace and stability.

During the Cold War, the United Nations could resort to multilateral peace operations only in the few cases when the interests of the Soviet Union and the West did not conflict. In the new strategic environment such operations can serve more often as a cost-effective tool to advance American as well as collective interests in maintaining peace in key regions and create global burden-sharing for peace.

---

* *U.S. Department of State, Washington, D.C., May 1994.*

Territorial disputes, armed ethnic conflicts, civil wars (many of which could spill across international borders) and the collapse of governmental authority in some states are among the current threats to peace. While many of these conflicts may not directly threaten American interests, their cumulative effect is significant. The UN has sought to play a constructive role in such situations by mediating disputes and obtaining agreement to cease-fires and political settlements. Where such agreements have been reached, the interposition of neutral forces under UN auspices has, in many cases, helped facilitate lasting peace.

UN peace operations have served important U.S. national interests. In Cambodia, UN efforts led to an election protected by peacekeepers, the return of hundreds of thousands of refugees and the end of a destabilizing regional conflict. In *El Salvador*, the UN sponsored elections and is helping to end a long and bitter civil war. The UN's supervision of *Namibia's* transition to independence removed a potential source of conflict in strategic southern Africa and promoted democracy. The UN in Cyprus has prevented the outbreak of war between two NATO allies. Peacekeeping on the *Golan Heights* has helped preserve peace between Israel and Syria. In *Former Yugoslavia,* the UN has provided badly-needed humanitarian assistance and helped prevent the conflict from spreading to other parts of the region. UN-imposed sanctions against Iraq, coupled with the peacekeeping operation on the *Kuwait* border, are constraining Iraq's ability to threaten its neighbors.

NEED FOR REFORM

While serving U.S. interests, UN peace operations continue to require improvement and reform. Currently, each operation is created and managed separately, and economies of scale are lost. Likewise, further organizational changes at UN Headquarters would improve efficiency and effectiveness. A fully independent office of Inspector General should be established immediately. The U.S. assessment rate should be reduced to 25 per cent.

Since it is in our interest at times to support UN peace operations, it is also in our interest to seek to strengthen UN peace-keeping capabilities and to make operations less expensive and peacekeeping management more accountable. Similarly, it is in our interest to identify clearly and quickly those peace operations we will support and those we will not. Our policy establishes clear guidelines for making such decisions.

ROLE IN U.S. FOREIGN POLICY

UN and other multilateral peace operations will at times offer the best way to prevent, contain or resolve conflicts that could other-wise be more costly and deadly. In such cases, the U.S. benefits from having to bear only a share of the burden. We also benefit by being able to invoke the voice of the community of nations on be-half of a cause we support. Thus, establishment of a capability to conduct multilateral peace operations is part of our National Se-curity Strategy and National Military Strategy.

While the President never relinquishes command of U.S. forces, the participation of U.S. military personnel in UN opera-tions can, in particular circumstances, serve U.S. interests. First, U.S. military participation may, at times, be necessary to per-suade others to participate in operations that serve U.S. interests. Second, U.S. participation may be one way to exercise U.S. influence over an important UN mission, without unilaterally bearing the burden. Third, the U.S. may be called upon and choose to provide unique capabilities to important operations that other countries cannot.

In improving our capabilities for peace operations, we will not discard or weaken other tools for achieving U.S. objectives. If U.S. participation in a peace operation were to interfere with our basic military strategy, winning two major regional conflicts nearly si-multaneously (as established in the Bottom Up Review), we would place our national interest uppermost. The U.S. will maintain the capability to act unilaterally or in coalitions when our most significant interests and those of our friends and allies are at stake. Multilateral peace operations must, therefore, be placed in proper perspective among the instruments of U.S. foreign policy.

The U.S. does not support a standing UN army, nor will we earmark specific U.S. military units for participation in UN operations. We will provide information about U.S. capabilities for data bases and planning purposes.

It is not U.S. policy to seek to expand either the number of UN peace operations or U.S. involvement in such operations. Instead, this policy, which builds upon work begun by previous administrations and is informed by the concerns of the Congress and our experience in recent peace operations, aims to ensure that our use of peacekeeping is *selective* and *more effective*. Congress must also be actively involved in the continuing implementation of U.S. policy on peacekeeping.

I. SUPPORTING THE RIGHT PEACE OPERATIONS

i. VOTING FOR PEACE OPERATIONS

The U.S. will support well-defined peace operations, generally, as a tool to provide finite windows of opportunity to allow combatants to resolve their differences and failed societies to begin to reconstitute themselves. Peace operations should not be open-ended commitments but instead linked to concrete political solutions; otherwise, they normally should not be undertaken. To the greatest extent possible, each UN peace operation should have a specified timeframe tied to intermediate or final objectives, an integrated political/military strategy well-coordinated with humanitarian assistance efforts, specified troop levels, and a firm budget estimate. The U.S. will continue to urge the UN Secretariat and Security Council members to engage in rigorous, standard evaluations of all proposed new peace operations.

The Administration will consider the factors below when deciding whether to vote for a proposed new UN peace operation (Chapter VI or Chapter VII) or to support a regionally-sponsored peace operation:

— UN involvement advances U.S. interests, and there is an international community of interest for dealing with the problem on a multilateral basis.

— There is a threat to or breach of international peace and security, often of a regional character, defined as one or a combination of the following:

— International aggression, or;

— Urgent humanitarian disaster coupled with violence;

— Sudden interruption of established democracy or gross violation of human rights coupled with violence, or threat of violence.

— There are clear objectives and an understanding of where the mission fits on the spectrum between traditional peacekeeping and peace enforcement.

— For traditional (Chapter VI) peacekeeping operations, a ceasefire should be in place and the consent of the parties obtained before the force is deployed.

— For peace enforcement (Chapter VII) operations, the threat to international peace and security is considered significant.

— The means to accomplish the mission are available, in cluding the forces, financing and a mandate appropriate to the mission.

— The political, economic and humanitarian consequences of inaction by the international community have been weighed and are considered unacceptable.

— The operation's anticipated duration is tied to clear objectives and realistic criteria for ending the operation.

These factors are an aid in decision-making; they do not by themselves constitute a prescriptive device. Decisions have been and will be based on the cumulative weight of the factors, with no single factor necessarily being an absolute determinant.

In addition, using the factors above, the U.S. will continue to scrutinize closely all existing peace operations when they come up for regular renewal by the Security Council to assess the value of continuing them. In appropriate cases, the U.S. will seek voluntary contributions by beneficiary nations or enhanced host nation support to reduce or cover, at least partially, the costs of certain UN operations. The U.S. will also consider voting against renewal of certain long-standing peace operations that are failing to meet established objectives in order to free military and financial resources for more pressing UN missions.

ii. PARTICIPATING IN UN AND OTHER PEACE OPERATIONS

The Administration will continue to apply even stricter standards when it assesses whether to recommend to the President that U.S. personnel participate in a given peace operation. In addition to the factors listed above, we will consider the following factors:

— Participation advances U.S. interests and both the unique and general risks to American personnel have been weighed and are considered acceptable.

— Personnel, funds and other resources are available;

— U.S. participation is necessary for operation's success;

— The role of U.S. forces is tied to clear objectives and an endpoint for U.S. participation can be identified;

— Domestic and Congressional support exists or can be marshalled;

— Command and control arrangements are acceptable.

Additional, even more rigorous factors will be applied when there is the possibility of significant U.S. participation in Chapter VII operations that are likely to involve combat:

— There exists a determination to commit sufficient forces to achieve clearly defined objectives;

— There exists a plan to achieve those objectives decisively;

— There exists a commitment to reassess and adjust, as necessary, the size, composition, and disposition of our forces to achieve our objectives.

Any recommendation to the President will be based on the cumulative weight of the above factors, with no single factor necessarily being an absolute determinant.

II. THE ROLE OF REGIONAL ORGANIZATIONS

In some cases, the appropriate way to perform peace operations will be to involve regional organizations. The U.S. will continue to emphasize the UN as the primary international body with the authority to conduct peacekeeping operations. At the same time, the U.S. will support efforts to improve regional organizations' peacekeeping capabilities.

When regional organizations or groupings seek to conduct peacekeeping with UNSC endorsement, U.S. support will be conditioned on adherence to the principles of the UN Charter and meeting established UNSC criteria, including neutrality, consent of the conflicting parties, formal UNSC oversight and finite, renewal mandates.

With respect to the question of peacekeeping in the territory of the former Soviet Union, requests for "traditional" UN blue-helmeted operations will be considered on the same basis as other requests, using the factors previously outlined (e.g., a threat to international peace and security, clear objectives, etc.). U.S. support for these operations will, as with other such requests, be conditioned on adherence to the principles of the UN Charter and established UNSC criteria.

III. REDUCING COSTS

Although peacekeeping can be a good investment for the U.S., it would be better and more sustainable if it cost less. The Administration is committed to reducing the U.S. share of peacekeeping costs to 25% by January 1, 1996, down from the current rate of 31.7%. We will also inform the UN of Congress's likely refusal to fund U.S. peace-keeping assessments at a rate higher than 25% after Fiscal Year 1995.

The Administration remains concerned that the UN has not rectified management inefficiencies that result in excessive costs and, on occasion, fraud and abuse. As a matter of priority, the U.S. will continue to press for dramatic administrative and management improvements in the UN system. In particular, the U.S. is working hard to ensure that new and on-going peace operations are cost-effective and properly managed. Towards this end, the U.S. is pursuing a number of finance and budget management reforms, including:

— immediate establishment of a permanent, fully independent office of Inspector General with oversight responsibility that includes peacekeeping;

— unified budget for all peace operations, with a contingency fund, financed by a single annual peacekeeping assessment;

— standing cadre of professional budget experts from member states, particularly top contributing countries, to assist the UN in developing credible budgets and financial plans;

— enlargement of the revolving peacekeeping reserve fund to $500 million, using voluntary contributions;

— Required status of forces/mission agreements that provide preferential host nation support to peacekeeping operations;

— prohibit UN "borrowing" from peacekeeping funds to finance cash shortfalls in regular UN administrative operations;

— revise the special peacekeeping scale of assessments to base it on a 3-year average of national income and rationalize Group C so that higher income countries pay their regular budget rate.

Moreover, the U.S. will use its voice and vote in the Fifth Committee of the General Assembly of the United Nations to contain costs of UN peace operations once they are underway.

IV. STRENGTHENING THE UN

If peace operations are to be effective and efficient when the U.S. believes they are necessary, the UN must improve the way peace operations are managed. Our goal is not to create a global high command but to enable the UN to manage its existing load more effectively. At present each UN operation is created and managed separately by a still somewhat understaffed UN Department of Peacekeeping Operations (DPKO). As a result, support to the field may suffer, economies of scale are lost, and work is duplicated. Moreover, the UN's command and control capabilities, particularly in complex operations, need substantial improvement. Structural changes at UN Headquarters, some of which are already underway, would make a positive difference.

A. The U.S. proposals include the reconfiguration and expansion of the staff for the Department of Peacekeeping Operations to create:

PLANS DIVISION to conduct adequate advance planning and preparation for new and on-going operations;

INFORMATION AND RESEARCH DIVISION linked to field operations to obtain and provide current information, manage a 24 hour watch center, and monitor open source material and non-sensitive information submitted by governments;

OPERATIONS DIVISION with a modern command, control and communications (C3) architecture based on commercial systems;

LOGISTICS DIVISION to manage both competitive commercial contracts (which should be re-bid regularly on the basis of price and performance) and a cost-effective logistics computer network to link the UN DPKO with logistics offices in participating member nations. This system would enable the UN to request price and availability data and to order material from participating states;

SMALL PUBLIC AFFAIRS CELL dedicated to supporting on-going peace operations and disseminating information within host countries in order to reduce the risks to UN personnel and increase the potential for mission success;

SMALL CIVILIAN POLICE CELL to manage police missions, plan for the establishment of police and judicial institutions, and develop standard procedures, doctrine and training.

B. To eliminate lengthy, potentially disastrous delays after a mission has been authorized, the UN should establish:

— a *rapidly deployable headquarters team,* a *composite initial logistics support unit,* and open, *pre-negotiated commercial contracts* for logistics support in new missions;

— a *data base* of specific, potentially available forces or capabilities that nations could provide for the full range of peacekeeping and humanitarian operations;

— *trained civilian reserve corps* to serve as a ready, external talent pool to assist in the administration, management, and execution of UN peace operations;

— *modest airlift capability* available through pre-negotiated contracts with commercial firms or member states to support urgent deployments.

C. Finally, the UN should establish a *professional Peace Operations Training Program* for commanders and other military and civilian personnel.

D. Consistent with the specific proposals outlined above, the U.S. will actively support efforts in the Fifth Committee of the General Assembly to redeploy resources within the UN to enable the effective augmentation of the UN DPKO along the lines outlined above. In addition, *the U.S. is prepared to undertake the following, primarily on a reimbursable basis:*

— detail appropriate numbers of civilian and military personnel to DPKO in New York in advisory or support roles;

— share information, as appropriate, while ensuring full protection of sources and methods;

— offer to design a command, control, and communications systems architecture for the Operations Division, using commercially available systems and software;

— offer to assist DPKO to establish an improved, cost-effective logistics system to support UN

peacekeeping operations;
— offer to help design the database of military forces
or capabilities and to notify DPKO, for inclusion
in the database, of specific U.S. capabilities that could
be made available for the full spectrum of peacekeeping
or humanitarian operations. U.S. notification in no way
implies a commitment to provide those capabilities,
if asked by the UN;
— detail public affairs specialists to the UN;
— offer to help create and establish a training program,
participate in peacekeeping training efforts and offer
the use of U.S. facilities for training purposes.

V. COMMAND AND CONTROL OF U.S. FORCES

A. OUR POLICY: The President retains and will never re-
linquish command authority over U.S. forces. On a case by case
basis, the President will consider placing appropriate U.S. forces
under the operational control of a competent UN commander for
specific UN operations authorized by the Security Council. The
greater the U.S. military role, the less likely it will be that the U.S.
will agree to have a UN commander exercise overall operational
control over U.S. forces. Any large scale participation of U.S. forces
in a major peace enforcement mission that is likely to involve combat should ordinarily be conducted under U.S. command and operational control or through competent regional organizations such
as NATO or ad hoc coalitions.

There is nothing new about this Administration's policy regarding the command and control of U.S. forces. U.S. military personnel have participated in UN peace operations since 1948. American
forces have served under the operational control of foreign commanders since the Revolutionary War, including in World War I,

World War II, Operation Desert Storm and in NATO since its inception. We have done so and will continue to do so when the President determines it serves U.S. national interests.

Since the end of the Cold War, U.S. military personnel have begun serving in UN operations in greater numbers. President Bush sent a large U.S. field hospital unit to Croatia and observers to Cambodia, Kuwait and Western Sahara. President Clinton has deployed two U.S. infantry companies to Macedonia in a monitoring capacity and logisticians to the UN operation in Somalia.

B. DEFINITION OF COMMAND: No President has ever relinquished command over U.S. forces. Command constitutes the authority to issue orders covering *every aspect* of military operations and administration. The sole source of legitimacy for U.S. commanders originates from the U.S. Constitution, federal law and the Uniform Code of Military Justice and flows from the President to the lowest U.S. commander in the field. The chain of command from the President to the lowest U.S. commander in the field remains inviolate.

C. DEFINITION OF OPERATIONAL CONTROL: It is sometimes prudent or advantageous (for reasons such as maximizing military effectiveness and ensuring unity of command) to place U.S. forces under the operational control of a foreign commander to achieve specified military objectives. In making this determination, factors such as the mission, the size of the proposed U.S. force, the risks involved, anticipated duration, and rules of engagement will be carefully considered.

Operational control is a subset of command. It is given for a specific time frame or mission and includes the authority to assign tasks to U.S. forces already deployed by the President, and assign tasks to U.S. units led by U.S. officers. Within the limits of operational control, a foreign UN commander *cannot:* change the mission or deploy U.S. forces outside the area of responsibility agreed to by the President, separate units, divide their supplies, administer discipline, promote anyone, or change their internal organization.

D. FUNDAMENTAL ELEMENTS OF U.S. COMMAND ALWAYS APPLY: If it is to our advantage to place U.S. forces under the operational control of a UN commander, the fundamental elements of U.S. command still apply. U.S. commanders will maintain the capability to report separately to higher U.S. military authorities, as well as the UN commander. Commanders of U.S. military units participating in UN operations will refer to higher U.S. authorities orders that are illegal under U.S. or international law, or are outside the mandate of the mission to which the U.S. agreed with the UN, if they are unable to resolve the matter with the UN commander. The U.S. reserves the right to terminate participation at any time and to take whatever actions it deems necessary to protect U.S. forces if they are endangered.

1. For simplicity, the term peace operations is used in this document to mean the entire spectrum of activities from traditional peacekeeping to peace enforcement aimed at defusing and resolving international conflicts.

APPENDIX I

DEFINING MISSIONS, SETTING DEADLINES: MEETING NEW SECURITY CHALLENGES IN THE POST-COLD WAR WORLD

BY ANTHONY LAKE*

I want to speak with you today about the most difficult issue any President has to address: when to use American force and to put young Americans in harm's way abroad. This is a good time for this discussion. Six weeks from now, the last of more than 20,000 American troops assigned to the U.N. mission in Haiti will come home. About an equal number are serving in Bosnia to help keep the hard won peace there. Both missions reflect answers to difficult questions about *when* to use force—and especially *how* to use it.

Let me start by putting my thoughts in a larger context. Halfway between the end of the Cold War and the start of a new century, we're living a moment of very real hope. Our nation is secure. Our economy is strong. All around the world more people live free and at peace than ever before.

But the promise of this moment is also matched by its perils— as the desperate and despicable acts of the enemies of peace in the Middle East have shown over the last week. Old threats like ethnic and religious violence and aggression by rogue states have taken on new and dangerous dimensions. And no one is immune to a host of equal opportunity destroyers: the spread of weapons of mass destruction, terrorism, organized crime, drug trafficking, environmental degradation. Individually, each could undermine our

* Remarks by the Assistant to the President for National Security Affairs delivered at George Washington University, March 6, 1996.

growing security. Together, they have the potential to cause terrible chaos around the world and in our own society.

Faced with both the promise and the problems of our time, there are those—on both the left and the right and in both political parties—who would have America retreat from its responsibilities.

Some proclaim that America must stay engaged—but they then would deny us the tools and the resources to match their rhetoric. These backdoor isolationists would stop us from working with others to share the risks and the costs of engagement. They would gut our diplomatic readiness and cut our assistance to those who take risks for peace around the world. They fail to recognize that the global trend toward democracy and free markets—and the opportunities it creates for our people—is neither inevitable nor irreversible. It needs our support, our resources and our leadership.

Others—call them neo-know-nothings—argue that with the Cold War won, it's safe to return to a Fortress America. It is not the American way to retreat or refuse to compete. We can't build a wall high enough or dig a moat deep enough to keep out the threats to our well-being—or to isolate ourselves from the global economy. As President Clinton said in his State of the Union address this year, we must confront these challenges now—or we will pay a much higher price for our indifference later.

The century that we have seen makes this truth very clear. After World War I, America withdrew from the world—leaving a vacuum that was filled by the forces of hatred and tyranny—and we paid the price in World War II. After World War II, we stayed involved, we worked with others and we led—patiently, persistently and pragmatically. And we helped create the institutions that secured half a century of security and prosperity for us all.

For the past three years, the Clinton Administration has built upon this bipartisan legacy of leadership by reducing the nuclear threat, supporting peacemakers, spreading democracy and opening markets. And I'm proud of the results—for our own people and for people around the world.

We stayed engaged with Russia and the other states of the former Soviet Union—despite our differences—because it is in the interests of the American people that we do so. Today, American cities and American citizens no longer live under direct targeting of Russian missiles. Ukraine, Belarus, and Kazakhstan are giving up the nuclear weapons left on their land when the Soviet Union collapsed. We are safeguarding nuclear materials and destroying nuclear weapons so they don't wind up in the wrong hands. And, we have taken the lead in securing, extending, or promoting landmark arms control agreements: START I and II, the Non-Proliferation Treaty, the Comprehensive Test Ban Treaty, the Chemical Weapons Convention.

We applied steady, patient pressure to North Korea. Now, it has frozen its dangerous nuclear weapons program. We're waging a tough counter-terrorism campaign with stronger laws; increased funding, manpower and training for law enforcement; sanctions against states that sponsor terrorism; and closer cooperation with foreign governments. Now, those responsible for the World Trade Center bombing are behind bars. We've foiled attacks on New York City and on our airliners abroad, and we've tracked down terrorists and brought them to justice around the world.

We sent our troops, ships and planes to the Persian Gulf when Saddam Hussein moved his forces closer to the Kuwaiti border. Now, Kuwait remains safe and the world's energy supply secure. We backed diplomacy with force in Haiti. Now, the dictators are gone. Haiti has celebrated the first democratic transfer of power in its 200-year history, and the flood of refugees to our shores has ended.

Our troops are standing up for peace in Bosnia. Now, its playgrounds are no longer killing fields. A dangerous fire at the heart of Europe is not raging as it had been for four years. The Bosnian people now have their first real chance for peace.

We are standing with those who are taking risks for peace—very real risks for peace—through good times, and as in the Middle East now, through bad times.

Now, in Northern Ireland, the determination of Prime Minister Major and Prime Minister Bruton is pushing the peace process back on track—and a date certain for negotiations and, we hope, a new cease-fire is on its way.

In the Middle East, we know, tragically, that fanatics will stop at nothing to kill the hope for peace. As you know, the President has ordered a series of steps to express our complete support for the peacemakers as they combat terrorism.

We must also not lose sight of the tremendous progress that has been made toward a comprehensive peace—or the fact that the overwhelming majority of people, Palestinians and Israelis, want peace. We will not rest until that desire becomes a reality.

What the terrorists want here is what we must not give them. We are going to be very tough and absolutely steadfast in the way we stand with Israel and the way we help the Palestinian Authority combat terrorism. But what the terrorists are trying to do is get us, in the process, to abandon the possibilities for peace itself, and to give up on peace. To abandon the peace process now in our very legitimate and natural anger at what has happened would be to do precisely what the terrorists want—it would give them the victory, a victory that must be ours.

And we negotiated a better deal for America as we opened markets abroad. Now, our exports are at an all-time high and hundreds of thousands more Americans have jobs at home. With Japan alone, this Administration has completed twenty specific trade agreements. The sectors covered by those agreements—from auto parts to medical equipment—have seen their exports increase by 80 percent. That's almost twice as much as exports from other sectors—which are also growing fast.

Not one of these achievements came about easily or automatically. They happened for a number of reasons. First, because we kept our military strong while adapting our alliance to new demands. Because we acted with others where we could and alone where we had to. Because we were patient enough to stick with diplomacy but prepared to use force. Because we rejected isolationism but refused to become the world's policeman. Because in each and every instance, we brought together our interests and values, and we acted where we could make a difference.

Some people, in a curious bit of nostalgia for the Cold War, complain that our policy lacks a single, overarching principle—that it can't be summed up on a bumper sticker. But while we are operating in a radically new international environment, America's fundamental mission endures. The same ideas that were under attack by Communism, and before that by Fascism, remain under attack today as we are seeing in the Middle East. Now, as then, we are defending an idea that has many names—tolerance, liberty, civility, pluralism—but shows a constant face: the face of the democratic society. Now, as then, our special role in the world is to defend, enlarge, and strengthen the community of democratic nations against all of these new threats and seizing these new opportunities.

Let me be very clear that in pursuing this mission, our interests and ideals converge. We know from experience that democracies rarely go to war with one another or abuse the rights of their people. They make for better trading partners. And each one is a potential ally in the struggle against the forces of hatred and intolerance—whether those forces take the shape of rogue nations, ethnic and religious hatreds, or terrorists trafficking in weapons of mass destruction.

What we have left behind are the certitudes and simplifications of the past—and that's not necessarily a bad thing. During the Cold War, policymakers could justify every act with one word: containment. We got the big things right—containment was the right policy and it succeeded, and we won the Cold War, and we are all far, far better for it. But even the best policy can become the worst straitjacket if it is pursued too rigidly and reflexively—as we saw in Vietnam.

Now, we have the opportunity to think anew about the best ways to promote America's interests and ideals. Our tools of first resort remain diplomacy and the power of our example. But sometimes, we have to rely on the example of our power. We face no more important questions than when and how to use it. From our experience in countering traditional aggression—as in the Persian Gulf—and contending with more novel crises—as in Haiti and Bosnia—there are some principles on the use of force that I would like to discuss with you.

First, let me cite one underlying and enduring principle: We will always be ready to use force to defend our national interests. Until human nature changes, power and force will remain at the heart of international relations.

This begs the question of just what those interests are that we will defend. I would cite seven circumstances, which, taken in some combination or even alone, may call for the use of force or our military forces:

— 1. To defend against direct attacks on the United States, its citizens, and its allies;

— 2. To counter aggression;

— 3. To defend our key economic interests, which is where most Americans see their most immediate stake in our international engagement;

— 4. To preserve, promote and defend democracy, which enhances our security and the spread of our values;

— 5. To prevent the spread of weapons of mass destruction, terrorism, international crime and drug trafficking;

— 6. To maintain our reliability, because when our partnerships are strong and confidence in our leadership is high, it is easier to get others to work with us, and to share the burdens of leadership; and,

— 7. For humanitarian purposes, to combat famines, natural disasters and gross abuses of human rights with, occasionally, our military forces.

Not one of these interests by itself—with the obvious exception of an attack on our nation, people and allies—should automatically lead to the use of force. But the greater the number and the weight of the interests in play, the greater the likelihood that we will use force—once all peaceful means have been tried and failed and once we have measured a mission's benefits against its costs, in both human and financial terms.

In Haiti, when we saw democracy stolen from its people, a reign of brutality take hold in our hemisphere, a flood of refugees to our shores, international agreements consistently violated, and efforts to resolve the impasse through negotiations and sanctions fail, the case for intervention was compelling. In Bosnia, the worst atrocities in Europe since World War II (a dangerous fire at the very heart of the continent), our commitments to our NATO allies, and a peace agreement the parties were calling on us to secure required us to act, and the President decided to do so.

But more than the "when" of using force, Haiti, Bosnia, and some other recent interventions highlight principles that get at a harder question, perhaps, and that is "how" we should use force.

First, threatening to use force can achieve the same results as actually using it—but only if you're prepared to carry through on that threat. The best-trained, best-equipped, and best-prepared fighting force in the world has a unique ability to concentrate the minds of our adversaries without firing a shot. In Haiti, when the military regime learned that the 82nd Airborne literally was on the way, those leaders got out of the way. In the Persian Gulf, as soon as President Clinton moved American forces into the region, Iraq moved its troops away from Kuwait. And by backing diplomacy with the presence of U.S. military forces to deter attack on the South, we convinced North Korea to freeze its dangerous nuclear weapons program.

A second principle is that the selective but substantial use of force is sometimes more appropriate than its massive use— provided that the force is adequate to the task, and then some. President Clinton refused to engage our troops in a ground war in Bosnia because he knew that no outside power could force peace on the parties. To do so would have risked a Vietnam-like quagmire. But this summer, the combination of NATO's heavy and continuous air strikes, Bosnian and Croat gains on the ground, and our determined diplomacy convinced the Bosnian Serbs to stop making war and start making peace. Now, our troops are in Bosnia not to fight a war through a massive intervention, but to secure a peace they produced through the deliberate, calibrated use of force.

A final principle is this: before we send our troops into a foreign country, we should know how and when we're going to get them out. Sounds simple, even obvious. But it is not an uncontroversial point. But carefully defined exit strategies for foreign interventions have not been a hallmark of our foreign policy in recent decades. Now they are—and that makes sense for America, for America's military, and for the people we're trying to help.

I don't want to be doctrinaire in asserting an exit strategy doctrine. When it comes to deterring external aggression—as in the Persian Gulf or the Korean Peninsula—or fighting wars in defense of our most vital security interests, a more open-ended commitment is necessary. But increasingly, our interests require that our military keep peace in the wake of internal conflicts. For these operations to succeed, tightly tailored military missions and sharp withdrawal deadlines must be the norm.

The logic is this: The first step is to give our Armed Forces a clear mission with achievable *military*—I repeat, *military*—goals, as President Clinton did in both Haiti and Bosnia. In Haiti, we asked our Armed Forces to return the elected government to power and restore a secure climate so that *civilians* could train a police force, hold elections, and begin reconciliation. In Bosnia, our soldiers are overseeing the implementation of the military side of the Dayton accords—separating the armies, maintaining the cease-fire, securing transferred territory—while civilian authorities help the Bosnian people rebuild their lives and their land. In both places, our troops are highly trained and heavily armed, with very clear rules of engagement. And the Executive Branch and Congress are united in their commitment to our military's goals and success, as they were in Operation *Desert Storm*.

Contrast these operations with Vietnam, Lebanon, and Somalia. There, clear and achievable missions for our military were not defined. In Vietnam, our society blamed our soldiers for a defeat that was not theirs. Because we neglected to ask the right questions and establish clear military goals from the start, our fighting men and women paid a terrible price, both in Vietnam and on their return home. We must never put them in that position again. Never. It just mustn't happen. The next step, then, having defined clear military missions, is to set deadlines for withdrawal based on the accomplishment of those missions. In Haiti, our military leaders informed the

President that our troops could complete their military tasks in about a year and a half, and in Bosnia in about one year—and they will.

Here's why setting deadlines is so important: Neither we nor the international community has either the responsibility or the means to do whatever it takes for as long as it takes to rebuild nations. There are many reasons for this.

First, providing a security blanket for an indefinite period without making clear it's on loan—and not for keeps—only gives those we are trying to help the comfort to believe that they can evade their own responsibilities for the future of their own societies. It creates unreasonable expectations that the hard work will be done for them not by them.

Second, assuming too much responsibility for a nation's future tends to undercut the very government you are trying to help. In Vietnam, the more we assumed responsibility for a weak Saigon administration, the more dependent it became—and the more open to charges it was a puppet regime beholden to foreigners. Unless you make clear that your mission is limited in scope and duration, you risk de-legitimating a government in the eyes of its own people and you will lose a conflict that is, at its heart, political, and not military.

Third, overstaying one's welcome ultimately breeds resentment of our presence and provides an easy target for blame when things go wrong. And believe me, that target will be us.

By carefully defining the mission and clearly setting a deadline, we serve notice that our only goal is to give governments and people the breathing room they must have to tackle their own problems. This "tough love" policy may sound harsh to some. It may strike others as a gamble. But consider the alternative: self-defeating efforts to take on responsibilities that are not ours—to create unsustainable dependencies instead of giving nations a chance to act independently. It is a dangerous hubris to believe we can build other nations. But where our own interests are engaged, we can help nations build themselves—and give them time to make a start at it.

I believe we can see the benefits of our exit strategy doctrine in Haiti and Bosnia. Given the chance, the Haitian people quickly focused on the ballot, not the bullet; on trade, not terror; on hope, not despair. In just a year and a half, with our civilian help, they have completed presidential, parliamentary, and local government elections; trained a police force that is as yet imperfect, but showing great progress. They have dramatically, despite problems, improved the human rights situation and begun to reverse the economic decline of the coup years. Haiti remains the poorest nation in the Americas. There is no guarantee democracy will take hold or the economy will prosper. But its people now have a real chance to build a better future for themselves and their children—and for the U.S. forces who have acted in Haiti with such strength and with such skill and are leaving when we promised they would, we can say "mission accomplished."

The same logic applies in Bosnia and the same opportunity lies before the people of Bosnia. Its people understand they have a window of opportunity that our military opened and will hold open for the remainder of this year to decide their future in peace: to freely choose their own leaders in elections later this summer; to begin to rebuild their roads and schools, their factories and their hospitals; to reunite children with their parents and families with their homes. At the end of this year, when our troops leave, we can reasonably hope that the people of Bosnia will have developed a greater stake in peace than war—that peace will have taken on a life and logic of its own. That is all that can be asked of us.

But let me make one point absolutely clear—the breathing room our military is providing in Haiti and Bosnia must be filled with the oxygen of economic reconstruction assistance. What we call civilian implementation is the vital and necessary companion to any peacekeeping operation. Our allies agree. That's why they are providing about 80 percent of the civilian assistance for Haiti and for Bosnia. The sooner people in conflicted countries recover the blessings of a normal life, the surer the chances our troops will leave behind them a legacy of peace and hope as they are doing in Haiti.

That's why Congress should now un-freeze the modest amount of outstanding development assistance for Haiti to fund primary education, child care, and immunizations. They should do it now. And that's why we are working with Congress on our request for $200 million to assist civilian reconstruction in Bosnia—money that will support economic revitalization and reform, the deployment of international police monitors, and our demining efforts. Money that is needed now.

In both Haiti and Bosnia, our Armed Forces are doing everything we have asked of them—and more. We should live up to their example on the civilian side in both the Executive branch and Congress. Their missions will only succeed if we do so. Holding back the dollars we need for relief and reconstruction doesn't serve our soldiers, it doesn't serve the people we're trying to help, and it doesn't serve our Nation's interests.

One of the great privileges of my job is to travel around the world and to see firsthand the extraordinary respect our Nation now enjoys. People look to us for leadership not only because of our size and our strength but also because of what we stand for— and what, as today in the Middle East, what we're willing to stand against. Now, perhaps more than any other time in our history, America has a unique ability to make a difference for our own people and for people around the world.

Our duty is to help use this power as wisely as possible—to steer by the stars of our interests and our ideals. As President Clinton has said, we can't be everywhere. We can't do everything. But where those interests and ideals demand it—and where we can make a difference—we must not hesitate to lead. We haven't— and we won't.

You must not hesitate, either. Many of you here today are embarking, I hope, on careers in foreign policy. Whether you do so as teachers or researchers, government officials or journalists, you will have an opportunity to weigh in on the great foreign policy questions of our time. Weigh in with passion, weigh in with argument— but above all, weigh in. America needs to hear your voices. It needs to feel your enthusiasm.

Right now, no question is more fundamental—and no outcome more important—than America's role in the world. We can succeed, this is an absolute certainty, only if we continue to lead—not merely be engaged, but lead. That is the lesson of what has come to be called the American Century. If we heed its call, we can remain a force for freedom and progress around the world as we are today, and for real security and prosperity at home. And the next century will be an American century, too. And the world will be a better place for it.

CHAPTER ONE

1. The most noted of this genre is Francis Fukuyama, *The End of History and the Last Man* (New York: Free Press, 1992). Not everyone was so optimistic at the time. See, for example, Lawrence Eagleburger, "Uncharted Waters: U.S. Foreign Policy in a Time of Transition," address delivered at Georgetown University on September 13, 1989 [unpublished], and John J. Mearsheimer, "Why We Will Soon Miss the Cold War," *Atlantic*, Vol. 266, No. 2 (August 1990), pp. 35–50. For more recent examples of geo-political pessimism, see Samuel P. Huntington, "The Clash of Civilizations?" *Foreign Affairs*, Vol. 72, No. 3 (Summer 1993), pp. 22–49, and Robert D. Kaplan, "The Coming Anarchy," *Atlantic*, Vol. 273, No. 2 (February 1994), pp. 44–76. The principal difference between Huntington and Kaplan is that Huntington sees future competition coinciding with large cultural divides—he cites seven or possibly eight—while Kaplan envisions a disorderly world characterized by numerous manifestations of localized banditry and violence.

2. Neither President Bush nor any senior official in his administration delivered a developed statement on the new world order. Bush presented a basic definition in his valedictory address at West Point on January 5, 1993: " . . . one of governments that are democratic, tolerant, and economically free at home and committed abroad to settling inevitable differences peacefully, without the threat or use of force." The full text of the address is in *Public Papers of the Presidents of the United States: George Bush, 1992–93*, Book II (Washington: U.S. Government Printing Office, 1993), pp. 2228–33. The relevant portions of the address are reprinted here in Appendix F.

3. See, for example, Alexander L. George, Philip J. Farley, and Alexander Dallin (eds.), *U.S. Soviet Security Cooperation: Achievements, Failures, Lessons* (New York: Oxford University Press, 1988), and Albert Carnesale and Richard N. Haass (eds.), *Superpower Arms Control: Setting the Record Straight* (Cambridge: Ballinger, 1987).

4. Daniel P. Moynihan, *Pandaemonium: Ethnicity in International Politics* (New York: Oxford University Press, 1993), p. 15.

5. In spring 1994, for example, China resisted U.S. efforts to isolate and pressure North Korea despite its refusal to cooperate fully with nuclear inspectors. Russia often refused to go along with U.S. desires to threaten the Serbs with military force in order to affect their behavior in Bosnia.

6. For some background on the evolving nuclear proliferation problem, see Leonard S. Spector, *Nuclear Ambitions: The Spread of Nuclear Weapons 1989–1990* (Washington: Carnegie Endowment, 1990); Robert D. Blackwill and Albert Carnesale (eds.), *New Nuclear Nations: Consequences for U.S. Policy* (New York: Council on Foreign Relations, 1993); and Zachary S. Davis and Benjamin Frankel (eds.), *The Proliferation Puzzle: Why Nuclear Weapons Spread (and What Results), Security Studies*, Vol. 2, Nos. 3/4 (Spring/Summer 1993).

7. Not everyone agrees with this vision. For something relatively upbeat, see Francis Fukuyama, "Against the New Pessimism," *Commentary*, Vol. 97, No. 2 (February 1994), pp. 25–29.

8. See George F. Kennan, "The Sources of Soviet Conduct," in his *American Diplomacy 1900–1950* (Chicago: University of Chicago Press, 1951), pp. 99, 104. For background see John Lewis Gaddis, *Strategies of Containment* (New York: Oxford University Press, 1982).

9. This sense of political and intellectual confusion is captured by Thomas L. Friedman, "It's Harder Now to Figure Out Compelling National Interests," *New York Times* (May 31, 1992), p. E5. The one attempt by the Clinton Administration to "solve" this problem of not having a successor to containment, the address by National Security Advisor Anthony Lake in which he described a policy of "enlargement," was a failure. Enlarging the circle of democracies is a worthy goal, but it does not provide a road-map for getting there, for dealing with difficulties along the way, or for determining priorities or trade-offs. See his "From Containment to Enlargement," an address delivered to the School of Advanced International Studies, Johns Hopkins

University, Washington, D.C., on September 21, 1993, reprinted in *U.S. Department of State Dispatch,* Vol. 4, No. 39 (September 27, 1993), pp. 658–64.

10. See Michael Clough, "Grass-Roots Policymaking," *Foreign Affairs,* Vol. 73, No. 1 (January/February 1994), pp. 2–7.

11. On just this point see Charles Krauthammer, "The Greatest Cold War Myth of All," *Time* (November 29, 1993), p. 86.

12. James Schlesinger, "New Instabilities, New Priorities," *Foreign Policy,* No. 85 (Winter 1991–92), pp. 23–24.

13. It is noteworthy that the Bush Administration felt compelled to address directly religious concerns (and/or concerns held by religious groups and people) during the Gulf crisis. See, for example, George Bush's speech of January 28, 1991, to the Annual Convention of National Religious Broadcasters, reprinted in *Public Papers of the Presidents of the United States: George Bush, 1991,* Book I (Washington: U.S. Government Printing Office, 1992), pp. 70–72.

14. Hugo Grotius, *De Jure Belli Ac Pacis,* Book II (New York: Ocean Publications, 1964), p. 170. This translation is by Francis W. Kelsey. The original was published in 1625. For a thoughtful essay on Grotius and his work, see Hedley Bull, "The Grotian Conception of International Society," in Herbert Butterfield and Martin Wight (eds.), *Diplomatic Investigations: Essays in the Theory of International Politics* (London: George Allen & Unwin, 1966), pp. 51–73.

15. See, for example, Stanley Hoffmann and Karl Deutsch (eds.), *The Relevance of International Law* (Garden City, N.Y.: Anchor Books, 1971).

16. The Clausewitz quotation can be found on page 87 of his *On War* in the version edited by Michael Howard and Peter Paret (Princeton: Princeton University Press, 1976). For a useful introduction to the writings of the major strategists, see Peter Paret (ed.), *Makers of Modern Strategy from Machiavelli to the Nuclear Age* (Princeton: Princeton University Press, 1986).

17. See *Field Manual 100–5: Operations* (Washington: Headquarters, Department of the Army, 1993), ch. 2.

18. Bernard Brodie, *Strategy in the Missile Age* (Princeton: Princeton University Press, 1965), p. 309. For additional examples of key works in this area, see Henry A. Kissinger, *Nuclear Weapons and Foreign Policy* (New York: Harper & Brothers for the Council on Foreign Relations, 1957); Robert E. Osgood, *Limited War: The Challenge to American Strategy* (Chicago: University of Chicago Press, 1957); Maxwell D. Taylor, *The Uncertain Trumpet* (New York: Harper & Row, 1960); Thomas C. Schelling, *The Strategy of Conflict*

(Cambridge: Harvard University Press, 1960); and Morton H. Halperin, *Limited War in the Nuclear Age* (New York: John Wiley & Sons, 1963).

19. This literature of limited war is related but still distinct from two others, one devoted to the possible use of battlefield nuclear weapons in "limited" nuclear wars, and a second devoted to arguing for limited nuclear options in major wars involving the superpowers.

20. See Schelling, *op. cit.*, and Robert Osgood, *Limited War Revisited* (Boulder: Westview, 1979), p. 11.

21. See Christopher M. Gacek, *Contending Approaches to the Use of Force: The "Never Again" and "Limited War" Schools in American Foreign Policy* (Stanford University, PhD dissertation, 1989). For two of the better retrospectives on Vietnam and its military lessons, see Bruce Palmer, Jr., *The 25-Year War: America's Military Role in Vietnam* (New York: Simon & Schuster, 1985), and Harry G. Summers, Jr., *On Strategy: The Vietnam War in Context* (Carlisle Barracks, Pa.: U.S. Army War College, 1981).

22. Relevant portions of the U.N. Charter are reprinted in Appendix A.

23. J.S. Mill, "A Few Words on Non-Intervention," in his *Essays on Politics and Culture* (New York: Doubleday, 1962), pp. 396–413.

24. See *The Harvest of Justice is Shown in Peace* (Washington: U.S. Catholic Conference, 1994), p. 16. Also see Peter Steinfels, "Catholic Bishops Proposing Active U.S. Policy Abroad," *New York Times* (October 28, 1993), p. A22.

25. A large literature devoted to this question (and, with few exceptions, sympathetic to the notion) has emerged in a relatively short period of time. For a sampling, see Laura W. Reed and Carl Kayson (eds.), *Emerging Norms of Justified Intervention* (Cambridge: American Academy of Arts & Sciences, 1993); *Right v. Might: International Law and the Use of Force* (New York: Council on Foreign Relations, 1991); Christopher Greenwood, "Is there a Right of Humanitarian Intervention?," *World Today*, Vol. 49, No. 2 (February 1993), pp. 34–40; Louis Henkin, "Notes From the President: The Mythology of Sovereignty," *American Society of International Law Newsletter* (March-May, 1993); Barbara Harff, "Bosnia and Somalia: Strategic, Legal, and Moral Dimensions of Humanitarian Intervention," *Philosophy & Public Policy*, Vol. 12, No. 3/4 (Summer/Fall, 1992), pp. 1–7; and David J. Scheffer, Richard N. Gardner and Gerald B. Helman, *Three Views on the Issue of Humanitarian Intervention* (Washington: U.S. Institute of Peace, 1992). For more cautionary or skeptical views, see the chapters by Michael Akehurst and Hedley Bull in Hedley

Bull (ed.), *Intervention in World Politics* (Oxford: Clarendon Press, 1984); Joshua Muravchik, "Beyond Self Defense," *Commentary*, Vol. 96, No. 6 (December 1993), pp. 19–24; Fareed Zakaria, "The Core vs. the Periphery," *Commentary*, Vol. 96, No. 6. (December 1993), pp. 25–29; Peter Rodman, "Intervention and Its Discontents," *National Review* (March 29, 1993), pp. 28–9; Dimitri K. Simes, "When Good Deeds Make Bad Policy," *Washington Post* (August 29, 1993), pp. C1–2; Richard Falk, "Hard Choices and Tragic Dilemmas," *Nation* (December 20, 1993), pp. 755–64; and Adam Roberts, "The Road to Hell . . . A Critique of Humanitarian Intervention," *Harvard International Review*, Vol. 16, No. 1 (Fall 1993), pp. 10–13, 63. For a brief primer, see Raymond W. Copson, *The Use of Force in Civil Conflicts for Humanitarian Purposes: Prospects for the Post–Cold War Era* (Washington: Congressional Research Service, 1992).

26. The text of Weinberger's November 28, 1984, speech to the National Press Club was released the same day by the Department of Defense as News Release No. 609–84. The bulk of the speech is reprinted in this volume in Appendix C. For some reaction at the time, see Richard Halloran, "Shultz and Weinberger: Disputing Use of Force," *New York Times* (November 30, 1984), p. B6.

27. Hart's guidelines were articulated as part of three speeches he delivered under the rubric of "enlightened engagement" to the Georgetown University School of Foreign Service in Washington, D.C., on June 11–13, 1986. For some press coverage at the time, see William Safire, "Gary Gets Engaged," *New York Times* (June 23, 1986), p. A15, and Bernard Gwertzman, "Hart Sees Shifts in Superpower Roles," *New York Times* (June 12, 1986), p. A21.

28. See two pieces by Colin L. Powell: "U.S. Forces: Challenges Ahead," *Foreign Affairs*, Vol. 72, No. 5 (Winter 1992–93), pp. 32–45, and "Why Generals Get Nervous," *New York Times* (October 8, 1992), p. A35. Excerpts of the first of these are reprinted in Appendix E. Also see Michael R. Gordon, "Powell Delivers a Resounding No on Using Limited Force in Bosnia," *New York Times* (September 28, 1992), p. A1.

29. Aspin's remarks, titled "The Use and Usefulness of Military Forces in the Post–Cold War, Post-Soviet World," were made on September 21, 1992, to the Jewish Institute for National Security Affairs in Washington, D.C. They are reprinted here in Appendix D.

30. The most complete statement by Bush on this question was his address at West Point on January 5, 1993. See Appendix F.

31. Christopher's testimony can be found in *Commerce, Justice, and State, the Judiciary, and Related Appropriations, FY94: Hearing* (Washington, D.C.: U.S. Government Printing Office, 1993), pp. 323–84.

32. Madeleine K. Albright, "Use of Force in a Post–Cold War World," address at the National War College, Washington, D.C., September 23, 1993, reprinted in *U.S. Department of State Dispatch*, Vol. 4, No. 39 (September 27, 1993), p. 667.

33. Bill Clinton, "Confronting the Challenges of a Broader World," address to U.N. General Assembly on September 27, 1993, reprinted in *U.S. Department of State Dispatch*, Vol. 4, No. 39 (September 27, 1993), p. 652. Excerpts of this speech are reprinted here in Appendix G.

34. See *The Clinton Administration's Policy on Reforming Multilateral Peace Operations* (May 1994). The text of this document can be found in Appendix H. For press reaction at the time, see Elaine Sciolino, "New U.S. Peacekeeping Policy De-emphasizes Role of the U.N.," *New York Times* (May 6, 1994), pp. A1, A7. Also see Chester A. Crocker, "Peacekeeping We Can Fight For," *Washington Post* (May 8, 1994), pp. C1, C4.

CHAPTER 2

1. For annotated lists or thumbnail sketches of many examples of use of force by the United States, see Ellen C. Collier (ed.), *Instances of Use of United States Armed Forces Abroad, 1798–1989* (Washington: Congressional Research Service, 1989); Daniel Y. Chiu and Anne M. Dixon, *The Context of Military Intervention: Past, Present, and Future* (Alexandria, Va.: Center for Naval Analyses, 1993); and Barry M. Blechman and Stephen S. Kaplan, *Force Without War: U.S. Armed Forces as a Political Instrument* (Washington: Brookings Institution, 1978).

2. On this last point, see Bruce W. Jentleson and Ariel E. Levite, "The Analysis of Protracted Foreign Military Intervention," in Ariel E. Levite, Bruce W. Jentleson, and Larry Berman (eds.), *Foreign Military Intervention: The Dynamics of Protracted Conflict* (New York: Columbia University Press, 1992), pp. 5–7. Closer to my approach is the official U.S. military definition of "military intervention," which also takes a broad tack: "The deliberate act of a nation or a group of nations to introduce its military forces into the course of an existing controversy." See *Department of Defense Dictionary of Military and Associated Terms* (Washington: U.S. Government Printing Office, 1994), p. 239; this publication is also known as JCS Pub 1–02.

3. Much of the background to the rescue attempt can be found in the memoirs of senior Carter Administration officials. See especially Gary Sick, *All Fall Down: America's Tragic Encounter with Iran* (New York: Random House, 1985), pp. 280–302; Stansfield Turner, *Terrorism and Democracy* (Boston: Houghton Mifflin, 1991), pp. 99–145; and Zbigniew Brzezinski, *Power and Principle: Memoirs of the National Security Advisor, 1977–1981* (New York: Farrar Straus Giroux, 1983), pp. 488–500. Also see Gary Sick, "Military Options and Constraints," in Warren Christopher, et. al., *Hostages in Iran: The Conduct of a Crisis* (New Haven: Yale University Press for the Council on Foreign Relations, 1985), pp. 144–72, and *Rescue Mission Report* (Washington: Joint Chiefs of Staff, 1980).

4. Address by Jimmy Carter to the World Affairs Council in Philadelphia on May 9, 1980, reprinted in *Department of State Bulletin*, Vol. 80, No. 2039 (June 1980), p. 7.

5. For background, see George P. Shultz, *Turmoil and Triumph: My Years as Secretary of State* (New York: Charles Scribner's Sons, 1993), pp. 101–14 and 220–32; Caspar Weinberger, *Fighting for Peace: Seven Critical Years in the Pentagon* (New York: Warner, 1990), pp. 135–74; and the so-called Long Commission report, known more formally as the *Report of the DOD Commission on Beirut International Airport Terrorist Act* (Washington: U.S. Department of Defense, 1983).

6. For background, see Janice R. Hanover, *Grenada: Issues Concerning the Use of Force* (Washington: Congressional Research Service, 1984); Shultz, *op. cit.*, pp. 323–45; Weinberger, op. cit., pp. 101–33; Hugh O'Shaughnessy, *Grenada: An Eyewitness Account of the U.S. Invasion and the Caribbean History that Provoked It* (New York: Dodd, Mead, 1984); Jiri Valenta and Herbert J. Ellison (eds.), *Grenada and Soviet/Cuban Policy: Internal Crisis and U.S./OECS Intervention* (Boulder: Westview, 1986); and Committee on Foreign Affairs, House of Representatives, *U.S. Military Actions in Grenada: Implications for United States Policy in the Eastern Caribbean* (Washington: U.S. Government Printing Office, 1984).

7. See "Remarks of the President and Prime Minister Eugenia Charles of Dominica Announcing the Deployment of United States Forces in Grenada"

(October 25, 1983) in *Public Papers . . . 1983*, Book II (1985), pp. 1505–08.

8. For background, see Weinberger, *op. cit.*, pp. 175–201; William J. Crowe, Jr., *The Line of Fire* (New York: Simon & Schuster, 1993), pp. 129–45; George Shultz, *op. cit.*, pp. 679–87; Tim Zimmermann, "Coercive Diplomacy and Libya," in Alexander L. George and William E. Simons (eds.), *The Limits of Coercive Diplomacy* (Boulder: Westview, 1994), pp. 201–28; and David C. Martin and John Walcott, *Best Laid Plans: The Inside Story of America's War Against Terrorism* (New York: Harper & Row, 1988).

9. Weinberger, *op. cit.*, p. 193.

10. See *Patterns of Global Terrorism: 1987* (Washington: U.S. Department of State, 1988), Pub. No. 9661, p. 6.

11. For background, see Crowe, *op. cit.*, esp. chs. 9–11; Caspar Weinberger, *op. cit.*, pp. 387–428; George Shultz, *op. cit.*, pp. 925–35; Committee on Foreign Relations, U.S. Senate, *U.S. Policy in the Persian Gulf* (Washington: U.S. Government Printing Office, 1988); Committee on Armed Services, U.S. Senate, *U.S. Military Forces to Protect "Re-Flagged" Kuwaiti Oil Tankers: Hearings* (Washington: U.S. Government Printing Office, 1987); Committee on Foreign Relations, U.S. Senate, *War in the Persian Gulf: The U.S. Takes Sides: A Staff Report* (Washington: U.S. Government Printing Office, 1987).

12. For background, see George Bush, "Letter to the Speaker of the House of Representatives and President Pro Tempore of the Senate on United States Military Assistance to the Philippines" (December 2, 1989), reprinted in *Public Papers . . . , 1989*, Book II (1990), pp. 1622–23; Dan Quayle, *Standing Firm: A Vice-Presidential Memoir* (New York: Harper Collins, 1994), pp. 136–38; and Bob Woodward, *The Commanders* (New York: Simon & Schuster, 1991), pp. 146–53.

13. For background, see William C. Bennett, "Just Cause and the Principles of War," *Military Review* (March 1991), pp. 2–13; Rebecca L. Grant, *Operation Just Cause and the U.S. Policy Process* (Santa Monica: Rand, 1993); Bob Woodward, *op. cit.*, especially pp. 83–195; Kevin Buckley, *Panama: The Whole Story* (New York: Simon & Schuster, 1991), esp. pp. 228–54; and Frederick Kempe, *Divorcing the Dictator: America's Bungled Affair with Noriega* (New York: G. P. Putnam's Sons, 1990).

14. For background, see Woodward, *op. cit.*, especially pp. 199–376; Michael A. Palmer, *Guardians of the Gulf: A History of America's Role in the Persian Gulf, 1833–1992* (New York: Free Press, 1992), pp. 150–238; Jeffrey Mc-

Causland, *The Gulf Conflict: A Military Analysis* (London: International Institute for Strategic Studies, 1993); Micah L. Sifrey and Christopher Cerf (eds.), *The Gulf War Reader: History, Documents, Opinions* (New York: Random House, 1991); Committee on Foreign Affairs, U.S. House of Representatives, *The Gulf Crisis: Relevant Documents, Correspondence, Reports* (Washington: U.S. Government Printing Office, 1991); Lawrence Freedman and Ephraim Karsh, *The Gulf Conflict, 1990–1991: Diplomacy and War in the New World Order* (Princeton: Princeton University Press, 1992); Rick Atkinson, *Crusade: The Untold Story of the Persian Gulf War* (Boston: Houghton Mifflin, 1993); Joseph S. Nye, Jr., and Roger K. Smith (eds.), *After the Storm: Lessons from the Gulf War* (Lanham, Md.: Madison Books, 1992); U.S. News and World Report, *Triumph Without Victory: The Unreported History of the Persian Gulf War* (New York: Random House, 1992); and James F. Dunnigan and Austin Bay, *Shield to Storm: High-Tech Weapons, Military Strategy, and Coalition Warfare in the Persian Gulf* (New York: William Morrow, 1992).

15. The text of Bush's remarks are in *Public Papers . . . 1990,* Book II (1991), pp. 1107–09.

16. Sanctions, while a form of intervention, are not a military intervention. It is the use of the military to enforce sanctions that makes it a military intervention.

17. The text of Bush's statement is in *Public Papers . . . 1990,* Book II (1991), pp. 1580–81.

18. See Victor Gold, "George Bush Speaks Out," *Washingtonian,* Vol. 29, No. 5 (February 1994), p. 40.

19. Many of the same works cited in the footnote providing background to the Gulf War discussion also contain some background to the war's aftermath. In addition, see Jane E. Stromseth, "Iraq's Repression of its Civilian Population: Collective Responses and Continuing Challenges," in Lori Fisler Damrosch (ed.), *Enforcing Restraint: Collective Intervention in Internal Conflicts* (New York: Council on Foreign Relations, 1993), pp. 77–117. For a critical view of U.S. policy at the time, see Committee on Foreign Relations, U.S. Senate, *Civil War in Iraq: A Staff Report* (Washington: U.S. Government Printing Office, 1991).

20. The April 5 announcement, "Statement on Aid to Iraqi Refugees," is reprinted in *Public Papers . . . 1991,* Book I (1992), pp. 331–32; the April 16 announcement, "Remarks on Assistance to Iraqi Refugees," on pp. 378–79 of the same volume.

21. See *Public Papers . . . 1992–93,* Book II (1993), pp. 1429–30.

22. For background, see John Zametica, *The Yugoslav Conflict* (London: International Institute for Strategic Studies, 1992); Misha Glenny, *The Fall of Yugoslavia: The Third Balkan War* (London: Penguin, 1992); John Newhouse, "Dodging the Problem," *New Yorker* (August 24, 1992) and "No Exit, No Entrance," *New Yorker* (June 28, 1993); Dusko Doder, "Yugoslavia: New War, Old Hatreds," *Foreign Policy,* No. 91 (Summer 1993), pp. 3–23; Samantha Power, *Breakdown in the Balkans: A Chronicle of Events January, 1989 to May, 1993* (Washington: Carnegie Endowment, 1993); George Kennan, *The Other Balkan Wars* (Washington, D.C.: Carnegie Endowment, 1993); Steven J. Woehrel and Julie Kim, *Yugoslavia Crisis and U.S. Policy* (Washington: Congressional Research Service, 1993); "The Road to Ruin," *Economist* (May 29, 1993), pp. 23–26; James B. Steinberg, "International Involvement in the Yugoslavia Conflict," in Damrosch (ed.), *op. cit.,* pp. 27–75; Ivo Banac, "Misreading the Balkans," *Foreign Policy,* No. 93 (Winter 1993–94), pp. 173–82; and David Gompert, "How to Defeat Serbia," *Foreign Affairs,* Vol. 73, No. 4 (July/August 1994), pp. 30–47.

23. Newhouse, "Dodging the Problem," pp. 66–67.

24. Excerpts of President Clinton's address (broadcast on February 19) are reprinted in *New York Times* (February 20, 1994), p. 10. For background into the change in U.S. policy, see Elaine Sciolino and Douglas Jehl, "As U.S. Sought a Bosnia Policy, the French Offered a Good Idea," *New York Times* (February 14, 1994), pp. A1, A6.

25. See Elaine Sciolino, "U.S. Termed Ready to Press Bosnians to Accept Division," *New York Times* (February 11, 1994), pp. A1, A6.

26. Secretary of Defense Perry ruled out the use of force in an appearance on April 3, 1994, on NBC's "Meet The Press."

27. See Christopher's February 23, 1994, testimony before the Senate Foreign Relations Committee. Perry's remarks (by far his most extensive on Bosnia) were delivered on March 10, 1994, in Washington, D.C., to the American Defense Preparedness Association. They were issued by the Pentagon as News Release No. 132–94.

28. On April 7, speaking at Johns Hopkins University in Baltimore, National Security Advisor Anthony Lake gave a major address on Bosnia in which he stated that "neither the President nor any of his senior advisors rules out the use of NATO power to help stop attacks such as those against Gorazde." The speech is reprinted in *U.S. Department of State Dispatch,* Vol. 5, No. 17 (April 25, 1994), pp. 226–29.

29. The text of the NATO ultimatum is in *New York Times* (April 23, 1994), p.6.

30. See Roger Cohen, "Bosnia Map: A Bitter Pill," *New York Times* (July 7, 1994), pp. A1, A4. Charles Redman, the U.S. envoy to the Bosnian peace talks, is quoted justifying U.S. willingness to endorse a settlement that allowed Serbs to enjoy most of the fruits of their aggression by saying, "We had to jump over the moral bridge in the interests of wider peace and of keeping Bosnia together." For a critical assessment of "contact group" diplomacy, see Albert Wohlstetter, "Creating a Greater Serbia," *New Republic,* Vol. 211, No. 5 (August 1, 1994), pp. 22–27.

31. For background, see Committee on Foreign Affairs, House of Representatives, *The Crisis in Somalia: Markup on S.J. Res. 45, Authorizing the Use of U.S. Armed Forces in Somalia* (Washington: U.S. Government Printing Office, 1993); Committee on Foreign Relations, U.S. Senate, *U.S. Participation in Somalia Peacekeeping: Hearing* (Washington: U.S. Government Printing Office, 1993); Raymond W. Copson and Theodros S. Dagne, *Somalia: Operation Restore Hope* (Washington: Congressional Research Service, 1993); William J. Clinton, *Report to the Congress on Somalia* (Washington: White House, October 13, 1993); Sidney Blumenthal, "Why Are We in Somalia?" *New Yorker* (October 25, 1993), pp. 48–60; and Jeffrey Clark, "Debacle in Somalia: Failure of the Collective Response," in Damrosch (ed.), *op. cit.,* pp. 205–39.

32. The text of Bush's remarks on December 4, 1992, are reprinted in *Public Papers . . . 1992–93,* Book II (1993), pp. 2174–76. It is important to note here that unlike the previous U.S. participation in Somali relief efforts pursuant to Security Council Resolution 751, which cited Chapter 6 of the U.N. Charter, this deployment pursuant to Resolution 794 was a mission of enforcement, and therefore under Chapter 7 of the Charter. For background on the Bush Administration's decision to intervene in Somalia, see Don Oberdorfer, "The Path to Intervention," *Washington Post* (December 6, 1992), pp. A1, A35.

33. Speech delivered to the Center for Strategic and International Studies, August 27, 1993, Washington, D.C. For press treatment of the speech, see John Lancaster, "Aspin Lists U.S. Goals in Somalia," *Washington Post* (August 28, 1993), p. A1.

34. For a graphic description of this battle, see Rick Atkinson, "The Raid that

Went Wrong" and "Night of a Thousand Casualties," *Washington Post* (January 30, 1994), pp. A1, A26, and (January 31, 1994), pp. A1, A10. For an analysis of what took place, see Michael R. Gordon and Thomas L. Friedman, "Disastrous U.S. Raid in Somalia Nearly Succeeded, Review Finds," *New York Times* (October 25, 1993), pp. A1, A10. For insight into intra-Administration (and intra-military) debates over policy and decisions that left U.S. forces with only modest levels of arms, see both Barton Gellman, "The Words Behind a Deadly Decision," *Washington Post* (October 31, 1993), pp. A1, A20, and Michael R. Gordon, "U.S. Officers were Divided on Somali Raid," *New York Times* (May 13, 1994), p. A8.

35. The full text of President Clinton's October 7 "Address to the Nation on Somalia" is reprinted in *Weekly Compilation of Presidential Documents*, Vol. 29, No. 40 (October 11, 1993), pp. 2022–25.

36. For a description of the pull-out of U.S. forces (as well as a useful summary what took place before), see Donatella Lorch, "What Began as a Mission of Mercy Closes with Little Ceremony," *New York Times* (March 26, 1994), pp. 1–2.

37. For useful background, see Donald E. Schulz and Gabriel Marcella, *Reconciling the Irreconcilable: The Troubled Outlook for U.S. Policy Toward Haiti* (Carlisle Barracks, Pa.: Strategic Studies Institute of the U.S. Army War College, 1994), and Ian Martin, "Haiti: Mangled Multilateralism," *Foreign Policy,* No. 95 (Summer 1994), pp. 72–89. Also see Dick Kirschten, "Haitian Headache," *National Journal* (March 13, 1993), pp. 620–24; Domingo E. Acevedo, "The Haitian Crisis and the OAS Response: A Test of Effectiveness in Protecting Democracy," in Damrosch (ed.), *op. cit.,* pp. 119–55; and Lawrence E. Harrison, "Voodoo Politics," *Atlantic*, Vol. 271, No. 6 (June 1993), pp. 101–07. The best descriptions of the evolution and making of U.S. policy under the Clinton Administration are Elaine Sciolino, "Failure on Haiti: How U.S. Hopes Faded," *New York Times* (April 29, 1994), pp. A1, A12, and Brian Duffy, "A Question of Options," *U.S. News* (May 23, 1994), pp. 26–30. Also see Eric Schmitt, "U.S. Making Moves for Haiti Action," *New York Times* (July 15, 1994), pp. A1, A6.

CHAPTER THREE

1. Alexander L. George and Richard Smoke, *Deterrence in American Foreign Policy: Theory and Practice* (New York: Columbia University Press, 1974), p. 11.

2. See Boutros Boutros-Ghali, *Agenda For Peace* (New York: United Nations, 1992), pp. 16–17.

3. Robert J. Art, "The Four Functions of Force," in Robert J. Art and Kenneth N. Waltz (eds.), *The Use of Force: Military Power and International Politics,* Fourth Edition (Lanham, Md.: University Press of America, 1993), p. 6.

4. Thomas C. Schelling, *Arms and Influence* (New Haven: Yale University Press, 1966), p. 72.

5. Scott D. Sagan, "From Deterrence to Coercion to War: The Road to Pearl Harbor," in Alexander L. George and William E. Simons (eds.), *The Limits of Coercive Diplomacy* (Boulder: Westview, 1994), p. 84.

6. See Alexander George, "The Cuban Missile Crisis: Peaceful Resolution Through Coercive Diplomacy," esp. pp. 124–25, and Bruce W. Jentleson, "The Reagan Administration Versus Nicaragua: The Limits of 'Type C' Coercive Diplomacy," esp. pp. 176–80, in George and Simons, *op. cit.* Also see Barry M. Blechman and Stephen S. Kaplan, *Force Without War: U.S. Armed Forces as a Political Instrument* (Washington: Brookings Institution, 1978).

7. James Cable, *Gunboat Diplomacy* (London: Chatto & Windus, 1971), p. 21.

8. A good short introduction to the subject is Brian Urquhart, "Beyond the 'Sheriff's Posse,'" *Survival,* Vol. 32, No. 3 (May/June, 1990), pp. 196–205.

9. William J. Durch and Barry M. Blechman, *Keeping the Peace: The United Nations in the Emerging World Order* (Washington: Stimson Center, 1992), p. ii.

10. See John Mackinlay, "Powerful Peace-Keepers," *Survival,* Vol. 32, No. 3 (May/June 1990), pp. 241–50.

11. Marjorie Ann Browne, *United Nations Peacekeeping Operations 1988–1993: Background Information* (Washington: Congressional Research Service, 1993).

12. For additional background on peacekeeping and how it has evolved, see William J. Durch, *The Evolution of U.N. Peacekeeping: Case Studies and Comparative Analysis* (New York: St. Martins, 1993); *The Blue Helmets: A Review of United Nations Peacekeeping* (New York: United Nations, 1990); Marrack Goulding, "The Evolution of UN Peacekeeping," *International*

Affairs, Vol. 69, No. 3 (July 1993), pp. 451–64; Mats R. Berdal, *Whither U.N. Peacekeeping?* (London: International Institute for Strategic Studies, 1993); and Dick Kirschten, "Missions Impossible," *National Journal* (October 30, 1993), pp. 2576–80.

13. See, for example, Michael Lind, "Peacefaking," *New Republic,* Vol. 209, No. 19 (November 8, 1993), pp. 14–17.

14. See Barry R. McCaffrey, "U.S. Military Support for Peacekeeping Operations," in Dennis J. Quinn (ed.), *Peace Support Operations and the U.S. Military* (Washington: National Defense University Press, 1994), p. 5.

15. See Ghali, *op. cit.,* pp. 20–25.

16. The Joint Chiefs of Staff defines environments as *permissive,* "in which host country military and law enforcement agencies have control and the intent and capability to assist operations that a unit intends to conduct;" *uncertain,* "in which host government forces, whether opposed to or receptive to operations that a unit intends to conduct, do not have totally effective control of the territory and population in the intended area of operations;" or *hostile,* "in which hostile forces have control and the intent and capability to effectively oppose or react to the operations a unit intends to conduct." See *Department of Defense Dictionary, op.cit.,* p. 275.

17. John Gerard Ruggie, "Wandering in the Void: Charting the U.N.'s New Strategic Role," *Foreign Affairs,* Vol. 72, No. 5 (November/December 1993), p. 28.

18. See Gerald B. Helman and Steven R. Ratner, "Saving Failed States," *Foreign Policy,* No. 89 (Winter 1992–93), pp. 3–20. The authors advocate re-creating U.N. trusteeships for failed states, using less tainted terms such as conservatorship or guardianship.

19. For background on the Liberia operation, see T.W. Parker, "Operation Sharp Edge," *U.S. Naval Institute Proceedings,* Vol. 117, No. 5 (May 1991), pp. 102–06. For background on the Liberian situation more generally, see David Wippman, "Enforcing the Peace: ECOWAS and the Liberian Civil War," in Damrosch (ed.), *op. cit.,* pp. 157–203.

CHAPTER FOUR

1. "To the Victors, the Spoils—and the Headaches," *Economist,* Vol. 320, No. 7726 (September 28, 1991), p. 24.

2. Hans Morgenthau, *American Foreign Policy: A Critical Examination* (London: Methuen & Co., 1952), p. 117.

3. Alexander L. George, "Domestic Constraints on Regime Change in U.S. Foreign Policy: The Need for Political Legitimacy," in Ole R. Holsti, Randolph M. Siverson, and Alexander L. George (eds.), *Change in the International System* (Boulder: Westview, 1980), p. 234.

4. Colin L. Powell, "U.S. Forces," *op.cit.,* p. 40.

5. Samuel P. Huntington, "Playing to Win," *National Interest,* No. 3 (Spring 1986), pp. 15–16.

6. For some fascinating insight into Japanese thinking at the time, see Fred Charles Ikle, *Every War Must End* (New York: Columbia University Press, 1971), p. 3. Also see Scott D. Sagan, "From Deterrence to Coercion to War: The Road to Pearl Harbor," in George and Simons (eds.), *op. cit.,* pp. 57–90. This is an excellent essay in an excellent volume.

7. Clausewitz, *op. cit.,* pp. 585–86.

8. The address, titled "The Ethics of Power" and delivered by then-Secretary of State George P. Shultz at Yeshiva University in New York on December 9, 1984, is reprinted in *Department of State Bulletin,* Vol. 85, No. 2095 (February 1985), pp. 1–3.

9. The sixty-day period can be extended for an additional thirty days in order to bring forces out of the theater. The text of the War Powers Resolution is reprinted here in Appendix B. For background on its provisions and implementation, see Ellen C. Collier, *The War Powers Resolution: Twenty Years of Experience* (Washington: Congressional Research Service, 1994). For one set of contributions on this controversial subject, see Gary M. Stern and Morton H. Halperin (eds.), *The U.S. Constitution and The Power to Go To War* (Westport: Greenwood Press, 1994).

10. *The Gulf War: Military Lessons Learned* (Washington: Center for Strategic and International Studies, July 1991), p. 42. On the lessons of Gulf War deterrence, see Janice Gross Stein, "Deterrence and Compellence in the Gulf, 1990–91: A Failed or Impossible Task?" *International Security,* Vol. 17, No. 2 (Fall 1992), pp. 147–79. Stein answers her own question about pre-August 2 deterrence by concluding that although the United States made mistakes in not communicating its intentions clearly, deterrence may well have been an impossible task because of Saddam's mindset.

11. John J. Mearsheimer, *Conventional Deterrence* (Ithaca: Cornell University Press, 1983), pp. 206–07.

12. Jack S. Levy, "Quantitative Studies of Deterrence Success and Failure," in Paul C. Stern, Robert Axelrod, Robert Jervis, and Roy Radner (eds.), *Perspectives on Deterrence* (New York: Oxford University Press, 1989), p. 100.

13. Paul Huth and Bruce Russett, "What Makes Deterrence Work: Cases from 1900 to 1980," *World Politics,* Vol. 36, No. 4 (July 1984), pp. 496–526.

14. For some background, see Steve Vogel, "U.S. Peacekeeping Troops in Macedonia Beefing Up Presence," *Washington Post* (May 17, 1994), p. A14.

15. Laurence Martin, "Peacekeeping as a Growth Industry," *National Interest,* No. 32 (Summer 1993), p. 7. For another skeptical view of the wisdom of intervening in internal conflicts, at least until they have largely burned themselves out, see S. J. Stedman, "The New Interventionists," *Foreign Affairs,* Vol. 72, No. 1 (Winter 1992–93), pp. 1–16.

16. See Charles William Maynes, "Containing Ethnic Conflict," *Foreign Policy,* No. 90 (Spring 1993), pp. 3–21, as well as Kamal S. Shehadi, *Ethnic Self-Determination and the Break-up of States* (London: International Institute for Strategic Studies, 1993).

17. See the chapter by John Shy on Jomini in Peter Paret (ed.), *Makers of Modern Strategy, op. cit.,* pp. 143–85, esp. pp. 170–71.

18. For similar conclusions, see both Charles Krauthammer, "Intervention Lite: Foreign Policy by CNN," *Washington Post* (February 18, 1994), p. A25, and Jessica Mathews, "Policy vs. TV," *Washington Post* (March 8, 1994), p. A19. For a prediction that viewers may be growing increasingly numb to the impact of televised pictures, see Walter Goodman, "Diminishing Returns in Misery Race," *New York Times* (August 19, 1993), p. B4.

19. For a similar conclusion, see Catherine M. Kelleher, "Soldiering On," *Brookings Review* (Spring 1994), pp. 26–29. For a fascinating discussion of this issue, see Committee on Foreign Affairs, House of Representatives, *Impact of Television on U.S. Foreign Policy* (Washington: U.S. Government Printing Office, 1994). The witnesses are Ted Koppel of ABC, Ed Turner of CNN, and the historian Michael Beschloss.

CHAPTER FIVE

1. David Fisher, "The Ethics of Intervention," *Survival,* Vol. 36, No. 1 (Spring 1994), p. 54. This is an important article that finds in the just war criteria grounds for using military force in many instances where intervention has been delayed or ruled out.

2. See, for example, Anthony Lewis, "A Lesson Too Late," *New York Times* (March 4, 1994), p. A27.

3. Samuel P. Huntington, *op. cit.,* p. 15. In the article, Huntington lists five principles that ought to guide American use of force: interventions designed to be as short as possible; operational plans to emphasize the offensive; the exploitation of high technology; use of overpowering force; and using military force to achieve military objectives, i.e., goals they are suited for.

4. Colin Powell is quoted arguing precisely this point, that a massive use of force is less risky for all involved, during planning for the Panama operation. See Woodward, *op. cit.,* p. 168.

5. Clausewitz, *op. cit.,* p. 598.

6. See Robert Osgood, *Limited War Revisited, op. cit.,* p. 48.

7. AWACS stands for Airborne Warning and Control System; JSTARS for Joint Surveillance Target Attack Radar System.

8. For a discussion of what the Gulf War revealed about the limits and potential for high technology, see Jeffrey McCausland, *The Gulf Conflict: A Military Analysis* (London: International Institute for Strategic Studies, 1993), pp. 62–64, and Les Aspin and William Dickinson, *Defense For a New Era: Lessons of the Persian Gulf War* (Washington: U.S. Government Printing Office for the Committee on Armed Services, House of Representatives, 1992).

9. For the flavor of this intense and at times bitter debate, see Theodore A. Postol, "Lessons of the Gulf War Experience with Patriot," *International Security,* Vol. 16, No. 3 (Winter 1991/92), pp. 119–71, and the correspondence between Postol and Robert M. Stein in *International Security,* Vol. 17, No. 1 (Summer 1992), pp. 199–240.

10. Department of Defense, *Conduct of the Persian Gulf War* (Washington: U.S. Government Printing Office, 1992), p. 181.

11. See Thomas A. Keaney and Eliot A. Cohen, *Gulf War Air Power Survey: Summary Report* (Washington: U.S. Government Printing Office, 1993) and James A. Winnefeld, Preston Niblack, and Dana J. Johnson, *A League of*

Airmen: U.S. Air Power in the Gulf War (Santa Monica: RAND, 1994).

12. Stanley Hoffmann, "Out of the Cold: Humanitarian Intervention in the 1990s," *Harvard International Review,* Vol. 16, No. 1 (Fall 1993), p. 9.

13. *Ibid.,* p. 62.

14. Michael Mandelbaum, "The Reluctance to Intervene," *Foreign Policy,* No. 95 (Summer 1994), p. 4.

15. Robert Cooper and Mats Berdal expand on this critical point and are worth quoting at length: "External interventions may succeed when goals are . . . based on well-defined national interests. In such cases, the intervening country will take sides and may be prepared for a long haul . . . In a more limited way, outside intervention can succeed when its objectives are to provide humanitarian assistance or to limit the scope of a conflict. What does not succeed is a confusion of the two. International forces can operate on the margin of consent obtainable among local actors . . . Alternatively, they can seek to *impose* a solution by military means. However, the two are different operations requiring different levels of commitment, different military deployments and different rules of engagement." See Robert Cooper and Mats Berdal, "Outside Intervention in Ethnic Conflicts," *Survival,* Vol. 35, No. 1 (Spring 1993), p. 138. Hans Morgenthau, writing nearly thirty years ago, makes a similar point. "Intervention must either be brutally direct in order to overcome resistance or it must be surreptitious in order to be acceptable, or the two extremes may be combined." See Hans J. Morgenthau, "To Intervene or Not to Intervene?" *Foreign Affairs,* Vol. 45, No. 3 (April 1967), p. 429.

CHAPTER 6

1. *Rescue Mission Report* (Washington: Joint Chiefs of Staff, 1980). This is not a universal view. One participant in the decision-making process told me he advised against the mission on the grounds that it was too difficult. In his view, logistical considerations precluded surprise and successful escape was highly unlikely. His bottom line: the disaster at Desert One saved the United States from a far greater tragedy in Tehran.

2. *Ibid.,* p. 33.

3. The best discussions of military alternatives are Gary Sick, "Military Options and Constraints," in Christopher, et. al., *op.cit.*, and Zbigniew Brzezinski, *Power and Principle: Memoirs of the National Security Adviser 1977–1981* (New York: Farrar, Straus, Giroux, 1985), pp. 470–500.

4. *Report of the DOD Commission on Beirut International Airport Terrorist Act, October 23, 1983* (Washington: U.S. Department of Defense, 1983), p. 41.

5. See Carla Anne Robbins, "As U.S. Looks at Haiti, Its Invasion of Panama Shows Limited Results," *Wall Street Journal* (August 3, 1994), pp. A1, A4.

6. An article appearing after the war argued that it met all six of Weinberger's guidelines regarding whether and how to intervene. Few situations in the future are likely to be so clear cut. See Thomas R. Dubois, "The Weinberger Doctrine and the Liberation of Kuwait," *Parameters*, Vol. 21, No. 4 (Winter 1991–92), pp. 24–38.

7. The Administration created some of its own difficulties by its overheated rhetoric that encouraged Iraqis to rise up against Saddam. It should be noted, however, that such language was the exception to a pattern of articulating more limited aims and that it was stated at a time in the crisis when Iraqis still had the chance to avoid a devastating war. It was not reinforced by private communications to the Iraqi opposition.

8. Two who claim that the United States ought to have pursued a policy of "occupation and pacification" are Robert W. Tucker and David C. Hendrickson. See their *The Imperial Temptation: The New World Order and America's Purpose* (New York: Council on Foreign Relations, 1992). Interestingly, much of the first half of the book is taken up with arguing that the United States should have stuck with sanctions and not gone to war in the first place.

9. The Bush Administration hurt itself by adhering too long to a policy that discouraged contacts with Iraqi opposition figures. Regular consultations with leading opposition figures inside and outside of Iraq would have provided the United States with a better understanding of their thinking and likely behavior and possibly provided U.S. officials with an opportunity to influence both.

10. See Julia Preston, "U.N. Moves Toward a New Role in Somalia," *Washington Post* (February 5, 1994), p. A14.

11. One who advocated such an approach is Walter S. Clarke, "Testing the World's Resolve in Somalia," *Parameters*, Vol. 23, No. 4 (Winter 1993–94), 42–58.

12. See Caleb Carr, "The Humanitarian Illusion," *New York Times* (September 16, 1993), p. A23.

13. Proof that the assessment of interests was no easy exercise can be found in the inconsistency of key observers. For example, in February 1993, Secretary of State Warren Christopher stated: "This conflict [in Bosnia] may be far from our shores, but it is not distant to our concerns . . . The continuing destruction of a new U.N. member state challenges the principle that internationally recognized borders should not be altered by force . . . The world's response to the violence in the former Yugoslavia is an early and crucial test of how it will address the critical concerns of ethnic and religious minorities in the post–Cold War world. The question reaches throughout Eastern Europe. It reaches to the states of the former Soviet Union . . . and it reaches to other continents as well." Contrast this with his remarks only months later on November 4, 1993, when Bosnia was not one of the six foreign policy priorities of the United States. Christopher's February 10, 1993, statement is reprinted in *U.S. Department of State Dispatch*, Vol. 4, No. 7 (February 15, 1993), pp. 81–2; his later remarks are in *Dispatch*, Vol. 4, No. 47 (November 22, 1993), pp. 797–802.

14. To get a feel for this debate, see Jeanne J. Kirkpatrick and Morton I. Abramowitz, "Lift the Embargo," *New York Times* (April 20, 1994), p. A19, and, on the other side, Claiborne Pell and Lee. H. Hamilton, "Don't Arm Bosnia," *New York Times* (May 5, 1994), p. A27.

15. A policy along these lines has been advocated by Richard Burt and Richard Perle. See their article, "The Next Act in Bosnia," *New York Times* (February 11, 1994), p. A35.

16. Gidon Gottlieb, *Nation Against State: New Approaches to Ethnic Conflicts and the Decline of Sovereignty* (New York: Council on Foreign Relations, 1993), p. 119. Also see "What the West Must Do in Bosnia," the text of an open letter to President Clinton signed by 100 prominent international figures including Margaret Thatcher and George Shultz, published in the *Wall Street Journal* (September 2, 1993), p. A12.

17. Even the military experts were divided on the question of what air power could accomplish. See Elaine Sciolino, "U.S. Military Split on Using Air Power Against the Serbs," *New York Times* (April 29, 1993), pp. A1, A6.

18. One advocate of a large-scale peace-making effort in Bosnia is John Steinbrunner. See his "The Quagmire of Caution," *Washington Post* (April 25, 1993), pp. C1, C4. Others, arguing that the ten-canton Vance-Owen plan was too complex to enforce, put forth a simplified partition plan of only four units. This would require considerable transfers of population and require massive

Western forces both to bring it about and to enforce it. See John J. Mearsheimer and Robert A. Pape, "The Answer," *New Republic*, Vol. 208, No. 24 (June 14, 1993), pp. 22–28.

19. The assessment of John Collins is worth considering in this regard: "Opportunities to apply U.S. and allied military power swiftly as well as decisively appear to be rare. Former Yugoslavia contains few target concentrations similar to those that centered on Baghdad. There are no clear military centers of gravity, such as Saddam Hussein's Republican Guard, against which to focus U.N./U.S. offensive efforts. Fluid movement by large land forces is infeasible anywhere, except on the northern plain. Potential opponents specialize in hit-and-run raids, ambushes, sabotage, hostage-taking, and terrorism, rather than traditional tactics that pit attackers and defenders head-to-head. Protracted operations, in short, seem more likely than swift, clean victory for either side, regardless of conflict intensity." See John M. Collins, *Balkan Battlegrounds: U.S. Military Alternatives* (Washington: Congressional Research Service, 1992), p. 14.

20. The problem with the safe-haven approach ultimately adopted (besides being too little, too late) is that the zones were too "soft"—Serbian military action continued unpunished—and what punishment there was proved to be far too modest. Also, it was unfortunate that the whole approach was tainted by simultaneous pressuring of the Bosnian Muslims to accept a permanent territorial settlement that they and many others viewed as illegitimate.

21. See his speech to the International Institute for Strategic Studies delivered in Brussels, September 10, 1993.

22. It is worth noting here the January 6, 1994 open letter to President Clinton sent by the Action Council for Peace in the Balkans. The authors, individuals of considerable prominence known for their pro-Bosnian, pro-interventionist stance, called for arming the Bosnians, a phased withdrawal of the U.N. forces on the ground carrying out humanitarian missions, and NATO air cover of Bosnian-conducted relief efforts.

23. On the question of flawed Bosnian diplomacy, see Edward Mortimer, "What We Should Have Done," *Financial Times* (January 6, 1993), p. 8. Also see David Gompert, "How to Defeat Serbia," *Foreign Affairs*, Vol. 73, No. 4 (July/August 1994), pp. 30–43. On the larger questions raised, see Amitai Etzioni, "The Evils of Self-Determination," *Foreign Policy*, No. 89 (Winter 1992–93), pp. 21–35, and Joseph S. Nye, Jr., "The Self-Determination Trap," *Washington Post* (December 15, 1992), p. A23.

24. See Susan L. Woodward, "Yugoslavia: Divide and Fail," *Bulletin of the Atomic Scientists,* Vol. 49., No. 9 (November 1993), esp. p. 26. Also see A. M. Rosenthal, "Bosnia: The Real Lessons," *New York Times* (February 22, 1994), p. A15.

25. The Clinton Administration began seeking such a resolution in July 1994. See Douglas Jehl, "Clinton Seeks U.N. Approval of Any Plan to Invade Haiti," *New York Times* (July 22, 1994), pp. A1, A8. U.N. receptivity to such an approach is strongly suggested in a report by Secretary General Boutros Boutros-Ghali in which he all but called for a U.N.-authorized invasion of Haiti followed up by either a U.N.-authorized or U.N.-conducted nation-building phase. See *Report of the Secretary-General on the United Nations Mission in Haiti* (New York: U.N. Document S/1994/828, 15 July 1994). The full text of Resolution 940 is printed in *New York Times* (August 1, 1994), p. A6.

26. Speaking on May 19, 1994, President Clinton listed six U.S, interests at stake. In addition to immigration and democracy, he mentioned proximity, drugs, the American community in Haiti, and the large number of Haitians living in the United States. See Douglas Jehl, "Clinton Explains Why He Might Use U.S. Army in Haiti," *New York Times* (May 20, 1994), pp. A1–2.

27. Examples of those sympathetic to an intervention include Randall Robinson, "Operation Island Storm?" *Washington Post* (May 15, 1994), pp. C1–2, and John Kerry, "Making Haiti's Thugs Tremble," *New York Times* (May 16, 1994), p. A17. For some dissenting views, see Thomas Carothers, "The Making of a Fiasco," *New York Times* (May 12, 1994), p. A25; Bob Dole, "Should U.S. Send Troops into Haiti?" *Washington Times* (May 15, 1994), p. B1; John R. Bolton, "The Case for Not Invading Haiti," *Washington Post* (May 17, 1994), p. A17; George F. Will, "Another Splendid Little Adventure," *Washington Post* (May 29, 1994), p. C7; and Brent Scowcroft and Eric D.K. Melby, "Invade Haiti? A Sure Way to Make a Bad Policy Worse," *New York Times* (June 1, 1994), p. A21. On sealing the Dominican border, see Ronald V. Dellums, "Squeeze the Dominican Republic," *New York Times* (July 24, 1994), p. E15. For a different (indirect) approach, see William Safire, "For a Haitian Legion," *New York Times* (May 9, 1994), p. A17. On the question of arranging international support for and participation in an invasion, see Howard W. French, "U.S. Hint of Force to End Haiti Crisis Draws Opposition," *New York Times* (May 13, 1994), pp. A1, A8; Steven Greenhouse,

"Governments are Joining Haiti Force," *New York Times* (June 8, 1994), p. A15; Elaine Sciolino, "Large Haiti Force is Weighed by U.S.," *New York Times* (June 25, 1994), pp. 1,6; and Bradley Graham, "Somalia Experience Haunts Pentagon Planning for Haiti Peacekeeping," *Washington Post* (July 12, 1994), p. A10.

CHAPTER 7

1. For a thoughtful examination of this matter, see Hedley Bull, *The Anarchical Society: A Study of Order in World Politics* (New York: Columbia University Press, 1977), esp. ch. 4.

2. See, for example, Charles Krauthammer, "The Lonely Superpower," *New Republic,* Vol. 205, No. 5 (July 29, 1991), pp. 23–27.

3. The most influential work on this question is that of Michael W. Doyle. See his "Kant, Liberal Legacies, and Foreign Affairs," *Philosophy and Public Affairs,* Vol. 12, No. 3 (Summer 1983), pp. 205–35, and Vol. 12, No. 4 (Fall 1983), pp. 323–53.

4. Some recent examples of the minimalist school include Christopher Layne and Benjamin Schwartz, "American Hegemony—Without an Enemy," *Foreign Policy,* No. 92 (Fall 1993), pp. 5–23; Alan Tonelson, "What is the National Interest?" *Atlantic,* Vol. 26, No. 1 (July 1991), pp. 35–52; Jonathan Clarke, "America, Know Thyself," *National Interest,* No. 34 (Winter 1993/94), pp. 19–25; and Doug Bandow, "Keeping the Troops and the Money at Home," *Current History,* Vol. 93, No. 579 (January 1994), pp. 8–13.

5. The original champion of this point of view was Paul Kennedy. See his *The Rise and Fall of the Great Powers: Economic Change and Military Conflict from 1500 to 2000* (New York: Random House, 1989). For a shorter and more recent example, see William G. Hyland, "Downgrade Foreign Policy," *New York Times* (May 20, 1991), p. A15. In reality, many minimalists are also declinists and favor using the resources saved for domestic public investment. Some minimalists—of a more conservative stripe—oppose such investment or simply want it spent on prisons rather than schools.

6. For criticisms of the declinists, see Richard Haass, "The Use (and Mainly Abuse) of History," *ORBIS,* Vol. 32, No. 3 (Summer 1988), pp. 411–19, and

Samuel Huntington, "The U.S.—Decline or Renewal?" *Foreign Affairs,* Vol. 67, No. 2 (Winter 1988–89), pp. 77–96. For an overview of this debate, see Charles A. Kupchan, "Empire, Military Power, and Economic Decline," *International Security,* Vol. 13, No. 4 (Spring 1989), pp. 36–53.

7. On the question of both retaliation in kind and strategic conventional options, see Eric Schmitt, "Head of Nuclear Forces Plans for a New World," *New York Times* (February 25, 1993), p. B7.

8. For background, see *Ballistic Missile Defense: Evolution and Current Issues* (Washington: U.S. General Accounting Office, July 1993), esp. pp. 43–49.

9. See Michael Walzer, *Just and Unjust Wars: A Moral Argument with Historical Illustrations* (New York: Basic Books, 1977), pp. 74–85.

10. The most comprehensive public statement of the Clinton Administration's thinking about the Korean problem is by Secretary of Defense William Perry. See his remarks to the Asia Society in Washington, D.C., on May 3, 1994, reprinted in *U.S. Department of State Dispatch,* Vol. 5, No. 19 (May 9, 1994), pp. 275–79.

11. Charles William Maynes, "A Workable Clinton Doctrine," *Foreign Policy,* No. 93 (Winter 1993–94), p. 13.

12. For background on the situation and U.S. policy, see Julia Preston, "Rwandans Confound U.N. Security Council," *Washington Post* (May 8, 1994), p.A25, and Paul Lewis, "U.S. Opposes Plan for U.N. Force in Rwanda," *New York Times* (May 12, 1994), p. A9. For an argument against intervention, see "Why Not Rwanda?" *New Republic* (May 16, 1994), p. 7. For a call to establish a safe haven, see Charles Krauthammer, "Stop the Genocide in Rwanda," *Washington Post* (May 27, 1994), p. A25. A strong criticism of Clinton Administration policy is Herman Cohen's "Getting Rwanda Wrong," *Washington Post* (June 3, 1994), p. A23. Also see Douglas Jehl, "U.S. Policy: A Mistake?" *New York Times* (July 23, 1994), pp. 1, 5.

13. Walzer, *op. cit.,* p. 86.

14. Pierre Hassner, "Beyond Nationalism and Internationalism: Ethnicity and World Order," *Survival,* Vol. 35, No. 2 (Summer 1993), p. 61.

15. One defense of the single half war approach is Michael E. O'Hanlon, *The Art of War in the Age of Force: U.S. Military Posture for the Post–Cold War World* (Westport: Praeger, 1992).

16. See Barton Gellman and John Lancaster, "U.S. May Drop 2-War Capability," *Washington Post* (June 17, 1993), pp. A1, A16.

17. For representative criticism, see Dov S. Zakheim, "A New Name for Winning: Losing," *New York Times* (June 19, 1993), p. 21. For the flavor of the debate, see Eric Schmitt, "Cost-Minded Lawmakers Are Challenging a 2-War Doctrine," *New York Times* (March 10, 1994), p. A22.

18. See *Future Years Defense Program: Optimistic Estimates Lead to Billions in Overprogramming* (Washington: General Accounting Office, July 1994). Not everyone agrees with this judgment. For some examples of those who argue that the United States is still spending too much on defense, see Lawrence J. Korb, "Shock Therapy for the Pentagon," *New York Times* (February 15, 1994), p. A21, and the editorial board of the *New York Times*, "More Is the Pity at the Pentagon," (February 9, 1994), p. A20. Also see Andrew F. Krepinevich, *The Bottom-Up Review: An Assessment* (Washington: Defense Budget Project, 1994).

19. On this point see Eliot A. Cohen, "Beyond 'Bottom Up'," *National Review*, Vol. 45, No. 22 (November 15, 1993), pp. 40–43. Also see *Report of the Defense Science Board Task Force on Readiness* (Washington: Department of Defense, June 1994).

20. See *Field Manual 100–5, op. cit.,* p. 13-1.

21. For discussion of this issue, see John H. Henshaw, "Forces for Peacekeeping, Peace Enforcement, and Humanitarian Missions," in Barry M. Blechman, et. al. (eds.), *The American Military in the Twenty-First Century* (New York: St. Martin's Press, 1993), pp. 397–430, and John P. Abizaid and John R. Wood, "Preparing for Peacekeeping: Military Training and the Peacekeeping Environment," *Special Warfare*, Vol. 7, No. 2 (April 1994), pp. 14–20.

22. A different version of concerned nations has been put forward by Charles William Maynes, who suggests looking to regional powers with both the inclination and strength to intervene to sort out their neighbors; see "A Workable Clinton Doctrine," *op. cit.,* pp. 3–20. Maynes would discipline this approach — one that he terms "benign realpolitik" but might be more simply defined as "regional policemen"—by requiring U.N. or regional authorization as a prerequisite. The problem with this is that no state will accept such a constraint when its national interests are at stake. The United States should think twice before it encourages such spheres of influence, which are all too easily abused.

23. For a criticism of this approach, see "Global Gunslinger, Global Cops, *New Yorker,* Vol. 68, No. 47 (January 11, 1993), pp. 4–5.

24. Support for this idea is expressed by Richard N. Gardner, "Collective Security and the 'New World Order': What Role for the United Nations?" in *Two Views on the Issue of Collective Security* (Washington: U.S. Institute of Peace, 1992), pp. 1–17; Gregory Harper, "Creating a U.N. Peace Enforcement Force: A Case for U.S. Leadership," *Fletcher Forum of World Affairs*, Vol. 18, No. 1 (Winter/Spring 1994), pp. 49–63; and in Final Report of the United States Commission on Improving the Effectiveness of the United Nations, *Defining Purpose: The U.N. and the Health of Nations* (September 1993). This report also favors creating a 5,000–10,000 person standing U.N. force.

25. Some steps are being taken in this direction. See Eric Schmitt, "15 Nations Offer Troops for U.N. Force of 54,000," *New York Times* (April 13, 1994), p. A12.

26. Proposals for a U.N. legion include Brian Urquhart, "For a U.N. Volunteer Military Force," *New York Review of Books,* Vol. 40, No. 11 (June 10, 1993), pp. 3–4, and Edward Luttwak, "Unconventional Force," *New Republic,* Vol. 208, No. 4 (January 25, 1993), pp. 22–23. Also see the two exchanges on the issue (subsequent to the Urquhart piece) in *New York Review of Books,* Vol. 40, No. 12 (June 24, 1993), and Vol. 40, No. 13 (July 15, 1993). See also Urquhart's "Whose Fight Is It?" *New York Times* (May 22, 1994), p. 15.

27. For some recommendations for U.N. reform, see "Heart of Gold, Limbs of Clay," *Economist* (June 12, 1993), pp. 21–24; "United Nations Peacekeeping: Trotting to the Rescue," *Economist* (June 25, 1994), pp. 19–22; the September 21, 1992, address by George Bush to the U.N. General Assembly, reprinted in *Weekly Compilation of Presidential Documents,* Vol. 28, No. 39 (September 28, 1992), pp. 1698–99; *Peacekeeping and the U.S. National Interest* (Washington: Stimson Center Report No. 11, 1994); and *The Clinton Administration's Policy on Reforming Multilateral Peace Operations,* reprinted in Appendix H of this volume.

28. See, for example, Eric Schmitt, "Bosnia Peace Move May Bring U.S. Commitment," *New York Times* (July 18, 1994), p. A2.

29. For a critical discussion of U.S. participation in such missions, see Mats R. Berdal, "Fateful Encounter: The United States and U.N. Peacekeeping," *Survival,* Vol. 36, No. 1 (Spring 1994). Also see Mark M. Lowenthal, *Peacekeeping in Future U.S. Foreign Policy* (Washington: Congressional Research Service, 1994).

30. Morton Halperin, "Guaranteeing Democracy," *Foreign Policy*, No. 91

(Summer 1993), p. 120. Halperin does include an exception that would allow the United States to act without a U.N. or regional mandate under the self-defense clause (Article 51) of the U.N. Charter.

31. For this same reason, advocates of humanitarian intervention should support it on its merits and not stretch the facts to make a case that a given situation warrants outside intervention because it poses a threat to international peace and security as required by the U.N. Charter.

ACKNOWLEDGMENTS

This is my fifth book, or sixth if one counts a volume I edited years ago with Albert Carnesale. If I have learned one thing as a result, it is that it is impossible to produce a book alone. Inevitably, many people provide assistance along the way. This is my chance to thank them.

I want to begin with Morton Abramowitz, President of the Carnegie Endowment for International Peace. Mort generously provided me a home after I left government. Once I arrived, he tolerated my getting involved in a host of enterprises while quietly encouraging me not to lose sight of this one. I also appreciate his pointed reactions to successive if not always successful drafts of this book.

Others at Carnegie also made a real difference. Edward (Ted) Amley and Sonia Katyal deserve pride of place here. Carnegie interns, they did yeoman work in providing background for case studies and in chasing down sources. The library staff—Jennifer Little, Susan Hanafin, and Christopher Henley—not only managed to find what I asked for but often identified useful items that I hadn't even known to request. Liz Jasper assisted in ways big and small and helped compile the appendices.

I want to express personal thanks to the members of the study group that read the manuscript in draft and met at Carnegie one day to rake me over the coals. Ably led by C. William Maynes, the group included Morton Abramowitz, James Dobbins, Michael Gordon, Morton Halperin, Jim Hoagland, Joseph Nye Jr., and Larry Smith. Anyone who knows these people will understand immediately that I have been more than fortunate to have critics such as these.

The same draft was also reviewed by Mark Danner, Leslie Gelb, Gidon Gottlieb, Daniel Kaufman, Charles Kupchan, Edward Luck,

Michael Oppenheimer, and Fareed Zakaria, all of whom participated in a second study group assembled in New York by Nicholas
Rizopoulos of the Council on Foreign Relations. To each of them,
I owe my sincere thanks, both for the quantity of time and the
quality of thought.

I also want to thank the others—Richard Betts, L. Paul Bremer,
Lynne Davidson, Alexander George, Gen. Joseph Hoar, Robert
Murray, Brent Scowcroft, and Lt. Gen. John Sheehan—who read
drafts of this manuscript and took the time to let me know what
they thought, often in considerable detail. Fred Cuny and Samantha Power critiqued the sections on the former Yugoslavia; Ian
Martin did the same for Haiti. Bruce Riedel commented on sections dealing with the Middle East and Persian Gulf. Again, the final result is much better for the help of all these people.

In the course of researching and writing this book, I benefitted
from the opportunity to attend conferences at other institutions that
touched on some of the subjects written about here. Most helpful was
a week spent at the Aspen Institute in summer 1993. I also want to
express my thanks to the Stanley Foundation, the Rand Corporation,
and the Olin Institute at Harvard University, which provided venues
for me to try out these thoughts while they were still tentative.

No book can ever be completed without editing and production
help. The copy editing of Rosemarie Philips saved me (as well as the
reader) from myself. Shane Green was good enough to go over the
manuscript and suggest where less could be more. Robert Wiser and
Lisa Markowitz did first rate design. Michael O'Hare was the able
shepherd of this production. To one and all goes deep appreciation.

Last, I want to thank my family: Susan for her support, Francesca
for her arrival, and Samuel Haass (to whom this book is dedicated)
for his motivation. Upon learning from his mother that his father
spent his time writing books, Sam would greet me at the end of the
day with the question, "All done Daddy?" For too long I had to
mumble "Not yet." It is nice to be able to answer "Yes."

Richard Haass
Washington, D.C.
August 1994

INDEX

THE BROOKINGS INSTITUTION

The Brookings Institution is an independent organization devoted to non-partisan research, education, and publication in economics, government, foreign policy, and the social sciences generally. Its principal purposes are to aid in the development of sound public policies and to promote public understanding of issues of national importance. The Institution was founded on December 8, 1927, to merge the activities of the Institute for Government Research, founded in 1916, the Institute of Economics, founded in 1922, and the Robert Brookings Graduate School of Economics and Government, founded in 1924.

The Institution maintains a position of neutrality on issues of public policy to safeguard the intellectual freedom of the staff. Interpretations or conclusions in Brookings publications should be understood to be solely those of the authors.

CARNEGIE ENDOWMENT FOR INTERNATIONAL PEACE

The Carnegie Endowment is a private, nonprofit organization dedicated to advancing cooperation between nations and promoting active international engagement by the United States. Founded in 1910, its work is nonpartisan and dedicated to achieving practical results. Through research, publishing, convening, and, on occasion, creating new institutions and international networks, Endowment associates shape fresh policy approaches. Their interests span geographic regions and the relations among governments, business, international organizations, and civil society, focusing on the economic, political, and technological forces driving global change. Through its Carnegie Moscow Center, the Endowment helps develop a tradition of public policy analysis in the states of the former Soviet Union and improve relations between Russia and the United States. The Endowment publishes *Foreign Policy,* one of the world's leading journals of international politics and economics, which reaches readers in more than 120 countries and several languages.